SLAVERY IN AMERICAN CHILDREN'S LITERATURE, 1790–2010

SLAVERY IN AMERICAN CHILDREN'S LITERATURE, 1790–2010

PAULA T. CONNOLLY

UNIVERSITY OF IOWA PRESS Iowa City

University of Iowa Press, Iowa City 52242

www.uiowapress.org
Printed in the United States of America

Design by Richard Hendel

The University of Iowa Press is a member of Green Press Initiative and is committed to preserving natural resources.

Printed on acid-free paper

ISBN: 978-1-60938-177-6
LCCN: 2012955015

To my parents,

JOE AND ISABEL CONNOLLY

CONTENTS

ACKNOWLEDGMENTS

Thank you to the many people who have helped me in large and small ways as I worked on this project. To Schley Lyons, former dean of the College of Arts and Sciences and to the University of North Carolina at Charlotte, I am grateful for a Faculty Research Grant and a reassignment of duties leave that allowed me time to work on the manuscript in its early stages.

I am grateful, as well, to the many librarians and staff members who have helped me to locate necessary texts and illustrations for my research. Special thanks to those at the University of North Carolina at Charlotte—Robin Brabham, Marilyn Schuster, and the staff at the Rare Books Room; the Interlibrary Loan team at Atkins Library; and Monica Alston of the English Department—all have been unfailingly helpful. I am also grateful to Edward Copenhagen of the Harvard Graduate School of Education, Tyler Gilmore of the University of North Carolina at Chapel Hill, Karen Hardie of High Point Public Library, Emilie Hardman of Harvard University's Houghton Library, Paul Hogroian of the Library of Congress, Karen May and the Association for the Study of African American Life and History, Aileen McNamara of the Free Library of Philadelphia, Megan Mulder of Wake Forest University, Jackie Penny of the American Antiquarian Society, Carolyn Shankle of the University of North Carolina at Greensboro, and the staff at the Boston Public Library. Microfilm of Confederate texts made by the Boston Athenaeum has also been invaluable.

I am fortunate to work in a field of generous scholars. Conferences of the Children's Literature Association and Modern Critical Approaches to Children's Literature have allowed me opportunities to work out my ideas in presentations and discussions with colleagues. I'm also grateful to colleagues who have offered suggestions on revisions and to friends (some also colleagues) whose sense of humor and generosity of spirit have immeasurably helped this project—and me. In this regard, many thanks are due to Frances Alexander, Cathy Anderson, Sue Diehl, Elizabeth Gargano, Terry Hoover, Tony Jackson, Jeffrey Leak, Jill May, James McGavran, Meg

Morgan, Anita Moss, Jen Munroe, Daniel Shealy, Katharine Capshaw Smith, Maya Socolovsky, Roberta Seelinger Trites, Mark West, and Greg Wickliff.

I am thankful for gracious and insightful editors at the University of Iowa Press, Elisabeth Chretien and Catherine Cocks. Thank you, as well, to the readers of the manuscript who provided important suggestions for its development.

My family's support and good humor are welcomed gifts. Thank you to my parents, Joe and Isabel Connolly, who are with me in spirit; to my sister Joyce, for her friendship, good sense, and coming to the rescue at the last minute; and to my husband, James—for everything.

A NOTE ON USAGE

Determining which terms to use in signaling race is often as problematic an issue as debates about race itself. I intentionally do not use the term "African American" until discussing time periods following the 1868 passage of the Fourteenth Amendment that granted citizenship to "all persons born or naturalized in the United States." I do this to acknowledge when legal citizenship was withheld or accorded by the federal government. At times, I use the terminology of specific authors under discussion, echoing, for example, the term "Negro" as authors of a specific time do, although to acknowledge that periodicity I often place terms in quotations. Typically, I use the terms "black" and "white" (lower case) to represent race, largely because the literary and cultural tropes discussed here most often define race in terms of color meant to represent opposition or marked difference.

The terms "slave" or "enslaved" are similarly under debate. I most often use "slave" because this study focuses on the ways slavery has been presented—as a viewed or read object—in literature. The term "enslaved" is used in specific instances to emphasize the conflict between condition and personhood, but my use of the term "slave" does not ignore that inherent tension.

SLAVERY IN AMERICAN CHILDREN'S LITERATURE, 1790–2010

INTRODUCTION

> One of the marveylous thynges that god useth in the composition of man, is coloure: whiche doubtlesse can not bee consydered withowte great admiration in beholding one to be white and an other blacke; beinge coloures utterlye contrary.
>
> —*The Decades of the Newe World* (1555)[1]

In 1619, after surviving capture and separation from their families, removal from their homelands, and forced transportation across the Atlantic, twenty Africans were sold to newly arrived colonists in Jamestown, Virginia. As the colonies developed, so too did slavery: by 1660, slavery was written into Virginia statute law and within little over a century later, the enslaved population across the colonies had increased to five hundred thousand. That population, deriving both from those kidnapped from Africa and others born in the Americas, continued to grow. Following the Revolutionary War—and despite the war's prefacing document avowing that "all men are created equal"—slavery became more socially, politically, and legally entrenched in the southern states, where the number of enslaved people would rise to nearly four million by 1861, just shortly before the Civil War.[2] For the millions of people brought to or born in America as slaves during those nearly two and a half centuries, there was little hope of manumission.

Beyond those fairly generalized facts, what slavery essentially *meant* in terms of its conditions, the experiences of those held under slavery, and the implications of race was highly contested. As politicians, scientists, and theologians debated racial hierarchies and slavery, antebellum literature entered the national discourse by framing contemporary theories with competing versions of "the peculiar institution" and those living under it, translating the anonymous generalization of "slave" into specific figures whom readers could variously admire, pity, laugh at, fear, or disdain. Called by one slavery advocate "the most powerful weapon" ("Duty" 242), literature—including both autobiography and fiction—was used by writers on all sides to justify their various positions, counter opposing arguments, and garner popular, and thereby political, support for their cause. But if literature in general was "the most powerful weapon" in the battle to engender sympathy for one's position about slavery, children's literature was an indispensable tool in that ideological arsenal. Indeed, children's literature and the figure of the child functioned centrally in debates about slavery, as they have in the literary and visual re-creation of slavery to the present day.

Slavery in American Children's Literature situates itself within this nexus of children's literature and racial mythmaking in America. Providing a literary history of over two hundred years of American children's literature, it examines the visual and verbal literary aesthetics of race making. Part recovery project, this study examines both well-known works and others that have ostensibly disappeared from contemporary cultural knowledge, but have nonetheless affected the American social consciousness in the creation and reiteration of racialized images. Interrogating how generations of U.S. children have been educated about slavery can tell us much, both about the development of the nation's racial debates and how literature has historically reframed existing tropes about slavery. This book thus is a study of the literary and cultural antecedents upon which current representations of slavery rest. At the same time, it examines how historical memory is reshaped to express contemporaneous racial politics. Examining children's literature about slavery ultimately provides an opportunity to explore notions of "American" identity, particularly in terms of who is or is not literarily enfranchised, as object and/or subject, and intra- and/or extranarratively. As literature teaches each successive generation what race means, it also teaches children what their function is in terms of race, citizenship, and personhood.

• • •

When, in 1788, Noah Webster wrote that the "only practicable method to reform mankind, is to begin with children," he was arguing the political implications—for him, the political necessity—of children's early education ("On the Education" 22, spelling modernized throughout). His assertion that the "education of youth is, in all governments, an object of the first consequence," in that "the impressions received in early life, usually form the characters of individuals; a union of which forms the general character of a nation" (1), aptly captured widely held beliefs about the moral, intellectual, and political implications of children's education. In political terms, the child represented the young republic's hope for a strong future, his success ensuring the continuance and prosperity of the new nation; in moral and intellectual terms, the child was believed to be reasoned, amenable to early instruction, and both educable and ethical.

Antebellum literature that laid the groundwork for engaged citizenship ranged from recreational novels, such as Jacob Abbott's *Rollo* series, which tutored children in the importance of patience, sympathy, honesty, and industriousness, to schoolbooks that presented lessons on early American history and the workings of the federal government. With admonitions for personal responsibility often standing alongside those to aid the poor and support temperance, children's literature from this era argued that the present state of the nation could be improved, and assured children of their efficacy as agents for such change. Yet, for all the suggested radical nature of literature which encouraged children's engagement in social reform, the vision of the child as hope for the nation's future was often a circumscribed one, largely offered by white, middle-class authors to white, middle-class children as a way to ensure a relatively comparable future.[3]

In the midst of this, one contentiously debated issue superseded any possibilities for national, and hence literary, agreement. Agitation about slavery had the potential to disrupt, if not destroy, generally accepted race and class hierarchies, as well as a nationally protected system of legalized enslavement. Supporters and detractors sought every advantage in their various campaigns to garner public opinion, and as they presented their cause to society at large, both anti- and proslavery advocates turned their attention specifically to children. Indeed, that American children's literature arose during a time of debates about slavery and race that were inextricably connected to issues of establishing the new nation places children's literature, from its beginnings, within a matrix of political, cultural, social, and literary influences focused on nation making.[4]

Blending sentimental and republican notions of childhood, abolitionists saw children as both the present and eventual instigators of a reformed nation, believing "if you make children abolitionists slavery must come to an end" ("To Juvenile Anti-Slavery" 8). Because of children's perceived innocence, their influence—that adults "may hearken what *you* say, / Though from *us* they turn away" (*Anti-Slavery Alphabet*)—made them particularly suited, many argued, to serve as "young moral reformers" ("Juvenile Anti-Slavery Society" 4). To encourage children to political activism, abolitionist literature like *The Slave's Friend* urged children to organize their own juvenile antislavery societies, write petitions to Congress, raise money for the abolitionist cause, and boycott products made with slave labor.[5]

More than children's moral and economic effect, it was their anticipated political influence as the nation's next generation of leaders that made them most powerful in the eyes of slavery advocates and critics. As a writer in *The Youth's Emancipator* argued, slavery advocates were more troubled by the prospect of abolitionist children, not adults. Such advocates, he asserted, believed abolitionists who were "old men will soon die off, and their influence will probably die with them; but these infants and children, who have the prospect of living many years, and exerting a great influence—those are the ones who will conquer us" ("Never Despair").

Proslavery writers agreed, but saw antislavery authors as the central problem, their books weapons with which to battle for the minds of children, an insidious way for abolitionists to gain control of the South's future. Slavery advocates, too, knew the importance of inculcating children to their position and also knew the dangers to their worldview if they did not. One slavery advocate argued this in an 1855 review, asserting: "There are few of those [books] published at the north which do not contain some sneer, or some attack on southern slavery. This is too apt to strike deep into the infant mind, and exert a pernicious influence in after years." The solution many believed clear: "no more useful task could be performed than the compilation of a series of southern schoolbooks, free from all taint of abolitionism" (Rev. of *A Southern Home* 668). As one educator explained, the goal of these new books would be to create strong Southern citizenship: "our entire youthful population, imbibing with their earliest ideas respect for their State, and for its greatest and most beneficent institutions [. . .] will be ready, as men and women, to serve its interests with more zeal and more intelligence than those who preceded them" (Hubbard 4). For such slavery proponents, children's literature offered potentially limitless possibilities both to protect their racialized view of nationhood and to justify their position, even to "millions of [. . .] descendants" from "unborn centuries" (Marshall, "Home Education" 666).

In the midst of such debates about the role of young, white

readers as reformers and future leaders of the nation, where was the black child? While the white child present intra- and extratextually in antebellum children's literature stood as a model of either pro- or antislavery action, the black child and adult were rarely acknowledged as intended audience, and thus literarily excluded from those deemed the nation's next leaders. Most frequently in antebellum children's literature, the black child was intratextually framed only, in rare instances as agent and hero, but most often as victimized or fortunate slave, depending upon the author's ideological perspective.

The figure of the slave was, of course, an essential one in literature about slavery, although no single figure would come to represent slavery. Instead, often vying images clashed with one another as those on different sides of the debate sought to present their version of slavery and the issues of race that underpinned it. In antebellum children's literature, for example, one meets characters fiercely independent who would "rise against their cruel masters" (Webster, *Little Reader's Assistant* 40) or others well content with slavery who are "happy" and "glad" (*Little Eva* 3, 4); some who are "scholar[s]" ("Lot Cary" 2), and others "ludicrous" (S., Peter) and "light-hearted" (Goulding, *Robert and Harold* [1852], 392). Such contrasting images also reflect the dynamic interplay between children's and adult literature, as antebellum children's literature often re-created images of slavery found in contemporaneous literature for adults. Moreover, literature for both audiences often echoed discussions about race that were occurring in the culture at large.

• • •

Views of slavery entered popular discussion via many means, including newspapers, political debates, lectures, and theological treatises. But, for the general public, literature—and three genres in particular—most successfully defined the slavery debates of the time: the autobiographical slave narrative; its ideological opposite, the proslavery plantation novel; and, often situated some place between the two, white-authored abolitionist fiction. As popular genres, the three formed a literary and ideological triad, each presenting distinct views of slavery, while at the same time linked to the others in a relationship of signifying counterpoints. That relationship was one antebellum writers often exploited as proslavery writers presented images of slavery to counter those offered by abolitionists, and vice versa.[6] In their translation and exploration of slavery debates, these genres helped to create iconic representations—of, for example, a thoughtful and rebellious Frederick Douglass, a happy and simple-minded Sambo, and a still-problematic Uncle Tom—that far outlasted the antebellum years.

In the process of reframing slavery debates, antebellum authors encapsulated race theories of the day as they sought to clarify, from their perspective, what race meant—specifically, what "white" and "black" meant as signifiers of personhood and citizenship. Fascinated by differences of skin color, theologians, philosophers, medical doctors, and early anthropologists, particularly in the eighteenth and nineteenth centuries, launched into myriad studies and hypotheses about the nature and very definition of humanity. While some argued that those designated "black" and "white" were thoroughly different species (and thus that those defined as "black" were not people at all), monogenists maintained both were the same species but nonetheless demonstrated undeniably essential differences. Pseudoscientific analyses to determine racial differences included studying crania, brain size, human hair, and even body lice. Particularly of interest to scientists was discovering the cause of varied skin color, and theories ranged from climatic effects to skin density. Theologians offered their own theories, some arguing that black skin signified a curse of servitude dating back to Noah's time. Whatever the focus or method of investigation, the results were the same: differences between Europeans and Africans—that is, between people who were classified as "white" and "black"—were defined as irreconcilably oppositional and set in hierarchical paradigms, with "whites" invariably at the top.[7]

Such pseudoscientific studies were particularly alluring to many white audiences because they cast an appearance of objective fact to the assurance of white supremacy. Moreover, racial differences determined by scientists and early anthropologists—including assertions of Africans' impaired intellect or insensitivity to pain and overwork—became the foundation for an array of distinctions that saw black Africans defined as "types" that made them particularly suited, some argued, for slavery. Slavery and race debates were thus linked symbiotically in the United States, as slavery became a reification of theories of racial superiority (on the side of European whites) and inferiority (on the side of African blacks); as Toni Morrison has pointed out, "it was not simply that this slave population had a distinctive color; it was that this color 'meant' something"

(49).[8] As a result, the implications of American slavery far outlasted its legal demise. Its grounding justifications, which had assigned a host of negative tropes to the designation of "black" or "African" had, as George Fredrickson has argued, "planted the seeds of disaster by creating a problem of race more fundamental and difficult to solve than the problem of slavery" (23).

• • •

Dana Nelson's argument that there is "an essential violence embedded in the very concept of 'race'" (xii) is reflected not only in many early race theories, but also in literature that has played an important role in the reiteration of images justifying slavery. If, indeed, "'race' as a knowable object [. . .] is constituted by every expression of that idea" (Nelson ix), exploring expressions of race—particularly in children's literature—offers important opportunities to understand how the literary construction of race has been central in the cultural education of successive generations of readers. This is perhaps nowhere more evident than in the literary retellings of American slavery for young audiences.

To say "children are the future" has admittedly become a pat expression to the point of pabulum. Yet the antebellum belief in children's importance as the nation's next generation of leaders still underwrites the nearly unbreakable triumvirate of children, education (including children's literature), and visions for the nation's future. Early in the twentieth century, W. E. B. Du Bois argued a more inclusionary paradigm of children who would engender "Democracy['s . . .] greater ends": "To this [success] there is but one patent way, proved and inescapable, Education [. . .] for the Immortal Child. And that child is of all races and all colors" ("Immortal Child" 209, 217). Reminiscent of Noah Webster's arguments in the late eighteenth century, Du Bois wrote that "all our problems center in the child. All our hopes, our dreams are for our children. [. . .] Is there anything we would accomplish with human beings? Do it with the immortal child" (213). It is, he asserted, "through children's eyes, then, [that] we look to a triumphant future" ("Immortal Children" 267).

Long after the antebellum years, the education of children has remained a central tool in shaping a national consciousness and political reality about race in America. Although some antebellum literature includes expectations of wide readership to encompass "black" and "white" children, the later broadening of authorship, readership, and especially those envisioned as potential leaders of the nation becomes all the more relevant in discussions of children's literature about slavery. The history of children's literature about slavery is, in many ways, a history of the intra- and extratextual construction of racial childhood in America. Shifting representations of slavery, particularly in the depicted agency of the slave figure, would come to reflect evolving definitions of the children who would be expected to participate in what Webster had once described as the hope to "reform mankind."

Whether consciously or as part of a now-shared cultural subconscious, American authors since the Civil War have consistently called upon images from one or more of the three primary antebellum genres about slavery—the slave narrative and abolitionist and plantation novels—in their depictions of slavery, slave characters, and race "types," variously accepting one or the other genres as the veritable source for understanding what slavery was and what race signifies. The number of studies about the influence of these antebellum genres on subsequent adult literature and its authors has been considerable, and includes Jean Fagan Yellin's *The Intricate Knot* (1972), Deborah McDowell and Arnold Rampersad's collection, *Slavery and the Literary Imagination* (1989), and Ashraf Rushdy's *Neo-slave Narratives* (1999). The effect of those genres on the racial socialization of children, however, has received much less attention. While Dorothy Broderick's *Image of the Black in Children's Fiction* (1973), Donnarae MacCann's *White Supremacy in Children's Literature* (1998), and Deborah De Rosa's *Domestic Abolitionism and Juvenile Literature, 1830–1865* (2003), all important books in the field, include discussions of slavery, there has yet been no study which comprehensively explores the changing representations of slavery and race in American children's literature. This study offers such an exploration. It also intersects with recent contributions in childhood studies—such as Mary Niall Mitchell's *Raising Freedom's Child* (2008) and Robin Bernstein's *Racial Innocence* (2011)—in its exploration of the cultural construction of childhood, in this case, the ways children are racially acculturated through literature about slavery. *Slavery in American Children's Literature* is built upon the premise that children's early education is politically significant, and that children's literature about slavery has been a means of both revealing and inscribing American racial politics.

This book is historically framed, both in its overall chronological examination of children's literature and in its investigation of how generations of authors have drawn upon the tropes and racial ideology of antebellum literature in their re-creations of slavery. A discursive circularity develops, wherein current literary discussions of race show themselves as successors to these antebellum genres. At the same time, these depictions of slavery reflect the influence of contemporaneous times. *What* images of slavery and race are adopted—whether drawn from the slave narrative *or* plantation novel *or* abolitionist novel *or* some permutation of those—is keenly affected by literary, social, and political contexts. Additionally intersecting this confluence of antebellum slavery discourses and the cultural inflection of later authorship eras is the accumulated literature on slavery, which has collectively reshaped, reinvented, and reinscribed these earlier images to create another generation's stories about slavery. Such interactions show individual works not as static or isolated texts, but rather as literature which interweaves and intersects, clashing and sometimes casting itself as counterweight to other common texts, particularly in this framework of competing ideological discourses about race.

Slavery in American Children's Literature thus explores images of slavery and race to make explicit the implicitly, if perhaps unconsciously, racialized images that have continued to define slavery and race for new generations of children. How, for example, does the literary representation of slavery become a meditation on freedom, race, and social identity, providing white readers with a landscape upon which to configure their own identity?[9] How does the slave's role as commodity become reinstated in literature that critiques commodification at the same time that it uses race as an opportunity to confirm social status? And how does the representation of the slave change, depending on issues of authorship or intended audience, particularly in the intervention of African American authors responding to culturally weighted racialized stereotypes or the inclusion of African American readership?

Especially because of the chronological breadth of this study, the works included cannot be exhaustive; readers will invariably note texts that could have been included, but were not. My selection of texts is meant to demonstrate representative works of specific ideological viewpoints about slavery and race. Particularly, I explore how images of slavery and race have been reshaped into significantly evocative and long-lasting cultural tropes, and then examine how they reflect larger literary trends, defined here as subgenres, such as antebellum radical abolitionist literature or twentieth-century neo-abolitionist novels. The study does, however, draw from a full range of children's texts—schoolbooks, magazines, poems, essays, short stories, picture books, and novels—to examine both worded and illustrated images of slavery. This range of genres acknowledges the span of readership ages (from very young children to adolescents) as well as the various forums through which stories of slavery and race have been communicated to children. This study then employs a close reading of texts while also placing them within their literary and cultural contexts.

The examination of children's literature begins with early works authored and published in the United States, moving through early slavery debates of the late eighteenth century to texts of the early twenty-first century. The more than two century period noted here has been divided into sizable eras marked by recognizable changes in racial politics, but one must be wary of assuming a neat literary evolution in which racist stereotypes disappear. One still finds, for example, contesting visions of slavery at the close of the twentieth century where apologist images from plantation novels linger alongside denunciations of slavery in neo-slave narratives.

Chapters are organized chronologically in terms of overall historical periodicity, and then each is divided into three subsections representing different and often competing articulations of slavery literature for children. Chronological discussion within chapters is not so strictly held, particularly because of the frequent simultaneity of literary discourse; that is, within marked periods some contesting representations of slavery encompass wide periods, others more narrow, and many frequently occur at the same time or overlap as one pushes against another in an attempt for ideological supremacy.

The first two chapters cover the antebellum period through the Civil War, focusing on anti- and proslavery writers, respectively. The first chapter, on abolitionist responses in children's literature, moves from activist literature that encouraged children's efforts for immediate emancipation to texts that conceded only gradual abolition. Such literature "signifies" (compare Gates, *Signifying*) on contemporaneous adult texts about slavery, particularly the slave narrative and abolitionist novel, while also reshaping those texts for a young, largely white audience. This chapter also explores how images that signal racialized hierarchies infiltrate abolitionist literature at all levels, making even the most radical of abolitionist literature a complex blend of social activism and conservativism. The second chapter turns to proslavery literature for children, exploring its expression of tropes from plantation novels and its role as a responsive refutation of pro-Northern and abolitionist children's literature. Proslavery children's literature collectively presents two ostensibly opposing representations—the rural fantasy of a plantation idyll and lessons in plantation management—that worked in tandem to teach young, white children their responsibilities as slave owners. By contrast, proslavery catechisms for young slaves at times both supported and countered the master's authority and pro-plantation ideals.

The next three chapters cover the years 1865–1919, 1920–1950, and 1951–2010. Chapter 3 moves from the close of the Civil War through Reconstruction to the early twentieth century. Beginning with texts written specifically for newly freed slaves, this chapter explores the tensions inherent in historical retellings as literacy is used as social control. It also investigates the influence of antebellum proslavery literature, particularly how postwar unease with emancipation is reflected and contained in the postplantation novel, one of the most popular genres for children of the time. Often as conflicted as antebellum abolition, postwar antislavery sentiment nonetheless also offered the first postslavery generation of African American–authored biographies that welcomed new audiences of African American children.

Chapter 4's study of texts published between 1920 and 1950 highlights a resurgence of overtly contesting visions of slavery, particularly through the influence of the Harlem Renaissance, which marked a literary breakthrough for African American authors writing with young African American readers in mind. During this time, while African American–authored biographies retell stories of slavery to focus on success in a postbellum world, images of the loyal and foolish slave are still firmly entrenched in children's literature, as evidenced in pseudoabolitionist adventures and neoplantation novels. This chapter examines how antebellum accounts are reshaped to tell different stories to different audiences, particularly how violence and rebellion are reframed to present contrasting depictions of slavery as paradigms for national leadership.

The final chapter, moving from the civil rights movement of the 1950s to the beginning of the twenty-first century, focuses on the re-creation of abolitionist fiction and the slave narrative in children's literature. In particular, neoabolitionist literature and the neo-slave narrative explore the ways antebellum tropes can be "newly" re-formed and interrogated. Diachronous literature, including fantasy, moves stories of slavery into new genres, while narrative techniques, such as polyphonic layering, replicate the responsive literary debates of slavery that have occurred in America over the past two centuries.

Slavery in American Children's Literature thus explores the question of how such literature has reflected and created myths of race and nationhood. It is a question of symbol, imagery, narrative perspective, literary antecedents, and racial politics; a question of how we tell a national tragedy to our children; a question of how images that first defined the racial hierarchies that enslaved millions and set up a legal system of white superiority are reiterated or investigated for successive generations of children. The history we tell becomes our new version of historical reality, and while it may or may not reflect what actually occurred during that historical period, it often can tell us much about how we view our present time—what our views, fears, biases, beliefs, and hopes are. This is a study about those fears and hopes.

CHAPTER 1

SLAVERY DEBATES FOR CHILDREN 1790-1865

ABOLITIONIST RESPONSES

> A female slave [. . .] was kneeling
> at the foot of a cocoa-tree. Chains hung
> from her wrists, and were fastened
> to her ancles.
> —"The Collection Box" (1836)

> He was about six feet in height [. . .]
> and was endowed with immense physical strength. [. . .]
> His expression was that of great intelligence. [. . .]
> He was a man who, even in a land of slavery, would
> be instinctively respected.
> —William Taylor Adams, *Hatchie, the Guardian Slave* (1853)

One of the central humanitarian issues of the antebellum period, abolition was also one of the most divisive issues of its time. It was a topic, too, that found expression in a wide range of antebellum literature for children, from poems and magazines to novels and schoolbooks. How authors navigated divergent audiences—such as young readers and their parents, and those who stood on opposing sides of the issue—often reflected varying levels of commitment to emancipation and racial equity. Some, wary of offending their readership, censored discussion of the topic, as was the case with authors of the American Sunday School Union's many publications who in 1832 were directed "on the delicate question of slavery, [to] abstain from all remarks; much injury may result from an indiscreet observation" (qtd in Avery 114). Indeed, children's authors could (and some did) suffer "injury" from taking an abolitionist stance, particularly by risking the ire and economic sanction of readers. Abolitionist, author, and editor Lydia Maria Child found this to be the case; the loss of subscribers and the consequent demise of the once-popular *Juvenile Miscellany* that she edited have been generally attributed to her antislavery stance.[1]

Antebellum children's literature reflected national debates about slavery which were argued in Congress, editorialized in newspapers, hypothesized about by scientists and theologians, and described in literature for adults. While abolitionist children's literature, by definition, includes literature supporting emancipation, the presentation of abolitionist sentiment in children's literature was neither ideologically cohesive nor uniformly critical. That, too, reflected abolitionist debates at large. "Abolitionism" is, in many ways, an umbrella term, encompassing a significantly broad spectrum of viewpoints. William Lloyd Garrison, one of the most influential activists of his time, reflected this in his own experiences. First accepting what he would eventually term the "popular but pernicious doctrine of *gradual* abolition," he later announced that on the subject of slavery, "I do not wish to think, or speak, or write, with moderation" ("To the Public," italics in original text unless otherwise noted). He instead became an ardent proponent of "radicalism" ("No Union"). Condemning what he called the "timidity" of other abolitionist positions, Garrison declared that "I will not equivocate—I will not excuse" but "shall strenuously contend for the immediate enfranchisement of our slave population" ("To the Public").

In *Slavery in American Children's Literature*, representations of abolition in antebellum children's literature are divided into three categories that loosely follow Garrison's discussion of abolition: radical, moderate, and conservative.[2] One might argue that abolitionist authors were interlocking partners in the cause to end slavery, but real ideological differences—particularly about the nature of race, the figure of the slave, and slavery itself—often placed them on opposite ends of an ideological divide. While, for example, radical abolitionists exposed U.S. slavery as unvaryingly exploitative, moderate abolitionists kept critiques of slavery offshore and diverted attention away from the American system. Further along the ideological spectrum, conservative abolitionists often argued that slavery had some beneficent effects, particularly as a necessary introduction of Africans to later emancipation in America. Despite such obvious difference, these divisions of abolitionist discourse for children also intersected as authors struggled with representations of racial interactions and hierarchies. Regardless of their varied commitment to abolition, radical, moderate, and conservative abolitionists developed narrative strategies—and created slave figures—that explored and most often contained slave narratives' expressions of black power.

RADICAL ABOLITIONIST LITERATURE

Radical abolitionist literature for children presented, as the term implies, a nonnegotiable view of slavery as an unquestionably cruel system under which people suffered tremendous injustices. Moreover, radical abolitionists placed slavery within a specifically American context to critique the failings of a government whose founding documents theoretically espoused liberty, yet in practice supported slavery. More passionate in their politics, more committed in their activism, and less wary of offending slavery sympathizers than moderate and conservative abolitionist writers, these authors often argued for racial equality and called for the immediate end to slavery. They also sought to radicalize young readers, encouraging them to actively participate in the abolitionist cause.

Although radical abolitionism ostensibly threatened existing political, social, and racial hierarchies, it was at times inflected with racial biases that maintained notions of white privilege. As much as radical abolitionists argued that abolition provided an opportunity for white activism, paradigms of white heroism were often constructed through oppositional representations of black need, passivity, and gratitude. One sees this, for example, in images of piteous, forgiving, and supplicant slaves. Although not as frequently represented, images of rebellious slaves (in the most radical of abolitionist literature for children) also offered a vision of heroic black activism. Amid varied slave images, radical abolitionist depictions of the violence endured by those enslaved were unswerving in their condemnation of slavery. Particularly in that way, radical abolitionist literature—in comparison to moderate and conservative abolitionist literature—was closest to the slave narrative in rhetoric and ideology.

The autobiographies or testimonies of those formerly enslaved were themselves the most radical of abolitionist literature, immensely popular with adult audiences who, as one abolitionist argued, were "itching [. . .] to hear a colored man speak, and particularly a slave" (qtd in Davis and Gates xvi). By breaking the silence of enslavement and asserting one's identity in a society that had racially excluded the enslaved from the ranks of citizenship and humanity, these testimonies offered what no white abolitionist could: first-hand accounts of what it was like to live under slavery.[3] These accounts contradicted those who argued the benefits of slavery or who asserted that Africans could not suffer unduly since "their griefs are transient [. . . .] and sooner forgotten with them" (Jefferson 134). In contrast, slave narratives offered explicit depictions of violence and showed that those who suffered the physical and psychological tortures of slavery did so in no way less keenly because of their race.[4] Moreover, while former slaves at times acknowledged aid from white sympathizers, they countered assertions of Africans' mental inferiority by describing their success in outwitting oppressors and escaping to freedom. Slave narratives thus described both the suffering and heroism of those enslaved. Together, these arguments supported the slave narratives' central political objective: immediate emancipation.

Radical abolitionist literature for children, largely authored by white abolitionists, often situated itself between descriptions of slavery offered in slave narratives and those in white-authored abolitionist novels for adults that show more obvious infiltration of contemporaneous race theories. Images of slave resistance, for example, which are often a hallmark of the slave narrative, struggle for expression in radical abolitionist literature for children as they do in white-authored radical abolitionist literature for adults. However, this literature remains "radical" precisely in the way it unvaryingly denounces slavery, affirms the humanity of those enslaved, demands immediate emancipation, argues for racial equality (even sometimes in the midst of implicit expressions of racial hierarchies), and often seeks to politicize children as young abolitionists. Moreover, it functions as the extreme and, perhaps, most complicated expression of abolitionism against which other authors, particularly slavery advocates, would offer their own representations of slavery.

For the most part, antebellum radical abolitionist literature for children was published by abolitionist organizations and antislavery presses. Titles such as *The Youth's Emancipator* (1842–1843), *The Anti-Slavery Alphabet* (1847), and *The Young Abolitionists* (1848) unmistakably declared their stand on slavery, and thus audiences most likely to read such works were at least somewhat receptive to the cause. Yet one of the earliest examples of radical abolitionism in children's literature was neither published by an antislavery press nor intended for a narrowly defined audience. That, in its own way, may make Noah Webster's *The Little Reader's Assistant* (1790) particularly radical. It is also one of the strongest antebellum examples of the ways children's literature evoked images from slave narratives.

Politics and children's education were largely synonymous to Noah Webster, whose immensely popular *American Spelling Book* (1787) sought to ensure the cultural and intellectual independence of the nation by standardizing American (as opposed to British) English in classrooms across the country.[5] Writing during the years of the U.S. government's formation—the peace treaty with England was finalized in 1783, the U.S. Constitution was ratified in 1788, and George Washington accepted the presidency in 1789—Webster was an influential political figure and ardent proponent of social justice. He was also an active abolitionist who would have been well acquainted with any number of antislavery tracts as well as with the testimonies of former slaves.[6] His abolitionism became, for him, a form of moral nationalism which he articulated to children in *The Little Reader's Assistant.* There, along with lessons in grammar, the newly formed federal government, and American history, Webster included two essays with an uncompromisingly abolitionist message.[7]

In the short six paragraphs of "Story of the Treatment of African Slaves," Webster synthesizes the cycle of slavery, beginning with African prisoners sold as slaves, then "chained together" (39), and brought to a ship for the torturous passage to the Americas. The "poor half starved negroes" who survive the sea journey then suffer the auction block, where remaining families are irrevocably separated. Plantations offer slaves no respite, and there "most of them die in a few years with fatigue and sickness and the rest live lives of severe labor and wretchedness" (40, spelling modernized throughout). Webster ends the essay in a direct address to readers, calling for their acknowledgment of racial equality, slavery's injustices, and asserting that God's "vengeance must fall" upon those who "commit this outrage" of enslaving others (41).

For those who had been kidnapped from Africa, that kidnapping and the ensuing forced ocean passage were quintessential representations of the horrors of enslavement, a microcosm of slavery itself. Ottobah Cugoano's *Thoughts and Sentiments on the Evil and Wicked Traffic of the Slavery and Commerce of the Human Species* (1787) and Olaudah Equiano's *The Interesting Narrative of the Life of Olaudah Equiano; or, Gustavus Vassa, the African* (1789) both detail the men's experiences in slavery,[8] particularly the suffocating violence aboard the slave ship where "a multitude of black people [were . . .] chained together [. . . .] and hourly whipped" (Equiano 22–23). There, "nothing [was] to be heard but the [. . .] smacking of whips, and [. . .] cries of our fellow-men" (Cugoano 15), and one could not escape the "stench of the hold [. . .] so intolerably loathsome" (Equiano 24).

One trying to find a consistent one-to-one correspondence between radical abolitionist literature for children and the slave narrative will often be disappointed. Nonetheless, as Webster re-creates the Middle Passage for young readers by describing fatal illness, mass murder, suicide, rebellion, and punishment, he demonstrates how some radical abolitionist texts were not only ideologically but also rhetorically aligned with slave narratives. Webster here evokes even similar phrases as those in Equiano's account. For example, his description—that "when they [kidnapped Africans] arrive at the ship, they are often crowded together in the hold in such numbers, as to breed a pestilential air, which causes sickness, and multitudes die on the passage" (39–40)—is strikingly similar to Equiano's account: "Now that the whole ship's cargo were confined together, it became absolutely pestilential. The closeness of the place [. . .] added to the number in the ship, which was so crowded that [this. . . .] brought on a sickness among the slaves, of which many died" (24–25).

In addition to revealing the suffering endured by the enslaved, slave narratives tell of their rebelliousness, even when it leads to the slave's death. In his narrative, for example, Cugoano describes an unsuccessful plot he and companions had devised to "burn and blow up the ship, and to perish all together in the flames" (Cugoano 15). Repeatedly, narratives describe that for those enslaved "death was more preferable than life" (Cugoano 15), and give accounts of those who "refused to eat or drink" (Cugoano 14) or "jumped into the sea" (Equiano 25) during the passage. More than an expression of hopelessness in the face of overwhelming oppression, suicide is presented as a means of rebellion, a way to escape slavery, effect personal liberation, and evade oppressors.

Webster captures this tenor of rebellion in "Story of the Treatment of African Slaves." Despite the object position of passive slaves inferred in the title, Webster describes slave agency and resistance: aboard the ship, some "rise against their cruel masters, and attempt to regain their liberty" (40). The price for such rebellion is dear, and as Cugoano describes "a cruel bloody scene" of retribution following their thwarted coup (15), Webster reports how, for their attempts, slaves are "stabbed on the spot, or beaten and mangled in the most barbarous manner." Webster describes, too, how others, "resolved to be free, plunge into the ocean, and thus happily escape a life of bondage" (40). Such images of death (in both slave accounts and white-authored abolitionist literature for children)—of "hundreds [. . .] sometimes thrown into the sea," of others who jump to their deaths, of the "multitudes" (Webster 40) who die of disease, and others whipped and beaten—also evoke the genocidal underpinnings of slavery.

Once in America, the auction block often represents the nexus of slavery's depravity, the site of irrevocable family separations and the public translation of people to property. There, as Equiano describes, "we were pent up altogether like so many sheep in a fold," and soon sold, "without scruple, [. . .] relations and friends separated, most of them never to see each other again" (27). In such scenes, the juxtaposition of animals with people—called here, by Equiano, not "slaves" but "relations and friends" and later "parents [, . . .] children, brothers [, . . .] sisters, [. . .] husbands [and . . .] wives" (28)—emphasizes the tension between the slave's treatment and inherent humanity, and thus signifies on "the metaphorical Great Chain of Being" (Gates, *Signifying* 167) to reassert the enslaved's place as fully human, and not—as racist ideologues would have it—a subrace, inferior to white Europeans.

Webster, too, implicitly comments on such tensions in his own description of the auction block, humanizing the "poor half starved negroes" by emphasizing how their familial connections are severed as "Parents are separated from children, and husbands are dragged from wives" (40). In the final paragraph, Webster also attempts to shatter the "otherness" of race as he asks his (implicitly white) readers:

> Are the negroes *brutes*? Or are they *men* like ourselves? What right hath *one man* to enslave *another*? Have not the negroes the same right to steal us, our wives and children, transport us

> to Africa, and reduce us to bondage, as we have to enslave them? If there is justice in heaven, vengeance must fall upon the heads of men who commit this outrage upon their own kind. (40–41)

Attacking not only the conditions of slavery, but also its fundamental assumption of racial hierarchy, Webster's use of italics emphasizes his recreation of the racial chain of being, moving "negroes" not only from "*brutes*" to "*men*," but to "*men* like ourselves," thus directing white readers to acknowledge racial equality. He then extends this revision of generally accepted racial hierarchies by attacking the racial insularity which keeps white, middle-class readers free from the threat of enslavement, encouraging his readers to imagine the possibility—indeed the moral justice—of being enslaved themselves.

In his second essay, "Lamentation of an Old Female Slave," Webster calls for reader sympathy by personalizing the figure of the slave through an abolitionist pseudonarrative, a fictional work designed to mimic a slave narrative. While Webster offers images of rebellion in his prior essay (its more distanced third-person point of view containing that agency in some measure), in this first-person pseudonarrative he presents a character who had been "faithful" in her master's service for fifty years, but now, as she describes it, "feebled [. . .] and [. . .] unable to labor, I am cast off to shift for myself" (44) and can only "wait with impatience for my eternal rest" (45). Actual slave narratives do portray such plights; Frederick Douglass, for example, would later describe how after a lifetime of slavery, his own grandmother, "racked with the pains of old age, and complete helplessness," was taken to a hut in the woods and "virtually turn[ed . . .] out to die" (*Narrative* 92). Yet slave narratives often counterbalance representations of trauma with those of resistance. In contrast, when abolitionist children's literature presents slavery from a slave's point of view through a pseudonarrative, expressions of cathartic power taking are frequently quelled, as here in "Lamentation." Despite that containment, in focusing on a character who tells her own story, describes the violence of slavery, and reminisces about the happiness of her childhood in Africa, Webster still confronts racialized stereotypes as well as the reader's possible cultural insularity.

The Little Reader's Assistant never came close to enjoying the success of Webster's spellers. Considering that Webster's textbooks typically populated schoolrooms across the country, it is likely the book's abolitionist stance contributed to its lack of success.[9] That was a risk radical abolitionist authors would continue to face. Nonetheless, as one of the earliest examples of radical abolitionism in U.S. children's literature, Webster's essays function as an important antecedent to the larger body of radical abolitionist children's literature which would begin in full force during the 1830s. While that later antebellum literature would describe slavery's violence to children, representations of slave rebellion that one finds in slave narratives and here in Webster's essays would be rare.

• • •

Only three years after the first edition of *The Little Reader's Assistant*, Eli Whitney's cotton gin was introduced to Southern farmers, ending any possibility that U.S. slavery would gradually die of its own accord. Essentially "revitaliz[ing . . .] slavery" (Foner and Garraty 242) by vastly increasing the production of cotton, the invention deepened the South's dependence not only upon the cotton industry, but also upon the slave labor that produced it. Although at the turn of the century, the slave population in the United States was just less than nine hundred thousand, by the beginning of the Civil War it had risen in the South to nearly four million (qtd in Kolchin 991). A number of congressional decisions, such as the 1820 Missouri Compromise, exemplified the nation's growing concerns about the balance of power between slave-holding and free states, and abolitionist and proslavery debates increased as slavery did.

Quakers founded the first antislavery society in the colonies the year before the signing of the Declaration of Independence, but in the 1830s, abolitionists organized as never before. The 1831 inauguration of the abolitionist newspaper *The Liberator* and the creation of the American Anti-Slavery Society two years later put the abolitionist movement on a national scale. Proselytizing was a major goal of the society, which established regional abolitionist groups; petitioned Congress to end slavery; and wrote, published, and distributed antislavery tracts. The 1830s have been defined as a time of "new" and "militant abolitionism," and abolitionism was, literally, an incendiary issue, from Nat Turner's famous 1831 insurrection to proslavery mob violence, such as that following Turner's rebellion and the 1837 murder of abolitionist-editor Elijah Lovejoy. Yet the abolitionism that typified the 1830s, particularly as expressed through Garrisonian politics, was nonviolent, "reject[ing] the use of all carnal weapons" ("Declaration"), while at the same time more organized and rhetorically fervent than earlier, regional abolitionism (hence the "militant" appellation).[10]

Children's literature functioned, in the midst of this, as an important tool for abolitionists to lobby their cause. *The Slave's Friend* (1836–1839), published by the American Anti-Slavery Society, in many ways exemplifies the ideology, rhetoric, and objectives of much radical abolitionist literature for children published during or after the 1830s. A small (3″ × 4¼″) sixteen-page magazine, *The Slave's Friend* was often distributed without charge to reach as wide an audience as possible (Edson 409). By its second year, editors could claim that about two hundred fifty thousand copies had been published and read by "at least fifty thousand children" ("Juvenile Anti-Slavery Society" 1–2). Each issue moves among brief essays, stories, exhortations, poems, biblical injunctions, statistics, and woodcut illustrations, and the general impression upon reading *The Slave's Friend* is of a multidimensional but singularly focused argument as one vignette after another presents the society's abolitionist agenda. Two central points in that agenda were to condemn slavery and encourage children's abolitionism.

A trademark of radical abolitionist literature was its unflinching portrayal of the violence of slavery and condemnation of racial prejudice—topics also central to slave narratives. Garrisonian radical abolitionist children's literature followed suit, and young children often read explicit descriptions of violence in *The Slave's Friend*: of, for example, a slave who was "pounded with a board full of holes, till his flesh came off" ("Starling" 3), and of sadistic slaveholders who assigned whippings for the merest of infractions—as in the case of a woman "whipt 99 lashes for neglecting to shut the piano at night" ("Isabella" 11). Radical abolitionist literature argued that no slavery was beneficial to the slave ("Rose and Miss Belle") and countered expectations of Western hegemony by offering positive descriptions of Africa, as in "Zamor and Hinda" (1838), where Africa is a utopian world of "beautiful flowers," "ripe fruits" (3), and peace, until the arrival of slavers.[11] Defining slavery as an explicit expression of racial bigotry, radical abolitionists also asserted the young reader's responsibility to fight against racism, while often retaining the reader's racial and class privilege. Essays in *The Slave's Friend*, for example, condemn educational exclusion ("Colored Children") and racist name calling ("Two Good Boys"), while encouraging a sense of noblesse oblige in injunctions such as, “be kind to people of color” (“To Juvenile Anti-Slavery” 9).[12]

Although black and white children in the antebellum North were not consistently granted the same rights to an education, the middle class of both races would have had access to many of the same books, and both black and white abolitionists supported the efforts of the American Anti-Slavery Society. As such, works like *The Slave's Friend* would in all likelihood have found their way into the homes of free blacks and abolitionist-minded whites in the North. Despite that, much radical abolitionist literature for children (and, for that matter, much radical abolitionist literature for adults) was intended for a Northern white audience, and most often a middle-class one. This is most evident, perhaps, in calls for whites to sympathize with slaves or in the modeling of white agency in the cause of abolition.

Since this was a readership insulated by economic privilege and, more fundamentally, protected from the possibility of enslavement because of race, the task of radical abolitionist authors was to disrupt that insularity as a way to counter race theories and tropes that defined “blacks” as less intelligent, less loving, even less sentient than “whites.” These authors thus sought to literarily rehumanize the figure of the slave. One way to develop reader sympathy was to present stories of enslaved children that not only emphasized the vulnerability of those enslaved, but also invited the young reader's concern for the plight of other children. *The Slave's Friend* often focused on enslaved children. There, one would read of “near 307 stolen children” (“Near” 3) and learn that “there are about six hundred thousand little boys and girls kept in slavery in the United States” (“Juvenile Anti-Slavery Society” 7).[13] More than statistics, radical abolitionists provided glimpses into the conditions suffered by enslaved children, often showing them bereft of their parents, as in the account of abolitionist Sarah Grimké who had witnessed “twenty children chained together, and driven through the streets [. . .] to be sold in New Orleans, never more to see their parents” (“Juvenile Anti-Slavery Meeting” 14). And when four excerpts of Charles Ball's narrative, *Slavery in the United States* (1837), were included in *The Slave's Friend*, each of them focused on the suffering of enslaved children and their forced separation from loving parents.

Another way in which abolitionists elicited the white reader's sympathy was through the white abduction story, a genre which precariously treads the boundaries of empathy and essentialism. White abduction stories extend the call to "put yourself in their place" ("Cart-Whip" 6) by showing a white character who is enslaved. The white reader, reading through this enslaved white character, hypothetically engages in a type of imaginative transference, a more keenly appreciated sense of the vulnerability and violence of slavery which the white reader might not otherwise imagine happening to him or her. It is akin to the objective Harriet Jacobs noted in her autobiography, *Incidents in the Life of a Slave Girl* (1861): of Northerners having a "realizing sense" of the conditions of slavery (1).[14]

Technically a "white" and "black" abduction story, Lydia Maria Child's "Mary French and Susan Easton," first appearing in the *Juvenile Miscellany* in 1834, tells of two young girls—one white, the other (free) black—who are kidnapped and sold as slaves. The girls are introduced as living in an Edenic forest world where they "had joyful times together" (186). Yet this world is idyllic precisely because it is isolated from the larger world of slavery that frames it. In the introduction, we learn that Susan's father "had once been a slave" (186), suggesting the tenuousness between freedom and enslavement, and foreshadowing the dangers lurking just outside their quiet woods. Such dangers are realized and their Eden soon destroyed when a passing "pedler" comes upon the girls at play, kidnaps them, and reveals himself to be a pedler, indeed, one engaged in human trafficking. By showing two children kidnapped, both of whom are legally free and differentiated only by race, Child explores issues of racial insularity and essentialism.

Child ostensibly shows the permeability of race as the pedler cuts and curls Mary's hair, then darkens her face with soot and grease until, as he determines, she is "almost as good-looking a *nigger* as t' other one" (192). In white abduction stories, white characters undergo an experience of slavery, feeling firsthand its violence. Both "black" and enslaved, Mary and Susan suffer beatings and enforced silence. When Mary is sold and insists, "I *am* a white child, and I *was* stolen" (195), she is ignored until—finally—tears reveal her white skin. The transformation out of slavery is thus incumbent upon a transformation out of blackness, as the revelation of Mary's white skin signals the legal inability of holding her as a slave and the plantation owner's intercession to reunite Mary with her family. Susan faces a far different fate. Typically, there is the rescue to freedom and family reunion in white abduction stories, but as "Mary French and Susan Easton" demonstrates, that rescue is usually reserved for white characters. Although Mary asks the plantation owner to help find Susan, the master and his family are unsympathetic to the fact that her friend was a free person, asserting that "*niggers* are used to being slaves" (198).

Moreover, while the French family is reunited, their "house [. . .] a house of joy" (202), Susan's father knows the cost of searching for his daughter: "a free colored man [. . .] was liable to be taken up and sold, or shot through the head for a runaway slave" (201). Initially representing a liminal, separated space, a fantasy of racial equality and freedom unrealized in contemporaneous America, their once-peaceful home has been destroyed, infiltrated by slavery's violence, and ultimately becomes a prison which Mr. Easton realizes he cannot leave. The wider world of America, differentiating and delegating the conditions of one's life according to race, is here a place that rescues white children but abandons black children to anonymous extinction. The concluding paragraph emphasizes this racial contrast, telling readers that while the French family is ensconced in "joy,"

> poor Mr Easton and his wife wept without hope. They never could gain any tidings of their lost child. She is no doubt a slave, compelled to labor [. . .] and whipped whenever she dares to say that she has a right to be free. Yet the only difference between Mary French and Susan Easton is, that the black color could be rubbed off from Mary's skin, while from Susan's it could not. (202)

The white abduction genre is often problematic in its representation of race. One could argue that its focus on the enslavement and recovery of a white character, to the general exclusion of black characters, is an implicit critique of existing racialized hierarchies, or that such presentations ultimately reinstate a sense of racialized hierarchy and accompanying insularity in the white reader. The genre probably accomplishes both. The narrative silencing of Susan speaks of power politics in a racialized world. Child's movement away from Susan's story could thus be argued to replicate the enforced anonymity and dehumanization enacted within slavery. White abduction stories may even establish a hypothetical racial equality, for the white character must equate (or be equated) with a black character, if only for a short time. By extension, the white reader racially identifying with Mary engages in a fiction which resignifies racial signifiers as Mary is recast as black or nonwhite. Such stories remind the reader that there is nothing intrinsically different between people designated as "black" and "white;" what protects the white reader from the exploitation of slavery is only a veil of cultural construction.

Yet as Child shifts racial signifiers by having Mary's face blackened, she eschews essentialism and racial appropriation by asserting the ultimate impenetrability of race: racial signification is not finally exchangeable and blackness remains a stabilized and immovable sign of oppression in antebellum America. In the focus on Mary's plight, particularly her reestablishment as a white child, the boundaries of race are firmly recovered. The central narrative arc of these stories, in which reclaiming whiteness is the means to identity and freedom, may show ways in which the genre contributes to a reader's renewed sense of racialized hierarchies. The fear—indeed, the danger—of the permeability of oppression is at the heart of such narrative race crossings, engendering an intranarrative and, for young white readers, a possible extranarrative relief in reclaimed whiteness and in the expunction of having been "stained" black.[15] The appreciation of racial privilege, which could potentially reinstate a desire for separateness on the part of the white reader, is, however, precisely the opposite of the overtly articulated objective of white abduction stories that ask for an acknowledgment of the unjustness of racial oppression and hierarchies.

Radical abolitionist literature for children that features adult slaves similarly argues the unjustness of racial oppression at the same time that it asserts essential distinctions that establish racial hierarchies. One especially sees this in adult figures of the forgiving and supplicant slave. Ostensibly presented as a moral icon, the forgiving slave responds to everything from name calling to whippings with moral superiority. Reflecting the sentimental and evangelical strains of abolitionism, the image also reiterates nineteenth-century race theories that designated Africans as, among other things, naturally religious (Fredrickson 103–109). One sees such propensity for forgiveness in J. Elizabeth Jones's *The Young Abolitionists* (1848) when a family of escaping slaves promises that "our freedom is all we ask. Though they [white masters] have made us very poor and forced us to work when we were sick, and whipped and beaten us, and sold away our children; yet we wish no harm to come upon *them*. If they will make us free, we will never hurt a hair of their heads, but always stand ready to defend them" (85).

A probable comfort to white readers assured that slaves harbor them no ill will, the forgiving slave (particularly when forgiveness is the central opportunity for agency on the part of enslaved characters) reveals how white-authored abolitionist fiction, including that for adults, often moves away from accounts in many slave narratives. This is evident, for example, in the contrast between Harriet Beecher Stowe's *Uncle Tom's Cabin* (1852) and *Father Henson's Story of His Own Life* (1849), the slave narrative upon which Stowe claimed to have based Uncle Tom's character. In his autobiography, Josiah Henson acknowledges his early identification with his master, but presents that as dishonorable complicity.[16] For Henson, his moral compass is righted when he fights against his master. Henson recounts, for example, how he would steal chickens, pigs, and sheep, "slaughtering [them] for the good of those whom [Master . . .] was starving. I felt good, moral, heroic" (22). By contrast, in Stowe's novel, although the ever-controversial Uncle Tom overturned contemporaneous racial hierarchies when he was cast as a Christlike figure never spiritually capitulating to the demonic Legree, he nonetheless asserts that it would be immoral to steal (even himself) from his master, and reaffirms the influence of Christianity in his duties as a slave: "I jist ask you, Mas'r [Shelby], have I ever broke word to you, or gone contrary to you, 'specially since I was a Christian?" (112).

Tom's faith, his unshakable forgiveness, as well as his overriding concern for Eva and young George, the children of his masters, provide, as George Fredrickson has argued of *Uncle Tom's Cabin*, "the classic expression of romantic racialism" (110). On the one hand, such romantic racialism proposed "that the Negro was the superior race [. . .] because his docility constituted the ultimate in Christian virtue." On the other, it "endorsed the 'child' stereotype of the most sentimental school of proslavery paternalists and [. . .] then rejected slavery itself because it took unfair advantage of the Negro's innocence and good nature" (102). In short, images of romantic racialism called for readers to simultaneously admire and pity self-sacrificing slaves. To encourage such sympathy, radical abolitionists often halved depictions in slave autobiographies that describe the slave as *both* victim and rebel. Frequently quelling possibilities for resistance, these authors often turned the slave into a fully suffering, ever-dutiful, and all-forgiving figure—hence, one easier for white readers to pity. This image also counters the "realizing sense" or appreciation of suffering that Jacobs had called for, replacing it with a hierarchical paradigm that validates the separation between white abolitionist and black slave.

Noah Webster's earlier depiction of slaves who "rise against their cruel masters, and attempt to regain their liberty" (*Little Reader's* 40) is rare in later antebellum children's literature.[17] Commendations of nonviolence were obviously a reflection of hegemonic values touted to children, but in abolitionist texts they also appeared as an interdictory response to the often graphically described violence perpetrated by slaveholders.[18] In contrast to that violence, young abolitionists were urged to "let truth and love / *Our* only weapons be" (*Anti-Slavery Alphabet*). Such mandates for nonviolence were not racially exclusive, and neither white abolitionists nor slaves were sanctioned to take up arms, even in self-defense.[19] Within a context of black agency, this literary absence of slave rebellion may have mollified white fears of race violence, creating a racial fantasy of black passivity in response to Nat Turner's 1831 insurrection. A desire to convert slaveholders may also have contributed to the development of this image. Moreover, while nonviolent images present forgiveness as a commendable moral value, the racial implications of this trope carried wider social significance. Passivity, victimhood, and race became synonymous—and even lauded—but only in black characters.

The racial tropes underlying this image of the "poor slave" are evident in one of the most recognizable visual icons of the abolitionist movement: the chained and kneeling slave whose arms are raised in supplication, at times to an unseen God, at other times to a white benefactor. This image, in varying renditions, appears frequently throughout the series run of *The Slave's Friend*[20] and serves as an intriguing counterpoint to more violent depictions, as in the woodcut accompanying Webster's "Story of the Treatment of African Slaves."[21] As Webster's visual vignette is paused in a moment of violence, the scene evokes the tension of racial oppression in the impending possibility of the white enslaver's assault on the four chained and slightly bent black figures.

In contrast, the image of the supplicant slave sublimates the racially adversarial nature of slavery in the presentation of a pleading slave and white savior. For example, a kneeling black woman, raising her chained arms to a white woman standing above her, ac-

FIGURE 1.1. *Illustration from* The Little Reader's Assistant *by Noah Webster. Courtesy of the Library of Congress.*

FIGURE 1.2. *"Am I Not a Woman and a Sister?" from* The Slave's Friend *(1838). Courtesy of American Antiquarian Society.*

companied by the inscription "Am I Not a Woman and a Sister?"—and another image of the time, of a male slave, similarly posed and asking "Am I Not a Man and a Brother?"—were ubiquitous icons for the abolitionist movement at large, and used for both adult and child audiences.[22] Eliciting the requisite pity of white audiences, the kneeling slave simultaneously suggests a direly felt request and consequent gratitude. Yet in its visual encouragement of abolitionism and emancipation, the icon also provided an indelible image that reaffirmed racial hierarchies, even—one could argue—those articulated as a racialized chain of being. In positioning the invitation (and necessity) for white aid, this tableau sets up a paradigm of dichotomous representations of race: of black helplessness and white agency, black piteousness and white heroism. Moreover, this representation of black passivity visually reaffirms other problematic radical abolitionist arguments: while the slave figure may be shown here as physically incapable of resistance, a young nineteenth-century reader might easily connect this to a larger framework of racialized tropes—that is, of slaves having a "peaceable disposition" (M. Thompson 119–120) or being somehow constitutionally unwilling or too emotionally weak to offer resistance. It is an image slave narratives would repeatedly reject.

The icon of the supplicant slave who is unable to act or fight on her or his behalf invites the possibilities of a white intercessor's heroic intervention. The call for racial equality—"Am I Not a Woman and a Sister?"—is thus undercut by the visual establishment of racialized hierarchy; as critic Paul Edwards has noted elsewhere, "black people were expected to be acted upon rather than take the lead themselves, and for some of the supporters of abolition, charity could be an act of self-gratification" ("Three" 195). In some ways—minus the visual chains and verbal request for recognition—this representation sets up a discomfortingly parallel image of proslavery plantation novels: of white benefactor (that is, the master) and grateful, black slave.

The centrality of white power is further evidenced in abolitionist texts where a white narrator, functioning as a fictional amanuensis, replaces black voices by recounting stories of slavery. Reminiscent of the problematic interference of the white point of view in early narratives which were dictated to or written by white abolitionists,[23] racial control in these radical abolitionist texts is at times heightened by accompanying depictions of white heroism. In Jones's *The Young Abolitionists*, for example, white, middle-class Mrs. Selden functions as a type of amanuensis as she tells her children stories about slavery. Later she evinces her heroism by protecting a family of escaping slaves. Using only the power of her "stately bearing and contemptuous tone" (defined, one suspects, by her racial and class status), she confronts a pursuing slave hunter so effectively that he "cowered" before her (89).[24] Like the heroic figure on the abolitionist emblem, Mrs. Selden has effectively saved the slaves, raising them up from their chains and helping them to freedom.

While radical abolitionists largely focused on representations of the forgiving and supplicant slave when depicting adults, the rebellious slave still found some expression, although certainly not as much. For example, although *Uncle Tom's Cabin* offers a quintessential example of romantic racialism, *Pictures and Stories from "Uncle Tom's Cabin"* (1853), written specifically for children, is in some ways more radical than its adult counterpart. Stowe never intended for *Uncle Tom's Cabin* to be read exclusively by adults. Indeed, in the conclusion of the serialized version of the novel, she addressed the children in her audience, offering them her "warmest love" and encouraging them to follow "the sweet example of little Eva" (*Uncle Tom's Cabin*, *National Era*, 1 April 1852).[25] Yet, Stowe must have believed children would benefit from a version of the novel tailored specifically for them because a year later *Pictures and Stories from "Uncle Tom's Cabin"* was published for young readers.[26]

Moving between prose and poetry, *Pictures and Stories from "Uncle Tom's Cabin"* follows the two central stories of Stowe's original novel: the plight of Eliza and her family as they escape to freedom and Tom's journey further south until he dies at the hands of the sadistic Simon Legree. As one might expect, plotlines which describe sexual exploitation are eliminated, and to strengthen young readers' interest, focus is tightened on the children: Harry, Eliza's young son; Eva, the reformer child and daughter of Master St. Clare; and Topsy, a slave whom Eva teaches "to be good" (26). Also, presumably for children's benefit (and unlike many issues of *The Slave's Friend*), violent scenes are tempered: Legree's beatings of Tom are here related offstage.

Tom's character remains essentially unchanged, yet in this much-abbreviated edition (of thirty-two pages, including illustrations), many racialized descriptions found in the original *Uncle Tom's Cabin*—of Africans as naturally sensual (253), domestic (162), timid (162, 165), childlike (135), and imitative (480)—have been taken out. Further, in excising descriptions and dialogue of slave traders, the children's version gives more narrative focus and authority to enslaved characters. For example, although in *Uncle Tom's Cabin*, Mrs. Shelby orders several slaves to aid Eliza by waylaying pursuing slave traders, in the children's version, the slaves "did what they could to detain the trader" (7–8) without the intercession of Mrs. Shelby, thus emphasizing their own initiative and rebellion. Through such seemingly slight narrative shifts and editing, *Pictures and Stories from "Uncle Tom's Cabin"* reframes Stowe's earlier novel to minimize racialized stereotyping and, at least to some degree, to highlight black agency.

More direct representations of the rebellious slave can be found in the short-lived *The Youth's Emancipator* (1842–1843), a four-page monthly initially published by the Executive Committee of the Oberlin Youth's Anti-Slavery Society.[27] An important center of social reform and abolitionism, Oberlin College admitted black and female students. The radical nature of *The Youth's Emancipator* reflects the influence of Oberlin's advocacy, particularly in its objective to inculcate abolitionist sentiment in youth and to present black-authored accounts that evoke representations of slave narratives. Although *The Youth's Emancipator* offers its share of descriptions of the "poor slave," it also presents slaves as active and effective opponents of slavery, providing young readers with accounts of those who have escaped, outwitted, and rebelled against their masters.

Featuring several excerpts of narratives and testimonies "purportedly" (Murphy 520) by former slaves, the magazine reasserts the centrality of the slave's voice and point of view and the authorship of his own story. In the magazine's first issue, for example, "Escape from Bondage in the State of New York" (1842) presents the story of a "middle-aged colored man [. . .] just as he wrote it" of his life in, and then his escape from, slavery (1). Capturing the rebellious tone often found in slave narratives, this account describes the narrator's confrontation with his master:

> having endured so much, I was resolved not to submit to any more abuse from him, and striking my spade in the ground, ordered him not to swear at me or touch me, and when he saw my firm and resolute stand, he turned and went into the house, and I followed, telling him that I never would do any more outdoor work for him as long as I lived. (2)

The Youth's Emancipator even argues the necessity for violence in the account of another man who had been caught while attempting an escape, then, as he recounts, "when I saw that he [the slave catcher] had hold of me, I wrestled from him, and then striking him in the face, he fell back into the stream. I then run for the woods." Unaccompanied by platitudes against violence, this act effects his freedom, for the man is then able to elude those who hunt him and arrive "in the land of freedom in safety" ("History of a Fugitive").

Unlike prescriptions to nonviolence in much Garrisonian abolitionist literature, these testimonies show not only the practical necessity of violence, but also the cathartic exuberance of besting one's adversary. In response to the question, "Have the Negros Any Minds?" (1842), and a slaver's anticipated response that "no [. . .] they were never made to be any thing else but slaves—they're a lower class of beings than white men," young readers are presented the "anecdote" of Sam who, not "provided with necessary food, [. . .] was in the habit of stealing—sometimes from his own master." Here, Sam has created a world centrally abolitionist in its struggle against the master's control. When a master "ingeniously" plots to catch Sam by placing a wolf trap in a hogshead, he unknowingly sets himself up against an adversary "more cautious than himself, and quite as ingenious."

Far from the forgiving or supplicant slave, Sam anticipates the master's plan and devises a counterattack. Moving the trap to the front of the smokehouse, Sam begins yelling as if he has been caught in it, and then stands back to watch while the master races in and, instead of seeing his success, "steps—with his naked foot—into the fatal trap." Like Brer Rabbit taunting Brer Bear, Sam then gloats as he "stopped only to give a ha! ha! with a word of counsel about catching a nigger in a '*bar*-trap,' and bade him good night." The narrator's ensuing critique of Sam seems both requisite and tepid, his praise far more genuine: "now it is not pretended that Sam did right—this is not the point now in hand; but think you that his master doubted that negros had minds?"

While the trope of submissive black slave and active white abolitionist constructed in much white-authored abolitionist fiction does not reveal real ways in which both free and enslaved blacks were engaged in abolitionist advocacy, in *The Youth's Emancipator*, the depiction of black agency broadens the frequently represented compass of antislavery to include black abolitionists. Not often recounted as readily as white abolitionist history, a long record of effective black activism and abolition nonetheless exists. Although often excluded from membership in white antislavery organizations, by the end of the eighteenth century, free blacks had organized freestanding mutual aid societies and activist churches on their own. Aiding escaping slaves through such organizations as the New York Vigilance Committee, petitioning the government for emancipation, and establishing abolitionist societies, including juvenile antislavery societies, black activists worked within black as well as white abolitionist communities to forward their goals.[28] Organized against slavery, they also sought to redress racial inequity; when federal and state legislation made public schools accessible to white students but excluded nonwhites, for example, black activists funded schools for black children, principally under the auspices of black churches.[29] Not depending on white abolitionists to speak for them, free blacks published their own testimonies, antislavery pamphlets, novels, and newspapers—the *Freedom's Journal* (1827) being the first but certainly not the last black-authored newspaper with a nationwide subscription base.[30]

Although depictions of black activists and rebellious slaves can be found in the corpus of radical abolitionist children's literature, they are far outnumbered by those of white agency and black submissiveness. It was a model meant to inspire young, white readers to active abolitionism, yet it was also one that suppressed representations of black activism and narratively excluded young, black readers from any agency of their own. Moreover, its inherent assertion of racial hierarchy made it a malleable image that would be shared by whites on either side of slavery's ideological divide.

MODERATE ABOLITIONIST LITERATURE

In a spectrum moving from radical to conservative abolition, the position of moderate as a mediation point between the two is obvious. Yet, it has in some ways more difficult boundaries to determine, particularly because moderate abolitionist texts for children were an often strange amalgam that vilified slavery and mitigated the scope of abolitionist inquiry. Moderate abolitionist literature was generally published by more mainstream presses and reached wider, less abolitionist audiences than did works written by radical abolitionists. Moderate abolitionists argued against slavery, but established parameters of discussion which excluded central elements of the radical abolitionist argument. For example, while radical abolitionist children's literature often foregrounded the reformer child as a model for abolitionist activity and attempted to engender reader sympathy by focusing on the plight of enslaved children and encouraging imaginative transference, moderate abolitionist literature generally eschewed such calls for both identification and activism. Instead, it offered a more distanced presentation of slavery for the young reader, both geographically and emotionally.

One of the most prolific and popular writers of his time, Samuel Goodrich exemplifies central elements of moderate abolitionism for children. Author and editor of over a hundred books, his reach was encompassing, both in terms of audience and genre. Particularly in "Peter Parley," his fictional author/narrator (and by whose name he became most well known), Goodrich offered a kindly avuncular white character who conversationally addresses young readers, telling them of adventures against a backdrop of ostensible lessons in history and geography.[31] Firmly rooted in assertions of the ideological, cultural, moral, and even genetic superiority of white Protestant Americans, Goodrich's books provided glimpses of a larger world while offering young white readers a ptolemaic assurance of their preeminent cultural, racial, and religious place within it.

A range of "other" people come in for Parley's (or Goodrich's) disapprobation: South American Indians are described as "ignorant and degraded" (*Tales of Peter Parley about America* 51), Arabs as "savage" (*Tales of Peter Parley about Africa* 96), and the Chinese as "ignorant and superstitious" (*Tales of Peter Parley about Asia* 55). Yet, as Daniel Roselle and Donnarae MacCann have each pointed out, it was not especially for those biases that Goodrich was criticized by his contemporaries (Roselle 76; MacCann, *White Supremacy* 67). Instead, it was his at times conflicted stance on slavery that caught the attention of critics. Proslavery Southerners argued that *Peter Parley* books "insult[ed] and misrepresent[ed] the institutions of the South," and denounced Goodrich who had "made large fortunes by the publication of [his . . .] Anti-Slavery School Books" (Heriott 651). That said, there was also much in Goodrich's oeuvre that could consternate radical abolitionists.[32]

Some of Goodrich's descriptions of African slavery echo unwavering denunciations made by radical abolitionists. One sees this, for example, in *The Tales of Peter Parley about Africa* (1830), where Goodrich describes how on that continent:

> The negroes [. . .] are constantly hunted [and . . .] torn from their homes, separated from their friends and families, and carried away into distant countries.
>
> There, deprived of their liberty, they labor for the luxury [. . .] of rich persons, who buy them. They die in a land of exile, and never know what becomes of their children or their friends, whether they are living or dead, happy or unhappy. (97–98)

In *Lights and Shadows of African History* (1844), a text for older children,[33] the description of the Middle Passage is similar to ones found in Cugoano's and Equiano's narratives, as well as in radical abolitionist texts such as Webster's "Story of the Treatment of African Slaves":

> Nothing in the history of human suffering can surpass the horrors of what is called the "Middle Passage," or the transportation of the slaves across the Atlantic. The miserable beings are crowded like cattle into the hold of the ship, in such numbers that a large portion of them necessarily die [. . .] by a want of ventilation. (290)

Reading such unequivocal statements—that "nothing in the history of human suffering can surpass the horrors" of the Middle Passage—one might understandably question these texts as moderate rather than radical. What sets Goodrich apart from radical abolitionists here—and what typifies moderate abolitionist writers—is denouncing slavery as cruel, but most often relegating depictions of those cruelties to sites *outside* the United States. As Ruth Elson has argued of such geographies, their abolitionist sentiment "is aimed not against slavery itself but against the international slave trade" (88), and since Congress had outlawed the importation of slaves in 1808, this focus on the international slave trade, to the exclusion of abuses within the United States, implicitly absolved Americans from slavery's violence (Murray 45). Thus, while the description above—of slaves transported to "distant countries" where they never know "what becomes of their children or their friends"—may evoke the sense of irrecoverable loss that one finds at the end of Child's "Mary French and Susan Easton," it also distances the reader's association with (or felt responsibility for) that loss by removing it from an American context. The reference to slaves being transported to "distant countries," for example, is never defined and any allusion to the United States is muted at best. Moreover, as is typical in moderate abolitionist children's literature, descriptions of slavery remain generalized, the author careful not to personalize enslaved individuals with whom the reader might too closely sympathize.

By confining denunciations of slavery to places outside the United States, moderate abolitionist writers also exploit national and ethnocentric notions of "otherness." Of necessity, descriptions of the Middle Passage implicate non-Africans as enslavers who make the ocean journey and bring those kidnapped to other continents. Yet even here, moderate abolitionists make every attempt to avoid implicating the United States in the slave trade. In *Lights and Shadows of African History*, for example, the Portuguese, Spaniards, English, and French are criticized for their role in the international slave trade. By contrast, the role of the United States regarding slavery is valorized, and readers learn that "the first objection to the slave-trade was made by South Carolina" (290) and the "United States [. . .] was the first power that abolished the foreign slave trade" (294). Thus, at the same time that there were as many as two and a half million people classified as the "slave population" in the United States (Kolchin 991), this history implies that the 1808 law eradicated America's involvement in slavery.

In moderate abolitionist texts, once the scene moves to the United States—as it must in *The Tales of Peter Parley about America* (1827)—slavery's effects are often mitigated. Although slavery in Africa is condemned as "inhuman and revolting" (*Lights and Shadows* 287), in America its conditions are considerably changed. Radical abolitionists would tell children that even slaves in ostensibly comfortable situations "never had one happy hour, or minute [. . . . because slavery] still [. . .] is a yoke and it *galls*" ("Rose" 11). Moderate abolitionist writers, by contrast, assert that a slave's state depends on his specific condition of slavery and that slaves can be "very happy" (48) with the right master. In *The Tales of Peter Parley about America*, for example, Goodrich (as Parley) recounts a friend's report of a visit to Charleston where he saw "negroes, men, women, and children, sold at public auction, as we sell goods" (47). Initially evoking images of slave narratives, Goodrich acknowledges that some slaves "who have cruel masters are wretched indeed," but also offers the palliative that "some of the negroes, who happen to have kind masters, are *very* happy" (48, emphasis added).

This contrast in the conditions of slavery is visually reinforced, as well. When the scene of slavery is in Africa—as in *The Tales of Peter Parley about Africa*—the cruelty of slavery is unambiguous in a woodcut showing white men forcibly taking children away from parents. When the setting shifts to America—as in *The Tales of Peter Parley about America*—Goodrich describes how in Cuba "negroes [. . . .] seemed to be very gay in their disposition, and generally happy. They are very fond of dancing" (48–49). Obfuscating whether the "negroes" are free or slave (slavery was not abolished in Cuba until the latter half of the century), he also directs readers to an accompanying woodcut, telling them, "here is a picture of negroes dancing" (49). Showing black characters playing musical instruments and dancing, the woodcut presents a joyful scene of leisure and liberation. The narrative proximity of this woodcut to Goodrich's assertion (one page earlier) that some slaves in the United States are "very happy" ultimately undercuts his criticism of the conditions of slavery under "cruel masters" and leaves the young reader with an overall visual and verbal assurance that slaves can lead quite happy lives.

Goodrich's work, taken as a whole, provides an intriguing example of conflicted images of abolitionist sentiment. Declaring that "every good person should condemn [slavery . . .] and use his efforts [. . .] to hasten the time, when there shall be no slavery in any land," Goodrich is careful to encourage, rather than insult, slave owners (a not uncommon practice for abolitionists) by virtually absolving them from responsibility: "No doubt, many good people [. . .] have slaves. But slavery is a bad system" (*Tales of Peter Parley about Africa* 112). Indeed, countering radical abolitionist arguments for emancipation that depict industrious blacks, Africans are described as exhibiting "constitutional indolence [. . .] which nothing but the most extreme terror can overcome" in *Lights and Shadows of African History* (307).

Such mixed messages continue in Goodrich's oeuvre. In *The Tales of Peter Parley about Africa*, readers are cautioned against racial discrimination: "people who treat free Negroes with harshness, unkindness, or inhumanity, are just as much to blame, as if they treated white people so. The color of the skin makes no difference. The obligation is universal, to do to another, as you would have another do to you" (113). Yet, as a collection, Goodrich's geographies unmistakably delineate people, then hierarchically order them according to racial classifications. In *The World and Its Inhabitants* (1845), for example, where race studies of crania size are recounted, readers are told that "the capacity of the cranium [is . . .] an index of intellectual power" (210). Of the five races studied, readers are assured that the "Caucasian variety, as a whole, stands greatly above all the rest" (208) and has "exhibited the moral and intellectual powers of human nature in their highest degree of perfection" (239). "Ethiopians," by contrast, rank "decidedly lowest in the intellectual scale" (207). In *Manners and Customs of the Principal Nations of the Globe* (1845), "the lead-

FIGURE 1.3. *Illustration from* The Tales of Peter Parley about Africa *(1830) by S. G. Goodrich. Courtesy of the Rare Book Collection, The University of North Carolina at Charlotte Library.*

FIGURE 1.4. *Illustration from* The Tales of Peter Parley about America *by S. G. Goodrich. Second Edition. Boston: S. G. Goodrich, 1829. Courtesy of American Antiquarian Society.*

ing features of the negro character" are defined as "improvidence, gentleness, and thoughtless gaiety" (287). In *Lights and Shadows of African History*, readers are instructed that "negroes [are] a weak and harmless race" (6) and that "the mass of its [Africa's] inhabitants have ever been shrouded in intellectual and moral darkness" (5–6). Thus while condemning racial justifications of slavery that "attempt to excuse this mean and dastardly conduct [of kidnapping

Africans], by representing them as brutes, rather than men" (*Tales of Peter Parley about Africa* 124), Goodrich's geographies nonetheless do just the opposite.[34]

Moderate abolitionist texts offer no model for young readers to engage in abolition. Instead, the reader's personal responsibility regarding slavery is often mitigated, since the texts define the worst abuses of slavery as those that occur offshore and that are sanctioned by foreign governments. By limiting the scope of inquiry, moderate abolitionist texts tempered the criticism of slavery and the possibility of reader engagement and activism, producing an often odd mix of criticism and palliative. Goodrich expressed such a blend of criticism and reticence when he wrote of his abolitionist views. Admitting that "slavery kicks against the law and the Constitution," he also absolved himself from political radicalism:

> We are not abolitionists, in that offensive sense [. . . .] We make no war on slavery where it is established. [. . .] Even if we hope for its gradual extinction, we hold that the best way is to commit it to the conscience, the wisdom and experience of those who are alone qualified to deal with it. . . . we make a broad distinction between constitutional and unconstitutional slavery [. . . .] We war not against slaveholders, but slave extensionists. (*New York Evening Post*, 15 October 1856, qtd in Roselle 139–140)

Presenting an antislavery message that was "offensive" to slavery advocates while falling short of Garrison's uncompromising commitment not to use moderation in the cause of emancipation, Goodrich's oeuvre demonstrates moderate abolitionism in that he "sought the middle ground and a possible compromise" (Roselle 139).

CONSERVATIVE ABOLITIONIST LITERATURE

Perhaps one of the clearest expressions of conservative abolition came in 1828 from Nathaniel Willis, influential editor of *The Youth's Companion*:

> All the pious people in the land [. . .] wish to make the slaves free; and are very sorry that their fathers ever put the yoke of bondage upon them. But it is not easy to set them free. They are unfit to take care of themselves and their families; many of them are very wicked; and if one million and a half should be made their masters at once, it would produce great confusion and misery in the

> country. Strange as it must seem, no doubt it is true, that mercy to the colored people themselves requires, that they should *for the present* continue as they are. But their masters, and the governments of the States, are certainly under every obligation to treat them with kindness, to give them literary and religious instruction, and to take every possible measure to give them their liberty in a gradual way. (Editorial 18 July 1828)

Opposed to radical antislavery activists, conservative abolitionists called for manumission only at a gradual if not glacial pace, and even that call was often tepid at best. Moreover, the personal accountability for racial oppression that stood at the heart of the radical abolitionist position is absent here, as, for example, Willis places the responsibility for "the yoke of bondage" upon ancestors. Indeed, in their racist depictions of Africans (without the influence of white culture) as dangerous and debased, conservative abolitionists often blamed slavery on the slaves themselves by portraying them as resistant to the possibilities of emancipation due to their own "wicked[ness]" and "unfit[ness]" for freedom.

Unlike moderates, conservative abolitionists focused on slavery within the United States, but their central concern was the perceived danger posed to white Americans in the event of mass emancipation. Although conservative abolitionists acknowledged slavery as a "great evil," that evil seemed only theoretical in the face of a greater one—the image of dangerous freed slaves—hence the conservative goal to "set the blacks free, and yet prevent their being injurious to the community" (Willis, Editorial 25 July 1828). Navigating between these conflicting views—of the injustice of slavery but the fear of the freed black—conservative abolitionists often argued for "prudent" emancipation following, as Willis proposes here, the slave's tutelage (Editorial 25 July). Thus for conservatives, freedom was dependent upon the slave's inculcation of white American values and, implicitly, upon the expulsion of specifically African attributes as defined in contemporaneous race theories.

Under this rubric, white activism involved educating slaves, rather than liberating them. In this way, conservative abolitionists often echoed slavery advocates in their claim that slavery could function as a potentially benevolent paternalism, a "mercy" that could benefit an otherwise uncivilized people. Here, the idealized master-slave relationship echoes proslavery assertions of attachment marked by paternal duty (on the part of the master) and loyalty (on behalf of the slave). Revealing the ways that pro- and antislavery ideologies sometimes shared the same racial perspectives, conservative abolitionist paradigms revised the white aid/supplicant slave model of radical abolitionists, transforming it to one in which slaves rise to freedom only under the tutelage of white masters. In the conflicted representations of conservative abolitionism, enslaved protagonists thus often appear as both heroic individuals *and* grateful slaves.

Two popular novels by important white authors of the time, *Hatchie, the Guardian Slave* (1853) by William Taylor Adams (writing under the name Warren T. Ashton, but best known by his pseudonym Oliver Optic) and John Townsend Trowbridge's *Cudjo's Cave* (1864), in different ways exemplify the ideology and conflicted presentations of slavery by conservative abolitionists. On the one hand, both novels present young readers with intelligent and powerful slaves as hero-protagonists who rebel against white oppressors. In this regard, these texts would hardly seem to tout "conservative" abolition, but instead evoke thoughtful and rebellious protagonists akin to representations in slave narratives. In fictional terms, these heroes seem similar to depictions in black-authored abolitionist novels like Frederick Douglass's protagonist in *The Heroic Slave* (1853), a novel for adults. Douglass's Madison Washington was fashioned after an actual man of the same name who, with a minimum of violence, commandeered an American slave ship in 1841, then redirected it to Nassau, where he and the ship's other slaves were given their freedom. Washington became, as critic William Andrews has pointed out, "a black revolutionary whom white Americans could admire [. . . . For] Douglass [. . . he was] a model of black militancy, aggressive in pursuit of his rights, but self-controlled in his use of violence" (Introduction 12).

Such a balance of aggression and self-control is central in depictions of the black hero-protagonists in *Hatchie, the Guardian Slave* and *Cudjo's Cave*. Both Adams and Trowbridge focus on slavery in the United States (unlike most moderate abolitionists) and provide stories which allow for an exploration of slaves' "fitness" for freedom. Countering popular race theories, their main slave characters are heroes who demonstrate their intellectual and physical superiority over whites. These are novels which, in this general sense, argue quite clearly for abolition, assuaging potential white anxieties by demonstrating the readiness of these slaves for emancipation.

On the other hand, while black-authored abolitionist novels of the 1850s, like Douglass's *The Heroic Slave* or William Wells Brown's *Clotel* (1853), remain focused on the dangers of white oppression,[35] both Adams's and Trowbridge's novels ultimately reassure their readers of the beneficial impact of slavery upon the slave. Their abolitionist messages are thus inherently conflicted, particularly in the ways they contain their respective black heroes. Underlying *Hatchie, the Guardian Slave* is a reluctance to accept the personal and social power of its protagonist in a free world; and the fantasy of black power is, in the end, sharply controlled. By contrast, Trowbridge allows his heroic slave freedom at the close of *Cudjo's Cave*, but underpinning that freedom is an assurance to readers that slavery must serve as a necessary apprenticeship for the African's movement into American free society, and that America is better off with some slaves dead than free. It is a political vision that argues simultaneously for and against abolition.

In *Hatchie, the Guardian Slave*, Adams weaves a tale of stolen wills, kidnappings, blackmail, disguises, and near murders. The main plotline follows the trials of the recently orphaned plantation heiress Emily Dumont, whose uncle attempts to disinherit her by forging a will that erroneously defines her not only as illegitimate, but also as a quadroon and hence a slave. In melodramatic fashion, Emily is variously kidnapped and freed as her uncle's plans to disinherit her are complicated by a duplicitous lawyer's schemes to marry her and, if need be, buy her as a slave in order to possess her. Although Emily's honorable suitor is a captain in the military, he is generally ineffective, and her repeated rescuing falls to the Dumont's loyal slave and the novel's hero, Hatchie.

The narrative potential for such a plotline to explore the condition and vulnerabilities of enslaved women is palpable, particularly when the disreputable lawyer Maxwell presents a bill of sale which, as he tells Emily, "gives me an undeniable right to your person" (152). Evoking the ideological possibilities of white abduction stories like Child's "Mary French and Susan Easton," Emily realizes that "she had seen slave-girls as fair and white as herself. She had heard of those who, with scarcely a drop of negro blood in their veins, were educated to pander to the appetite of depravity. She had seen them in the streets of New Orleans, in no manner differing in appearance from the best-born ladies" (151–152). Yet Emily's reflections offer no real call for the reader to imagine the unjust plight of enslaved women; she—and Adams—view the vulnerability of enslaved black women only as a reference point for Emily's situation.

Although slavery may be detestable for the white Emily who suffers "the odium of having been a slave" (77), that is not the case for Hatchie, who sees no disgrace in his enslavement. Just the opposite. The narrator does acknowledge that "the general condition of negro slaves at the South is the most degraded in which humanity can exist," but, noting that "there are some exceptions to the rule" (81), focuses on the Dumonts, who "loved even [their . . .] slaves" (111), especially Hatchie, whom Emily "regarded more as a friend than a slave" (44). Indeed, Hatchie's depiction shatters radical abolitionist representations of the victimized or supplicant slave. The rhetorical rumination "alas! what could a slave do against the powerful machinations of such a villain as Maxwell?" (282) becomes ironic in a novel in which a slave is the active hero, an omniscient figure who repeatedly overhears and foils nefarious plots. Upsetting race hierarchies and countering conservative claims, like those of Willis that slaves are debased and "unfit" for freedom, Hatchie displays not only "an intelligence far superior to his condition" (81), but one also far superior to other characters. Hatchie knows what the others do not and when he enlists the aid of sympathetic whites, they both immediately trust him and follow his direction.

Facing the banalities of cruel men, Hatchie always retains his composure in heroic form. When, for example, the white lawyer Maxwell excoriates Hatchie as a "craven! woolly-headed coward!" Hatchie's response is both measured and threatening: "be calm, Mr. Maxwell; do not waste your last moments in idle invectives" (177). Hatchie is a man with "great muscular power and skill" (211), and in his quest to save Emily he uses not only physical strength, but everything from knives to pistols. Unlike George Harris in *Uncle Tom's Cabin*, Hatchie never relents or forgives his adversaries, and he even enacts a feigned lynching of Maxwell. In this role reversal of established racial hierarchies, he tells the lawyer, "you are entirely in my power" (176), then secures a noose around Maxwell's neck, pulling the rope "gently at first, but gradually increasing the pressure upon the prisoner's throat."[36] Maxwell soon capitulates: "the

FIGURE 1.5. *Illustration from* Hatchie, the Guardian Slave *(1853) by William T. Adams [W. T. Ashton, pseud.]. Boston: B. B. Mussey and R. B. Fitts. Courtesy of American Antiquarian Society.*

slow torture was too much for the attorney's fortitude" (178), and he answers Hatchie's questions.

Moving far afield from Garrisonian radical abolitionists who eschewed violence because it was a sign of degradation (both in terms of the perpetrator's depravity and the recipient's pain), as an adventure novel *Hatchie, the Guardian Slave* revels in violence. Suspense, which is predicated upon imminent threat, exploits violence as titillating, as in this scene where Hatchie uses a threatened lynching as lugubrious "slow torture." In a genre that mandates an active, physical hero and portrays violence as a means of just retribution, personal catharsis, and a sign of manhood, this adventure lauds Hatchie's full scope of agency and controlled violence. Diametrically opposed to the supplicant slave figure, Hatchie does not need the aid of white intercessors; rather, they—particularly Emily and her fiancé—need his aid.

Yet while Hatchie's intelligence and agency appear to undercut racial tropes, he is, after all, not full African, but instead a "mulatto." In nineteenth-century racial paradigms, whites, or Anglo-Saxons, were defined as having "a spirit of individual enterprise and resourcefulness, and a capacity for practical and reasonable behavior" (Fredrickson 98). In *Uncle Tom's Cabin*, for example, when George Harris (also mulatto) defends his family against the assault of slave hunters, Stowe ascribes his physical and emotional heroism to his white ancestry, for it was from that "he had inherited a set of fine European features, and a high, indomitable spirit" (182). The figure of the mulatto was also often used in abolitionist texts as a way to engage the empathy of white readers as well as their ire—even if only from a racist standpoint of defining who should or should not be enslaved. In Adams's novel, although the injustice of Emily's enslavement is based on the fact that she is white, Hatchie's status as mulatto engenders no concern about his enslavement; even in Emily's racist terms, that white admixture of blood does not signal his slavery as unjust. Instead, Hatchie's status as mulatto serves to explain his heroism, ultimately reinstating contemporaneous race theories that privileged Caucasians.

The problematic characterization of Hatchie is highlighted by its contrast with Douglass's heroic Washington. In *The Heroic Slave*, after the ship's captain has been killed and Washington takes command of the ship, Douglass has him say to the white crew members, "I have complete command of this vessel. All resistance to my authority will be in vain" (67). Ironically, while Adams's hero has similar power over the white lawyer Maxwell—as when he tells him "you are entirely in my power" (176)—Hatchie never argues for his freedom, any desire for which he has long since sublimated in order to serve Emily. When one of Hatchie's aides tells him, "I hope soon to meet you in the land of liberty," Hatchie responds, "I shall never leave my mistress. [. . .] I feel that I was sent into the world for no other purpose than to protect and serve her. Liberty away from her has no charms for me" (112–113).[37] Hatchie's ultimate objective is thus not to secure his own freedom, but Emily's, and as he reinstates her race, legitimacy, fortune, and birthright as mistress of Bellevue, Hatchie is not merely "guardian slave" to his white mistress, but more broadly to the institution of slavery itself.

One has in Hatchie a character who would answer Nathaniel Willis's concerns about the effects of emancipation. Hatchie is a slave clearly "fit" for freedom. Yet he is also one who eschews freedom in favor of faithful service as his raison d'être. In the end, William Taylor Adams's presentation is a keenly conflicted one. He presents an enslaved character one would not meet in proslavery texts: Hatchie is the unqualified hero of the novel, evincing superior intellect and ability as he successfully battles villainous whites. Yet, at the same time, Adams sharply contains Hatchie's power. When lawyer Maxwell attempts to remind Hatchie of his place in a slave society, telling him, "your master—," Hatchie evades such control by correcting him: "I have no master." Yet he immediately redefines himself as a slave (and a willing one), telling Maxwell, "Miss Emily is my mistress" (179). Thus the slave's power is both played out against the cruel lawyer, as if a catharsis of slave rebellion against white oppressors, then contained in a narrative paradigm that defines slavery as an honorable alliance between mistress and slave.

One might suppose it is precisely because of Hatchie's power that Adams contains him as a willing and loyal slave. The depiction of a freed slave punishing white oppressors both radically rescripts racial hierarchies and evokes images of the "Nat" slave stereotype, which haunted white imaginations following Turner's rebellion in 1831.[38] Instead, Adams allows Hatchie nearly unmitigated agency in achieving his goals, then assures readers that he acts only to defend slavery itself. The novel becomes, in some ways, a half fulfillment of the declarations of slaves in Jones's *The Young Abolitionists*; in that radical abolitionist novel, escaping slaves calm potential fears by assuring the protagonist (and young, white readers) that "if [masters . . .] will make us free, we will never hurt a hair of their heads, but always stand ready to defend them." While those slave characters affirm that "our freedom is all we ask" (85), in *Hatchie, the Guardian Slave* the protagonist slave does not even ask—or desire—to be freed from slavery.

In *Cudjo's Cave*, John Townsend Trowbridge also offers readers a strong, intelligent hero-slave, but in contrast to Hatchie, Trowbridge's Pomp gains his freedom by the novel's close. Yet Trowbridge tightly defines emancipation here, and in this novel "appropriated by children" (Bingham and Scholt 199), when white Quaker schoolmaster Penn Hapgood is assaulted by secessionists and brought to the eponymous "Cudjo's Cave" to recuperate, the labyrinthine plot allows Trowbridge an opportunity to articulate a vision of conservative abolitionism. More specifically, he sets up a spectrum of three slave types to argue who should—and should not—be allowed freedom.

As the novel begins, readers meet Toby, who had once been a slave of the Villars family but is now their freed servant. A minstrel figure, his self-importance punctured by exaggerated dialect and physicality, Toby is the "faithful black" (77) who consoles readers worried that emancipation "would produce great confusion and misery" (Willis, Editorial 18 July). He seems an echo of the supplicant slave, forever grateful to whites who have aided him. At the close of the novel, for example, Toby gives his wages to the impoverished Villars, but refuses their gratitude: "If you's gwine to tank anybody, ye better jes' tink and tank yersef! Who gib ol' Toby his freedom, an' den 'pose to pay him wages? Reckon if 't hadn't been fur dat, massa, I neber should hab de bressed chance to do dis yer little ting fur de family!" (495). Like Adams's Hatchie, Toby reaffirms kindly relations between slave and master. Unlike Hatchie, Toby never takes violent action against white oppressors and so becomes a more likely literary candidate for freedom; here, he provides white readers the comforting promise that if only they will pay wages, their slave/servants will remain loyal and even gratefully return those wages when needed by "massa."

With Toby as his only frame of reference, the sick and dazed Penn mistakes the two black men who have helped him for the Villars's servant, thinking "there seemed to be two Tobys, one good and the other evil" (113). When Penn later regains full consciousness, he describes the "twin Tobys" as unequivocal opposites:

> What a contrast between the two! There was Toby the good, otherwise called Pomp, dignified, erect, of noble features; while before him cringed and grimaced Toby the Malign, alias Cudjo, ugly, deformed, with immensely long arms, short bow legs resembling a parenthesis, a body like a frog's, and the countenance of an ape. (118)

That the three men are mistaken as one figuratively situates them as three parts of a single whole. With Toby as the median point, Pomp, Toby, and Cudjo form an evolutionary spectrum that provides Trowbridge an opportunity to present a conservative abolitionist argument that both critiques and supports slavery. The tri-persona also encapsulates central racial tropes of the African/slave as philosopher, clown, savage; or similarly, hero, fool, animal.

More polemical in its overt antislavery statements than *Hatchie, the Guardian Slave*, *Cudjo's Cave* ostensibly upsets racial hierarchies by depicting Pomp as an intelligent, heroic figure. He is, as critic Dorothy Broderick has pointed out, the "superspecimen" (110) in intellect, reason, and physicality. Portrayed as a figure of "imposing stature [. . . .], magnificently proportioned, [. . .] and black as ebony" (Trowbridge 117), he is "proud" (118), with "features lighted up with intelligence and sympathy" (120). Others recognize his authority as well, and white Unionists along with Cudjo follow his lead. In contrast to Toby's minstrelsy and strongly inflected dialect, Pomp's antislavery speeches, delivered in heroic style and with formal diction, become "a masterpiece of logic" (Broderick 20). His speeches also evoke a sense of humanity, justice, and equanimity in the face of rapacious power. No fool, he is in many ways the hero of the novel. A "powerful and intelligent black," Pomp prefers his life in the cave to enslavement: "it is a savage, lonely, but not unhappy life I lead—far better for a man like me than servitude here, or degradation at the North" (133).

In contrast to Pomp, who is "a man," there is Cudjo who, the narrator tells us, is "more like an ape [with his . . .] gibberings, his antics, his delight in mischief" (122–123). Like Penn, at first glance Pomp believes Cudjo is an animal until, as he recounts, "I perceived that my animal was something human. It climbed the tree, ran out on one of the branches, leaped, like a squirrel, to some bushes [. . .] and soon pulled itself up to the top" (133). "Savage" and "grotesque" (116), the "wild beast" (144) Cudjo is an evolutionary mistake. Clearly animal-like, even that status is muddled in Cudjo, who is ultimately indefinable, less a specific animal than a composite of them (here, frog, ape, squirrel). While the description of Pomp as "the perfect specimen of a gentleman" (122) elevates his status, the conflation of Cudjo with animals counters slave narratives and radical abolitionist literature. In those texts, slaves' treatment as animals is decried (particularly in scenes of slave auctions), separating the slave's condition from the person himself, thus retrieving the slave's humanity. In contrast, on Trowbridge's chain of being, Cudjo's descriptions reinstate proslavery assertions of slaves as animal-like.

Pomp and Cudjo function as more than simple opposites. Trowbridge's repeated description of them as a "double being" (115) and "double individual" (113–114) links them in a visceral way as doppelgängers. Although both are racially African, they represent two ends of an evolutionary scale. Trowbridge—and Pomp—define their central point of difference as the civilizing force of slavery. Cudjo is the true "native African" still in his natural state (hence, the repeated animal imagery associated with him), "brought to this country a young barbarian; and he has barely got civilized—hardly got Christianized yet!" (137). Yet Pomp, born in American slavery, declares that "I was so fortunate as to be brought up by a young master who was only too kind and indulgent to me [. . .]. He went to Paris to study medicine, and took me with him. I passed for his body servant, but I was rather his friend" (125–126). Cudjo's experiences in slavery have been vastly different; although he had a "tolerably good" master (134), the overseer beat him cruelly. Yet such treatment is not sufficient to shake Pomp's belief that Cudjo's birth and freedom in Africa were inherently debasing and in all probability responsible for Cudjo being a "brute" (120).[39]

Thus, while the narrator, and particularly the characters Pomp and Penn, offer strong arguments for emancipation, and the plot climaxes with the defeat of slavery advocates, the characterizations of Pomp and Cudjo implicitly argue the civilizing effect of slavery. A doppelgänger in its truest sense, Cudjo is what Pomp might have been without the intervention of slavery. By setting up such an evolutionary hierarchy of black characters and placing it within the terms of American slavery, Trowbridge's overt abolitionist arguments are disassembled by the racism which marks conservative abolitionism. Moreover, in Pomp's description of his servitude as less "body servant" than "friend," he reiterates proslavery notions of slavery as a personal attachment between master and slave. The problem, as Pomp—and Trowbridge—posit it, is not that Pomp was ever enslaved, but that the intentions of his master (who had freed Pomp) were thwarted when another man duplicitously kept him in slavery. Pomp is, in many ways, as grateful to his "true" master as Toby is to the Villars.

Cudjo's Cave admits that slavery cannot cure all ills; that Cudjo is a "native African" seems an almost insurmountable barrier to his being civilized. Cudjo dies at the end of the novel, locked in a "deadly embrace" with the cruel overseer who had once beaten him, as they fall to their deaths in the cave (455). There is no hope, no future for Cudjo in America, and readers may be relieved such an "ape" is not set free. But for Pomp, American-educated and Parisian-trained, emancipation is a logical progression following his apprenticeship under a "kind" master. Enslavement here becomes a foundation for citizenship and Trowbridge's vision allows manumission only for those who are "fit" for freedom after the tutoring of a good master.

• • •

Notwithstanding their varying commitments to emancipation, radical, moderate, and conservative abolitionists synthesized essential elements of the abolitionist debate. From the range of rebellious, forgiving, victimized, and supplicant slaves of radical abolitionist literature to the ambivalent position of moderates and the concerns about fitness for freedom that occupied conservative abolitionists, these writers presented iconic images of slavery. *The Little Reader's Assistant*; *The Slave's Friend*; *The Young Abolitionists; Peter Parley* books; *Hatchie, the Guardian Slave*; *Cudjo's Cave*—these and other texts described in this chapter are not ones that current children or adolescents read or even, in all likelihood, know anything about. Yet the images created in these and similar abolitionist texts for children are nonetheless ones that today's readers are intimately familiar with, for as defining expressions of race and slavery they have been re-created in various forms to the present day. They are also images that would be explored by slavery advocates who hoped to counter what they feared was the "pernicious influence" (Rev. of *A Southern Home* 668) of any and all abolitionist literature on their children.

CHAPTER 2

SLAVERY DEBATES FOR CHILDREN 1830–1865

PROSLAVERY RESPONSES

It seemed a pity to leave the
beautiful country with its [. . .]
negro children, the daddies and maumahs, [. . .]
and all the freedom of a rural life [. . .].
—Caroline Gilman, "The Return" (1834)

When a man sells land he writes a deed for it;
when he sells a negro, he writes a bill of sale.
—M. B. Moore, *The Dixie*
Elementary Spelling Book (1864)

While "North" and "South" are commonly used shorthand markers for antebellum anti- and proslavery sentiment, neither unwaveringly fits its respective designation. As much as Northern abolitionists had varying commitments to immediate emancipation, there were also an uncounted number of Northerners who agreed with slavery or disavowed abolition altogether, as did New England minister Nehemiah Adams, who described slavery as potentially "the perfection of human happiness" (92). Children could also find proslavery stories in Northern publications, as one sees in "The Water-Melon Boats" (1847), which describes for readers of *The Youth's Companion* the "delightful times" (58) had by a planter's children and their slaves. And, of course, Northern racism—even when expressed through an ostensibly abolitionist frame—contributed to white supremacist arguments that justified slavery.

Collectively, white Southerners, too, held varying views. Sarah and Angelina Grimké, who grew up in a South Carolina slave-holding family, for example, became well-known abolitionists; Sarah's eyewitness account of the treatment of enslaved children even appeared in *The Slave's Friend* ("Juvenile Anti-Slavery Meeting" 14). Pockets of rebellion by white citizens—such as in Jones County, Mississippi—revealed violent disagreements about slavery and secession. And while one's allegiance during the war was not necessarily a sign of one's position on slavery, that the number of white Southerners who fought in Union armies totaled over a third of those who fought in Confederate armies indicates that the South did not hold an indisputably unified view against Unionist ideals, including slavery.[1]

That said, the South's principal literary contribution to the slavery debate—the plantation story—was unquestionably proslavery. As the debate intensified on a national scale, particularly in the 1830s following Nat Turner's rebellion and with the rise of radical abolitionism in the North, proslavery ideology became a mainstay of antebellum Southern literature. As one slavery advocate argued, "in an age when the power of the pen exceeds that of the sword, purse and tongue," literature could serve as a crucial "weapon[. . .] for [. . .] defence" against abolitionist attacks ("Duty" 246). Plantation stories provided just such a weapon. Although today's general readers are likely to at least be familiar with Frederick Douglass's *Narrative* and Harriet Beecher Stowe's *Uncle Tom's Cabin*, if not to have read them, it is unlikely many would have heard of John Pendleton Kennedy's *Swallow Barn; or, A Sojourn in the Old Dominion* (1832). Yet many critics believe it helped to "inaugurate" the plantation novel.[2] Offered, as author Kennedy described it, as "an antidote to the abolition mischief" (qtd in Osborne xl),[3] it and the other plantation and proslavery domestic novels that followed would come to define stereotypes of slavery and race that have lasted to the present day. Although the versions of Southern slavery they propagated proved to be popular exports to Northern audiences, not as readily shared with Northern neighbors were other representations of slavery—including slave codes, auction notices, advertisements for runaway slaves, bills of sale, and advice about slave management—that revealed the harsh realities of day-to-day plantation life for those enslaved.[4]

Proslavery children's literature reflected similarly vying representations. Yet, there is not a particularly "radical, moderate, and conservative" paradigm to follow in exploring proslavery antebellum and Confederate Southern children's literature, because—unlike abolitionism in the North—Southern proslavery representations in children's literature did not encounter resistance from general readers. There was not, for example, a "radical" form of proslavery racial representation that argued a drastic change to the status quo. Proslavery literature, for the most part, argued in favor of the status quo (or, more accurately, an idealized past), certainly so in its acceptance of slavery.

The expression of racial representations in antebellum Southern children's literature differed depending on genre, and three categories of proslavery literature—the plantation story, the proslavery adventure novel, and Confederate schoolbooks—contributed distinct tropes to slavery literature, each shaped by their intended effect on young, white readers, largely those from the master class. Although each genre fundamentally focused on training the next generation of slave owners, they did so by offering different visions of slavery. Plantation stories for children incorporated lessons of slave management against a backdrop of plantation life as idyllic repose; proslavery adventure novels extended the sphere of the plantation and influence of the slaveholder to a wider world; and Confederate arithmetics revealed realities of slave life far from the reputed ideals of proslavery fiction. What they collectively offered was a repertoire of racial tropes and slave figures—as variously foolish, needy, loyal, fortunate, or objects of exchange—to argue proslavery perspectives.

While Confederate schoolbooks were directed toward whites, and generally those of the master class, slaves also received proslavery education, most directly, of course, through their treatment by whites and their day-to-day lives in slavery. Some also received religious education sanctioned by masters who touted the virtues of servitude. Although certainly not the only lesson young slaves learned in the quarters, proslavery religious catechisms functioned as both a counterpart and counterpoint to the plantation stories offered to white children of the master class.

PLANTATION STORIES

The plantation story provided Southerners an opportunity for cultural self-definition, a way to wrest literary hegemony from Northern writers whom many in the South believed were singly defining the terms of slavery. Offering an arcadian idyll seemingly insulated from outside chaos, this genre idealized the plantation as a protected space and model of Southern civility. Ostensibly ignoring the racial strife of such contemporaneous events as Nat Turner's revolt (which occurred only nine months before the publication of *Swallow Barn*), these fictional plantations offer their inhabitants security, comfort, and racial harmony based on the regularization of hierarchies and the maintenance of a benevolent system of slavery.

The two Southern antebellum genres that principally articulated the plantation myth for adults were the plantation novel and the proslavery domestic novel. Both argued the morality of slavery, but while the typically male-authored plantation novel most frequently described the plantation as an idyll of repose, the female-authored proslavery domestic novel offered a more critical examination of power structures, particularly in its discussion of the authority and obligations of husbands and slaveholders. In *Recollections of a Southern Matron* (1838), for example, Caroline Gilman asserts that a good husband should also be a good master, and argues that men and women should fulfill their responsibilities as dutiful slaveholders, spouses, and parents, conquering intemperate behavior and providing a stable environment for one's family and slaves. Although the plantation novel's tone was often more lighthearted and the proslavery domestic novel more didactic, both genres gained popularity in the South and North as they argued that slavery was a moral good when overseen by judicious masters.[5]

Despite their seeming remove from current events, the genres nonetheless attempted to answer abolitionist arguments at every turn. Where slave narratives assert the often sadistic cruelty of white masters, plantation novels argue the ideal of kind masters who sacrifice their own best interests to care for slaves. Where slave narratives repeatedly reveal slaves' victimization, plantation novels show their "contentment and good humor" (J. Kennedy 452). Where Equiano presents a heroic and intelligent figure, plantation stories describe slaves as "essentially parasitical," having "the helplessness of a child,—without foresight, without faculty of contrivance, without thrift of any kind" (J. Kennedy 453). And while the racial chain of being which equated Africans with animals was excoriated by radical abolitionists, it was a staple of plantation novels where, as in *Swallow Barn*, slaves are variously described as "untamed monkeys" (308), blackbirds (454), and a "pack of antic and careless animals" (310).[6]

While this may give the impression that the plantation story's overt focus is on slavery, the figure of the slave often remains in the background, appearing only to provide entertainment or assurance of loyalty to fictional masters and white readers alike. Nonetheless, slave figures are necessary characters in defining the parameters of white racial identity in stories where the literary construction of "whiteness" resolutely depends upon the representation of "blackness" as oppositional: black foolishness is contrasted with white wisdom; black indolence with white responsibility; black superstition with white religiosity; black fear with white courage; and, ultimately, in the figure of the slave and master, black self-abnegation with white self-possession. Indeed, in these novels it is the possession of slaves, particularly in vast numbers, that becomes an essential marker of white social status, political power, and emotional satisfaction.

While current readers may not be familiar with either genre, they would likely recognize the racial characters the genres made famous: the foolish, lighthearted "Sambo"; the loving and sometimes pestering "Mammy"; the aged, sentimentalized "Aunt"; and the loyal, but slightly incompetent "Uncle" (character tropes not unfamiliar in Northern literature).[7] By way of racial contrast, the genres also furnished readers with the dutiful and generous plantation mistress as well as the judicious, patient master. Both genres defined slavery as a system based on attachment rather than commerce,[8] which not only provided a convenient contrast to Northern industrialism and wage labor (E. Moss 2, 67), but also a range of characters types—such as the Mammy, Uncle, and the master and mistress as parental figures—that defined slavery as an amicable pseudoextended family.

The focus on attachment also shaped language about slavery, as evident in the common proslavery exchange of "slaves" for "negroes." By linguistically erasing "slavery" as a sign of oppression in an abolitionist context, this rhetorical sleight of hand obfuscated the commodifying relationship of slave to master while still acknowledging its essential dependence on racial difference. Plantation stories which focus on slavery as a system of attachment thus often reveal inherent tensions as masters simultaneously care for slaves while being meticulously careful not to transgress racial boundaries.

It was Caroline Gilman, perhaps more than any other antebellum writer, who translated the plantation genre for children. An influential spokesperson for Southern slave-holding culture and a slaveholder herself, Gilman would present commonly touted themes—such as responsibility and kindness—through the prism of a Southern perspective, particularly a Southern slave-holding one.[9] Her four-page weekly newspaper, *The Rose Bud*, which Gilman edited and largely wrote, was the nation's first children's magazine to be published in the South (Avery 85). First appearing in August 1832, only a few months after the publication of *Swallow Barn*, a year after Nat Turner's revolt, and amid contentious nullification debates,[10] the children's weekly was poised at the crossroads of sectionalizing debates and confrontations. Although Gilman assured readers that *The Rose Bud* would avoid "controversy" to focus on stories, poems, and essays for children's "pleasure and improvement" ("Editor's Address"), that *The Rose Bud* and its successors, *Southern Rose Bud* and *The Southern Rose*,[11] were consistently proslavery implicitly asserts Gilman's perspective that slavery is not a controversial issue. Properly managed, it was to her an ethical, orderly, and generous system of kindly race relations.

The didactic impetus underlying Gilman's representations of slavery for children is in encouraging proper management of slaves, and hence supporting the continuation of Southern slavery. Her goal to present stories for "pleasure and improvement" also defines her representations of slavery for children: Gilman heightens the idyll of plantation life by aligning it with childhood pleasures at the same time that she instructs young readers in the proper behavior of masters and mistresses. An ideological primer for her later proslavery domestic novels, Gilman's rendition of the plantation story for children becomes a site of education and moral lessoning, situating the plantation as a place where white children practice being masters and mistresses, even as they experience the dangers of mismanagement and irresponsibility. As such, the plantation simultaneously serves as both idyll and training ground for young masters. In these stories, slave characters serve as little else than objects for that training—both intranarratively for white characters, and extranarratively, for white readers of the master class.

As is typical of plantation genres' placement of slavery in their margins, Gilman's stories and poems for children that include depictions of slavery number only a handful. Nonetheless, even when appearing as only a brief narrative interpolation, slavery as a positive good underlies *The Rose Bud*'s representation of the South. Gilman's presentation of slaves—as loyal, foolish, at times mischievous, but more often needing a master's protection—echoes representations in plantation fiction for adults. As there, in *The Rose Bud* the figure of the "slave" is often used as a type of shorthand to provide local color. For example, in the first installment of the six-part essay "Sullivan's Island," as a white family prepares for a day's excursion, a basket of their goods will be carried by "their only attendant, a country negro, who as a great favour, was permitted to go and see 'dem big boat, what trow up fire'" ("Sullivan's Island" 13). Although such a short description suggests the unimportance of the slave's presence, the passage is layered with signs of racial hierarchy. The common proslavery linguistic invisibility of the term "slave," for example, is simultaneously countered by the character's visible use of dialect. Even if young, white readers could reasonably imagine being impressed with the sight of a large boat, the segregating effect of the negro's dialect has marked him as "other," and thus would keep readers from identifying with him.

While radical abolitionists typed slaves through romantic racialism as religious, sacrificial figures (as with Uncle Tom), in proslavery texts, any romanticizing of slaves moves them further down—not up—the chain of being, particularly connecting them to the natural world. This occurs here as the negro is defined as an unsophisticated country rustic. This "country negro['s]" servitude is described unironically as a sign of a white family's noblesse oblige as he is "permitted" to accompany them. Servitude (hence, slavery) is thus defined by the narrator as "a great favour" on the *master's* part. The unnamed negro is narratively subsumed into this perspective, for he also views servitude as a treat that will allow him to see wondrous things. Overall, the brevity of such interpolations about happy slaves bespeaks a confidence of the master class, presenting slavery as a narratively unremarkable and understood element of society.

In the plantation tradition, the central idyll of the plantation is its isolation from the larger world, particularly as it serves as an arcadian respite for visiting whites otherwise taxed by a busy, bothersome world.[12] A place "where rural joys prevail," the plantation is "a lovely," almost liminal place (Gilman, "Ballad" 150). Functioning as a geographic and racial version of the separation of spheres, it is a private counterpart to the public world of business and politics. Here, leisure predominates for white visitors and black residents alike where the plantation's depicted insularity heightens its arcadian idyll.

As much as a respite on the plantation revives weary white visitors of the master class, one suspects it is not the plantation's scenery alone that has this effect. The fictional slaves' inferiority and adulation become a heady mix that reaffirms white characters' racial and personal importance, and allows them the strength, energy, and confidence to return to the outside world. One sees this in Gilman's most substantial plantation story for children, the twelve-part "The Country Visit" (1834), which tells of young Clara and her brothers who travel from the city for "Spring holidays" to Oak Hall Plantation. That slaves function as identifying markers of the plantation idyll is evident here where they serve as the entrance and exit frame of the children's visit: "a large number of the slaves were awaiting their arrival" ("Arrival"), and when the children leave, "the negroes stood in a row to let the carriage pass [. . .] and the negroes said 'by'te little massauhs, by'te little missis'" ("Return"). As the symbolic centerpiece of plantation visits, slaves represent an isolated natural world.[13] Yet the romantic possibilities that an individual may achieve a type of transcendence in his connection to nature are denied black characters who are carefully contained by racialized prescriptions that forbid them the possibilities of higher states of awareness than whites. In "The Country Visit," for example, the slave's connection with nature is demoted to an alignment with animals as Gilman describes slave children who welcome the white children to the plantation as "leaping and singing about [. . .] like so many monkeys" ("Arrival"). By contrast, white children achieve a type of secularized divinity in their roles as young masters and mistresses, shown through the adoration of grateful slaves and the child master's/mistress' power.

Although the plantation in "The Country Visit" is a holiday for visiting white children who have temporarily left their schoolbooks behind, it becomes another type of schoolroom for them, a training ground where they play at adulthood. As young children might use dolls to practice their anticipated roles as parents, so young white children here play with slaves (more as objects than as companions) in anticipation of their roles as plantation masters and mistresses. Not divine in any romantic sense, the proslavery child is a socialized and socializing force, a defender of the racialized status quo, and exemplary student of her parents' tutoring.

In "The Country Visit," Gilman depicts Clara's parents as kindly, moral, and protective, offering a stabilizing hierarchical order to their children and slaves alike. Slave narratives would denounce the proslavery conflation of "master/mistress" and "father/mother," exposing the proslavery metaphor of benevolent paternalism as a literal expression of sexual exploitation.[14] In plantation novels, however, the conflation of master/parent carries no suggestion of miscegenation, but only the assurance of kind masters who provide for slaves in the most selfless of ways. In proslavery children's literature, such depictions heighten the assurance of slavery's beneficence as young readers are encouraged to imagine these caring masters and mistresses as being his or her own parents. As plantation caretakers, these parents tutor white children in the ways of the master class.

Socializing play is evident when young Clara plays at her mother's role as slave mistress: "Clara was very fond of seeing her mama give out fish and tobacco [. . .] to the slaves, and she wondered how her mama could give to each so exactly alike" ("little Negroes"). As Gilman does to some extent in her later domestic novels for women, she here shifts the plantation novel's paternal proslavery paradigm to a maternal one. The shift is evident in Clara's role as protagonist as well as in the influence of her mother as mistress, active model, and tutor for the daughter who represents the next generation of female slave owners. As Elizabeth Moss points out, the "southern domestic heroine [. . . maintains] the complex role of wife, mother, and plantation administrator. A gracious hostess, competent housewife, and sympathetic mistress, she ministered to the physical and spiritual needs of her white and black families and, in so doing, ensured the moral and social stability of the South" (36). Both Clara and her mother fulfill this role here. Clara's mother assures her daughter she will eventually be included in the family's tradition: "when you are sixteen years old, [. . .] you must help me as I did your grandmamma."[15] Not willing to wait, Clara asks her mother "if she might *treat* the little negroes" now ("little Negroes").

As an expression of mastery over slaves, "treat[ing] the little negroes" requires more than Clara's noblesse oblige. In a slaveholding context, the achievement of the master class' white identity requires contrasting black subservience, and in this scene Clara exacts deference for her "treats":

> Clara told ["the little negroes" . . .] to sit on the grass in a circle, and she stood in the middle and shared the biscuits and sugar [. . .].

> They were all beginning to eat, when Clara said, "stop." They obeyed her like so many soldiers.
>
> "Get up," said she, and up they all scrambled [. . .].
>
> "Now," said she, "make cutchy." They understood her better than our readers, for the girls all made curtesys [*sic*], and the boys flung back their right feet, or kissed their hands, and some of them said, "Tank you, my little missis."
>
> Then Clara said, "Eat." And they began without delay [. . .]. ("little Negroes")

Here, the slaves—themselves young and receiving training in the art of slavery from their future mistress—present themselves as sentient dolls, windup toys who respond to their owner's every command, or even—on a racial chain of being—as pets who obey their mistress' commands for food. Educational historian Lawrence Cremin's account that "when the master and mistress would visit [, . . .] the [slave] children were taught appropriate modes of submissive bowing and curtsying" (431) captures this scene of Clara giving "treats" as she teaches subservience to young slaves. She enacts her role as a slaveholder by having slaves enact their prescribed roles. Like her mother and grandmother before her, Clara is already a "southern domestic heroine," and Gilman demonstrates that the presumed "moral and social stability" of the master class depends upon a racialized stability of expressed black inferiority and gratitude in the presence of white authority.

Clara's use of slave dialect in this scene reveals both her power and the limits of sympathy in children's proslavery fiction. As she moves from the Standard English she uses when speaking to other white characters to her address to the slaves—"here! [. . .] Pompey, [. . .] go tell all you broder and sister come ere, I been got someting good for em" (183)—Clara demonstrates her ability to move between defined "white" and "black," "master" and "slave" linguistic space, and hence models how slaveholders may communicate with slaves through code switching (Bakker 274). Not a moment of real exchange or identification, when the young mistress momentarily moves into fictionalized black linguistic space, she remains in authority, maintaining "mastery over dialect" (Kenny 75) to direct slaves before returning to the racialized safety of white linguistic space. Thus, at a moment of potential bridging, racial boundaries are never in danger of being transgressed, particularly because fictionalized slaves do not show a similar fluency moving between white and black speech (also see Kenny 75). Such a carefully maintained separation at the very moment of feigned linguistic bridging serves as a counterpoint to the imaginative transference of such abolitionist works as "Mary French and Susan Easton." Indeed, Clara's code switching is minimized in commands. Expressed without dialect interference, Clara's precise commands—"stop," "get up," "eat"—remain succinctly and unambiguously in the master's language. The young slaves, good students of their mistress-teacher, readily understand the mistress' imperative and "scrambled" to obey ("little Negroes").

In educating children of the master class, one of Gilman's central concerns was, as she would later argue, that the "temptations of power should be diligently pointed out, passion repressed, purity enforced [. . . . So] should every father prepare his son, at the South, for the little kingdom over which he is to reign in wisdom and love" (*Recollections* 202–203). In "The Country Visit" Clara proves herself a successful apprentice mistress not only in her regulation, but also in her protection of young slaves. In one episode, as she, her brothers, and the "little slaves" take turns on a swing, one brother disrupts their otherwise harmonious (although still hierarchical) play: "George was a rogue, and wished to swing them ["the black babies"] high and frighten them." When Clara and her other brother intercede on behalf of the slaves, the crying slave child then "*sidled* up to Clara, and stood by her for protection" ("Swing"). Revealing the ways that white power was similarly evinced in abolitionist and proslavery rhetoric, this scene of the white intercessor offering protection to a needy slave evokes images of the abolitionist icon of the protective white guardian. Here, however, as the protective guardian becomes an idealistic icon for slavery propagandists, it is the kind mistress who becomes the savior of grateful slaves.

At times Gilman acknowledges the petty rebellions of slaves—of Jim who is slow to respond to his young master's commands ("Planter's Son" [1832]) or Toney who, sotto voce, mocks his young master's vanity ("New Boots").[16] In both cases, Gilman presents slaves who puncture the presumption of the master's unquestioned authority and who, at least momentarily, resist proslavery assertions of slaves' dimwittedness and inability to maintain a separate identity from their masters. Although slaveholders feared slaves who resisted their presumed hegemony—Nat Turner's revolt being the most nightmarish scenario to the master class—plantation genres largely deal with those fears by diminishing slave rebellion to individual examples of a slave's humorous overreaching and incompetence. In her plantation stories for children, Gilman depicts such rebellions as harmless as long as masters are honorable and kind.

Emulating the judicious masters of plantation novels for adults, young slave owners learn to view minor slave rebellions with patience and even bemusement.[17] Gilman teaches young masters and mistresses that the danger of responding with violence can be dire. In "The Planter's Son," when the slave Jim "either did not, or affected not to hear his young master['s order to tend to a horse]," young master William's "little stock of patience was exhausted." When he raises a whip to strike the slave, he mistakenly hits his own brother. At first glance, the scene seems evocative of abolitionist claims that the slave is one's brother, yet Gilman never argues that the slave is the master's equal. Rather, readers of the master class learn that noblesse oblige and proper plantation management are both a moral and practical response, benefiting one's self-interest. Although minor slave resistance suggests that slaves may reveal moments of independence, such depictions are rare; the slave's rebellion is short-lived and slaveholder hegemony soon restored. Gilman, for example, ends with the slave's avowal that "nudder time, me gaun fetch mass Billy horse" (18). Moreover, in the illustration of "The Planter's Son," Jim's rebelliousness is deflated, even in the midst of the seeming tragedy. His apparent horror and exaggerated readiness to exit the scene suggest his recalcitrance will not be repeated.[18] In this story, where Gilman cautions against privileged slave owners who may be "slightly injured by the early exercise of power" (17), children of the slave-holding class learn it is they—not slaves—who have both agency and responsibility, they who must learn to curb their tempers to manage a well-ordered plantation—in short, they who must not rebel.

Although, as Elizabeth Moss argues, Gilman's domestic fiction shows that the author "remained firmly convinced that the plantation system nourished a ["virtuous"] communitarian ethic" (67), the "social distance" (Kenny 73) required of masters to slaves is another of Gilman's lessons in interracial interaction. One sees this in the emotional remove of white children from "Mammies," or female slaves who would have an expected functional and emotional sway over their white charges. In "The Country Visit," for example, when "old Sue" tries to wake the white children, they resist her as they

FIGURE 2.1. *"The Planter's Son" from* The Rose-Bud Wreath *(1841) by Caroline Gilman. Courtesy of the Rare Book Collection, The University of North Carolina at Charlotte Library.*

never would their parents: "'Get up, little maussahs,' said [Sue . . .], 'he bery late.' 'It is no such thing,' grumbled George with his eyes shut." A nagging Mammy figure, Sue has no real authority over these white children, and they respond to her only so far as they are rewarded for it—in this case, the brothers finally rise when promised Sue's johnnycakes ("Second Visit").

In a more emotional scene, Clara later visits "her old favorite, maum Nelly [. . . who] had been the Nurse of the plantation, but was now too infirm to do that duty." Informed by different gender expectations, Clara is kinder to her old maum than her brothers are to Sue. During the visit, Nelly tells the young girl that she expects soon she "will lie yonder under de pines, but my soul will go to God Almighty" ("Old Nelly"). Despite the elegiac tone of this leave-taking, when Clara and her family finally leave the plantation—and the slaves, including Nelly, come to bid them goodbye—"Clara remembered what [Nelly . . .] had said about lying beneath the pine-trees, and she [. . .] wanted to cry, but the coachman snapped his whip and the carriage rolled on, and Clara began to think about the city" ("Return"). In this emotional turnaround, Clara's momentary grief at Nelly's imminent death quickly dissolves into her engagement with city life.

That Nelly will soon die emphasizes Clara's coming-of-age. That Clara's thoughts of the city quickly replace her thoughts of Nelly shows how children's plantation stories ultimately assert the at-best transitory effect of even once-significant slaves. Such a separation—of whites (particularly young children) who return to the wider world, while most slaves remain behind on the plantation (even, as with maum Nelly, to die)—presents slaves as romantically insulated in ways that do not elevate them. They do not leave the plantation because they lack the agency that white characters enjoy and because they define the plantation as an inseparable part of its landscape; they are, in these stories, an essential part of the racial makeup of a plantation. Plantation masters need slaves; in proslavery children's plantation stories, that need is not for their labor, but for the ways that they define, through contrast, what it means to be white and powerful. It is, perhaps, in this leave-taking that the argument of slavery as a relationship based on attachment wears most thin. That the obsolescence of individual slaves occurs within an insulated landscape housing an innumerable number of slaves assures their easy replacement. Moreover, the emotional remove of white protagonists from their early slave caretakers shows that any influence of an attachment to the slaves occurs only because of the white child's youth; it must be outgrown for one to become a master or mistress.

• • •

It may seem odd to classify slaves' education as part of the plantation myth, but regarding much of the religious education afforded slaves and sanctioned by the master, that was the case. Religious education was a means to spiritually colonize slaves, to inculcate their obedience to masters more earthly than divine. Sanctioned religious education for slaves took place at Sabbath schools in towns and, more frequently, on the plantation where masters could oversee proceedings. Both slave children and adults attended religious meetings, although children were a special focus of missionaries.[19] To avoid the ire of masters who feared slaves gaining literacy, much instruction was offered only through the spoken word, as the extensive title, *A Catechism to Be Taught Orally to Those Who Cannot Read; Designed Especially for the Instruction of the Slaves, in the Prot[estant] Episcopal Church in the Confederate States* (1862), indicates.

In the antebellum South, literacy was carefully prescribed. Masters feared losing control of slaves who might learn to read seditious literature or write their own passes to freedom. Many Southern slave states enacted laws making it illegal for slaves to learn to read and write, and for anyone (white or black) to teach them. Although probably between five to less than ten percent of the slave population achieved literacy, they did so often through their own ingenuity and at great risk.[20] Fearing the link between literacy and liberation, some states enacted laws against free black persons having access to abolitionist literature. In 1831, for example, Georgetown, Maryland, passed an ordinance prohibiting "any negro or mulatto person [. . .] from receiving [. . .] or to circulate, any [. . .] publication [. . .] calculated to excite insurrection or insubordination among the slaves" (*History of Schools* 309–310).[21]

Free blacks in the South did, nonetheless, have some access to formal education; some cities, such as New Orleans, had a sizeable enough population of affluent free blacks able to financially support private education for their children.[22] It would be likely that free black students, like Southern white students, would have used Northern textbooks—like *McGuffey* readers and *Peter Parley* books—that populated classrooms across the nation. Whatever potentially seditious material (such as the abolitionist newspaper, *The Liberator*) may have been brought into the classroom would have been kept secret from the surrounding slave-holding and white population. In many ways, however, abolitionist literature was not necessary for sedition; for the black population, either free or enslaved, learning to read and write was itself an essentially seditious act. For the free population, it countered popular race theories that asserted black intellectual inferiority. For the slave population, it offered a practical means of escape and rebellion.

Rarely, some slaves, with written permission from their masters, were admitted into Southern schools (Curry 159). More commonly, if slaves were allowed education, their masters permitted religiously oriented schooling on the plantation. Missionaries intent on not angering slave owners, who nevertheless brought Christianity to the plantation so that slaves would be among the "saved" (C. Jones, *Catechism* 38), tread a careful path and offered an often ambivalent message. In *The Religious Instruction of the Negroes* (1842), Rev. Charles Colcock Jones encouraged ministers to court the approval of masters and to refrain from any preaching that might lead to the "insubordination" (192) of slaves. Ministers hoping to preach to slaves often assured masters—as did Thomas Bacon in 1749—that "the direct Tendency of the Gospel-Doctrine is to make [. . .] Negroes the better Servants [i.e., slaves] in Proportion as they become better Christians" (T. Bacon 81). Rev. Jones would concur, arguing that the "Gospel recognizes the condition in which the Negroes are, and inculcates the duties appropriate to it" (*Religious* 198).

Sanctioned religious instruction for slaves also reveals tensions lying under the surface of the plantation myth. An inherently conflicted genre, catechisms for slaves argue the divinely granted right of masters to rule over slaves, asserting that "*Masters and Mistresses* are God's Overseers" (T. Bacon 92). For example, a section titled "Duty of Servants to Masters" in *A Catechism for Colored Persons* (1834) instructs slaves that "servants must *honor and obey* their Masters and Mistresses, and do their best to please them in all things" (C. Jones 95). A recitation exercise calls upon slaves to respond to the question, "is it right for the Servant to runaway; or is it right to *harbor* a runaway?," with an unambiguous "no" (94). As much as religious education argued that the master was God's intermediary and that slaves must obey masters, it supported the plantation idyll.

At the same time, some catechisms for slaves counter the plantation myth by critiquing slavery practices and asserting racial equality before God. *A Catechism for Colored Persons*, for example, declares masters' responsibility to slaves in its admonition that the master is "duty bound to take care of the Servant [even] when he is old and unable to work, and when he is sick or a cripple" (C. Jones 92); argues the sanctity of marriage for all persons (87–88); and includes the question, "does He [God] favor the Master more than the Servant, *because* he is the Master? A[nswer]. No." Here, slaves are taught that God will ultimately judge master and slave "according to his works" (93). Like the conflicted religious ideology inscribed upon Stowe's Uncle Tom, catechisms for slaves both support servitude and undercut its racial hierarchies. That masters were promised no special compensation in heaven because of their racial or social status chafed some slave owners; one, for example, complained to a preacher, "is it Possible that any of my slaves could go to Heaven, & I must see them there?" (qtd in Young, Introduction 26).

In plantation fiction, religious education is part of a romanticized vision of slavery. Gilman's "The Country Visit" presents it as a mark of interracial accord, as when Clara and her family "assembled at prayers, and those of the servants [i.e., slaves] who wished," joined them ("Arrival").[23] In the proslavery adventure novel, *Robert and Harold* (1852), master Dr. Gordon offers weekly religious instruction to his slaves (Goulding 225), showing him as a gracious master while at the same time arguing the proslavery perspective that one of slavery's benefits is that it Christianizes slaves. Yet, as one sees in Gilman's "The Country Visit," even ostensibly harmonious representations of religion can suggest subtextual resistance to slavery. As Gale Kenny points out, that Gilman's slaves sing "Master Jesus is my Captain, / He is my all in all, / He give me grace to conquer, / And take me home to rest" (Gilman, "Singing Hymns") hints at "the subversive meanings slaves invested into their lyrics" to which white auditors—and perhaps Gilman herself—were "oblivious" (Kenny 72).

Signaling both religious inculcation and allegiance to a divine (not earthly) master, the song "Master Jesus Is My Captain" suggests the "linguistic virtuosity" (Kibbey 180) of slaves whose songs and stories were embedded with double meanings, one ostensibly amenable to white oversight, the other subtextually coded with expressions of rebellion and escape. Unrecognized by listening slaveholders, such expression positioned whites as deafeningly illiterate, unable to understand the codes of black resistance.[24] The plantation myth—like the uncomplicated Sambo which it touted—provided an unintentional covering for such subversive expressions. Young slaves received often dueling educations: religious instruction vetted by masters and instruction by slaves for slaves. Within the slave community, the master's religion was transformed to disempower justifications of slavery and racial superiority, to define slaves as God's "chosen people." Coded spirituals, folk and trickster tales, and secular and escape songs all became part of the lexicon of slave quarters.

This subversive education taught young slaves not only practical lessons in plantation survival, but also provided them with "a world apart" from that commandeered by their masters (Levine 80), creating for them a psychological respite, an oppositional paradigm of identity and community, and opportunities for rebellion.

Slave stories, like Brer Rabbit tales, could be told in the presence of whites because masters did not expect slaves to have the necessary sophistication for linguistic virtuosity and because the stories they told and songs they sung seemed ostensibly unremarkable and often fitted prescriptions of the plantation myth. Subversive expressions of religious education could use the plantation myth as cover for rebellion. Thus, in the act of ostensibly assenting to the unassailability of white hegemony and the racial harmony of plantation slavery, slaves' understanding of the religious education offered to them encouraged the counterculture they developed within their communities, separate from the management—and even knowledgeable purview—of white masters.

THE PROSLAVERY ADVENTURE

Described as "without a doubt, the most important children's book produced in the Confederate States" (Kennerly 229), Francis Robert Goulding's *Robert and Harold; or, The Young Marooners on the Florida Coast* (1852) was the most successful Southern antebellum book for children, enjoying an international readership, multiple editions, and popularity well into the postbellum years when Joel Chandler Harris would declare the book "a classic" (Introduction, *Young Marooners* iii).[25] The novel offers a Robinson Crusoe–like tale of four white, slave-holding children (Harold and his cousins Robert, Mary, and Frank) who shipwreck on an island where they have adventures, rescue a slave, and live off the land until finally reunited with their parents several months later.

As much as the slave narrative and abolitionist creations, like Douglass's *Heroic Slave*, Trowbridge's Pomp in *Cudjo's Cave*, or George in Stowe's *Uncle Tom's Cabin*, present heroic, black slaves, Goulding counters the slave narrative by revisioning slavery as play and diminishing the heroic slave to impotence, leaving instead white heroes whose adventures are the mainstay of the novel. In the plantation story—as the term implies—it is the geographical location that defines slavery, and the master is a generally staid representation of that insularity. Further, in plantation stories, the quarantined space of the plantation suggests that slavery could not survive exposure to the wider world. Adventure novels, by contrast, typically present a more energized world and focus on individual prowess, especially in the face of unexpected adversity. More confident in its assertions of white supremacy than the plantation story for either adults or children, the antebellum proslavery adventure for children breaks the boundaries of the plantation genre as white protagonists geographically move "far beyond" the plantation (Goulding [1852] 185).

Compared to the proslavery adventure story, Gilman's earlier plantation stories seem a retreat from the energies, confidence, and scope of Goulding's child protagonists. Although Gilman's young Clara and her brothers leave the plantation for a busier town life, their abilities remain contained and they are not yet fully even "masters" of themselves. In contrast, Goulding's children do not merely play at being master and mistress during their island adventure. Although their parents' influence is apparent in the skills and logic the children have acquired from them and often put into action, the dominion of these white children ultimately surpasses their parents whom the children rescue near the close of the novel. In ideological terms, the children take the plantation with them as they colonize and master a larger, otherwise uncivilized world. In doing so, the proslavery adventure presents a clearer fantasy of white racial superiority than the plantation story, as it exchanges arcadia for untamed worlds, insularity for exploration, and supervised training for self-reliance. In that and in their exercise of independence, resourcefulness, and authority on the island, the children become not merely the next generation of dutiful slaveholders. Rather, they invigorate the scope and definition of the master class itself.

While the plantation novel describes slavery as a contented state of grateful slaves and kindly masters, the genre at times suggests moments of slaveholder anxiety. There is, one could argue, fear around the margins of the plantation novel. In *Swallow Barn*, for example, ruptures in the idyll of plantation life can be found in subtextually displaced narratives. In a scene that metaphorically speaks to racial anxiety, Kennedy describes how the otherwise peaceful plantation suffers the nightly invasions of a possum who threatens to "attack the young fowls and cut their throats" (398). Following a lengthy hunt led by a loyal slave, the possum is caught and peace finally restored to the plantation. The narrator's comment about this "nocturnal adventure"—that "the presence of darkness conjures up in every mind an indefinite sense of fear [. . .] to which we are strangers in the daytime" (399)—invites a psychological reading. This "indefinite sense of fear" bespeaks racial angst—here, fear of the slave. The "daytime" world of this plantation may offer no dangers, but the threat of a waiting "nighttime" serves as a metaphor of racial revolt and dangerous loss of white control. The message is clear: to leave or give up the plantation would be a dissolution, for white masters, into chaos.[26]

By contrast, in the antebellum *Robert and Harold*, Goulding declares that white masters face no danger they cannot ably meet, even if they leave the plantation. Lauding the stabilizing effects of colonization by white slaveholders, *Robert and Harold* shows the self-sufficiency of the four children as they explore and domesticate an uninhabited island. Dangerous bears and panthers prowl the island, but unlike the lingering anxieties of masters in *Swallow Barn*, the children here self-assuredly stalk, trap, kill, skin, and eat their prey. Particularly for the titular heroes, the journey serves as a rite of passage, and as young Frank celebrates a birthday on the island, his older brother Robert offers to teach him how to use a gun, "so as to kill whatever you wish" (389). Survival on the island and its concomitant entrance to manhood here require the ability to dominate one's surroundings. The island functions, as does the journey of the children, as a microcosm of slavery in the white characters' mastery of their world. The children become an unstoppable force. Buoyed by the robust confidence of childhood (and class), their faith in God's guidance, and the training they have received from Dr. Gordon (uncle to Harold and father to the other children), the children assure readers of the moral, intellectual, and natural justice of their position as young slaveholders.

Set in 1830 Florida, the novel begins with the declaration that while the parents had been "accustomed all their lives to the service of slaves, [they] had educated their children to be as independent as possible of unnecessary help" (15). It is, readers soon learn, fortuitous that these children were raised not to depend upon slaves, for with the exception of talents in cooking and singing, Goulding's slaves-called-servants are markedly incompetent. Indeed, the children's unintentional expedition is precipitated by the ineptitude of their "servant [/slave]" William. When Dr. Gordon momentarily returns to the house, he instructs William to attend to the boat that the four children have just boarded. William promptly loses control of the boat and then falls overboard, leaving the children alone and pulled out to sea by an errant devilfish. By contrast, once the children land at a distant, uninhabited island, they show remarkable self-sufficiency in quickly setting up a shelter and providing for themselves. Later, when their "negro carpenter" Sam arrives on the island in a failed attempt to rescue them, he has suffered a broken arm and leg, and, as Harold points out, "instead of helping us, he wants us to help him" (164).

While Sam does not figure prominently in the novel (in terms of the number of scenes in which he plays a significant role), his character is nonetheless essential in providing a racial foil for the white children, especially for Robert and Harold. His character functions on a metaphoric level to define contrasting white identity, and on a literal level, to provide a slave for these young masters. Although an adult, Sam's race and servitude underwrite his repeated emasculation as he is carried to the camp where he is fed and cared for by the children who later also rescue him from drowning. From the beginning of his initial rescue, Sam is ineffectual at best. When the boys find him and he tells them "I 'fraid it will kill me to move," Robert and Harold know better and quickly build a makeshift stretcher to "gently" remove him to their shelter (170). As the weakened slave is carried into the children's civilized space, they sacrifice their own comfort to provide Sam with medical aid, food, and shelter. In short, they model the proslavery argument that masters are generous stewards of slaves otherwise unable to provide for themselves. Indeed, when Sam is greeted at their camp, his weakness and the necessary intercession of Robert and Harold are emphasized as "poor Sam tried to answer, but his voice was too weak. Robert and Harold answered for him" (171).

In a genre in which the plot depends upon the absence of adults so that children can enjoy their adventures and develop self-reliance, Sam's character becomes a perfect foil; he may be an adult but he is an inadequate one. More than this character simply fulfilling childhood fantasies of power, the essential designation of Sam as black expresses fantasies of white supremacy. Although Sam's advice as a carpenter is solicited as they build a boat, he generally disappears from the story when the children are working out problems and is most frequently present to voice fears, offer gratitude, and reveal his superstitions (410) and the religiosity he acquired as one of

Dr. Gordon's "plantation negroes" (225). Even Robert and Harold realize that Sam is unable to defend either himself or the youngest children, and they are afraid to leave camp even temporarily, deciding that it is "so manifestly improper to leave the two younger ones [. . .] unprotected, except by a lame, bedridden negro, who was unable to protect himself" (283).

As much as Sam functions as a racial foil to define Robert and Harold as masters, he also serves to define their passage into manhood, which is placed in a specifically racial context. The boys can do what Sam cannot in terms of hunting and providing for others. They are wise while he is foolish; they are self-reflective while he is superstitious; and—in the accumulation of racialized traits—they are white "massas" while he is a self-described "nigger" (313). Although the children never use the term "slave" or "nigger," Sam uses the latter word liberally, both in reference to himself and to other blacks. The reader is continually reminded that blackness is a state of inability, of incompetence, of need, and of request for and dependence upon white ability and protection. Adventure stories that focus upon the white male protagonist's passage into manhood define that manhood as control of oneself, of nature, and of men—control the slave Sam never has.

At its core, the proslavery adventure novel is a racial fantasy of power. It would be of little consequence were Robert and Harold to best other children, white or black. Although at the novel's close the children do rescue Dr. Gordon from a wrecked boat, the father/uncle/slaveholder's guidance has been useful to them throughout their adventures; any more radical overthrowing of a white adult male, particularly the likes of Dr. Gordon, would disrupt the novel's implicit assurances of white master efficacy and hegemony. As a result, the central foil-pairing for racialized adventure novels becomes the white male child and the black male adult, the latter functioning as the white child's incompetent sidekick. The trope, which would be a long-lasting one, diminishes the adult black slave not merely to serving as a child's slave, but more insidiously to child status himself.[27] Race and manhood thus become synonymous in this novel where white boys can achieve manhood while black male adults cannot. Constructed as neither independent nor effective, not struggling against enslavement and never questioning his master, this literary emasculation of black men was perhaps the most direct assault on the slave figure presented in slave narratives.

Goulding also uses Sam's dialect and the children's contrasting use of Standard English to argue white superiority. Sam's dialect is often emphasized through the use of italics and asterisked translations, suggesting its impenetrability by educated white readers. Unlike Clara in Gilman's "A Country Visit," Dr. Gordon's children and nephew never condescend to speak in dialect, and their occasional usage of formalized speech dramatizes the chasm between the "massa" and "negro." Dialect as a sign of inferiority is most clear, perhaps, when Sam offers obsequiously excessive gratitude to his young masters: "Tankee, Mas Robert! Tankee, Mas Harold! Tankee, my dear little misses! Tankee, Mas Frank too! Tankee, ebbery body! I sure I bin die on dat sand-bank, 'sept you all bin so kind to de poor nigger." Although only fourteen years old, Robert responds with the masterly noblesse oblige and formalized speech typically found in adult plantation novels: "no more of that, Sam, [. . .] you were hurt in trying to help us; it is but right we should help you" (177). In Goulding's fiction, Sam's acknowledgment of his vulnerability without the protection of the slave-holding children serves as a justification for slavery itself. Having the slave characters assert that themselves—and having the slave character use the term "nigger" self-referentially—has the additional advantage of assuring white readers of even the slave's acceptance of white superiority.[28]

This unquestioned acceptance of white superiority and mastery also underlies the novel's narrative trajectory. As another significant counterpoint to the slave narrative, the objective of the children and their slave is to return to the plantation and reunite with the kindly father/master, Dr. Gordon. As in plantation novels, Goulding's work shows the feeling of slave to master as one of real affection. When Sam learns that the children are on the island, for example, he says how he "lub" (168) them and wants "to see dey sweet face" (170). Of his master, Dr. Gordon, Sam also avows his love and even adoration (184). That Goulding's slaves evince no rebellions—petty or otherwise—emphasizes how white control is never punctured in the proslavery adventure novel, as it is to varying degrees in plantation stories. Moreover, unlike plantation stories, in *Robert and Harold*, the master's children do not need emotional distance from their caretaker-slaves; they—not slaves—are the competent caretakers and they are never under slaves' protection.

The adventure genre, with its narrative impetus of masculine power, exploration, authority, and control over nature and whatever functions as the exotic, is a particularly apt one to transmit the racial hierarchies of proslavery fiction to children. The slave might function as an almost indistinguishable part of the natural landscape were it not for his indispensable role as racial foil. The development of the white protagonists' heroism, intelligence, and dominance—ultimately, of his masculinity and passage to young manhood—is buttressed by the narrative diminution of the black adult male figure. That diminution and the assertion of white authority is also evident in the novel's subtitle—*The Young Marooners*—where Goulding replaces a black experience of rebellion and heroism with a pleasant excursion for privileged white children.

Early in the novel, Dr. Gordon tells the children, "The word 'maroon' is of West Indian origin [. . .]. It meant at first a free negro. But as those who ran away from their masters became virtually free for the time, it came afterwards to mean a runaway negro. To maroon therefore means to go from home, and live like a runaway negro." He proposes that the children join him for a short maroon. When they remain silent, he reframes his proposal: "to maroon means also to go to some wild place, where there is plenty of game or fish, and to live upon what we can obtain by our own skill" (59). The children then happily accede to his plans.[29] Dr. Gordon's redefinition of terms parodies a central focus of slave narratives: the escape from slavery. The journey of slaves who had sought escape through their wits and physical resources, often encountering harrowing challenges and, for many, death, becomes not simply appropriated by white children. Instead, Goulding's novel touts a proslavery position which denies both slavery and the slave. In this way, the proslavery adventure tale functions in responsive opposition to the slave narrative as it erases the danger to the slave, diminishes the slave figure himself, and repositions the white character as hero.

Such depicted heroism stands at the core of *Robert and Harold*, which promises young readers that they can move beyond the plantation to confidently colonize a wider world, both taming and dominating nature—beast and slave alike. Goulding depicts such colonizing as powerful, virile, ennobling, and cathartic; the white child, already a knowledgeable master, can both kill and control nature, yet show kindness to ever-needy slaves. The genre offers white children a lesson of power and dependence based upon immoveable racial designations. In these ways, the proslavery adventure for children becomes the strongest fantasy of white racial superiority and the most confident expression of proslavery ideology in antebellum literature.

CONFEDERATE SCHOOLBOOKS

Unlike the exuberant confidence of *Robert and Harold*, where slaveholders' children command a world far beyond the plantation, by the 1860s many slave owners were embroiled in debates about succession and abolition. In addition, increasing anxieties about possible war and slave rebellion left many of them concerned about the future of their way of life. Feeling besieged by Northern newspapers, magazines, and literature, editors of some of the major Southern journals argued that Southerners (unlike the brave Robert and Harold of Goulding's novel) were not colonizers but rather colonized, dependent upon Northern publishers who had garnered the national market and, by doing so, the nation's ear.[30] As much as critics of Northern literature were concerned about its "pernicious" effect on Southern adult audiences ("Disenthralment" 355), they worried more about its anticipated effect on young readers.

Before the Civil War, most of the books read by Southern children were written and published in the North. Although some Southern educators argued against the regional biases of schoolbooks that ignored Southern geography and culture, they were more concerned about what attention these books *did* give to the South, particularly about slavery. From "anti-slavery textbooks" such as the *Peter Parley* series to Webster's *Dictionary*, with its definition of "slave" as a "person *subject to the will of another*, a drudge" (Heriott 653, 655), slavery advocates argued that Northern books were "dangerous to Southern youth" and, by extension, to the South, its families, and its future (Heriott 652). One critic argued that Southern children had "scarcely a book to study, except such as are written with a view to arraying children against their parents [. . .] or such as are [. . .] published by establishments which are as hostile to our interests as the maddest fanatic" (Marshall, "Southern Authors" 520). The South's "worst enemies" (Heriott 650) had entered the classroom and for those who feared the "suicidal policy" (Marshall, "Home Education" 664) of having Northern schoolbooks in Southern classrooms, the solution seemed clear: "no more useful task could be performed than the compilation of a series of southern school books, free from all taint of abolitionism" (Rev. of *A Southern Home* 668).[31]

With the beginning of the Civil War and the blockades which prevented the importation of Northern goods, publishing homegrown schoolbooks served not only an ideological imperative, but a practical necessity in the South. Nonetheless, Southern-published books were more easily argued for than achieved. Before the war, only four major publishers operated in the South, and during the war, the scarcity of paper, ink, and other printing supplies made production difficult. So, too, did the fact that Southern publishers were often forced to shut down as Northern troops advanced. Considering these problems, Southerners maintained a fairly strong publishing record during the war. While Southern publishers produced only a few recreational books and magazines for children, the belief that children's education was an essential defense for Southern slave-holding society was evident in the fact that Southern educators "undertook a crash program" of textbook publication, producing over a hundred schoolbooks during the few years of the Confederacy (Marten, *Children's* 52).[32]

The attention to Southern culture varied in these schoolbooks. Some publishers merely reprinted popular Northern schoolbooks in expurgated form; an advertisement on the back cover of Levi Branson's *First Book in Composition* (1863), for example, assured readers that the North Carolina–based Branson, Farrar would publish "The Elementary Spelling Book, Revised from Webster and adapted to Southern Schools [. . . .] leaving out all Yankee phrases and illusions [. . .] as were necessary to make it fully Southern." Other textbooks were original contributions, written and published entirely in the South. Of those, some were comparable in content to apolitical schoolbooks published in the North, while other titles—such as *The Geographical Reader for the Dixie Children* (1863, M. B. Moore) and *The First Reader, for Southern Schools* (1864)—provided instruction in Southern culture and ideology, as well as in traditional subject areas.

Like much of Gilman's antebellum work for children, most Confederate schoolbooks do not focus on slavery. Nonetheless, lessons about slavery do appear across the spectrum of textbook genres and subject areas. Indeed, specific types of textbooks influence the depiction of slavery, particularly because the subject matter's pedagogical focus or genre's expectations often frame *how* race is made significant to students. When primers and readers include descriptions of slavery, for example, they often attempt to recapture the antebellum proslavery idyll of slaves protectively ensconced in the plantation. The war and its attendant economic deprivations provide an informing context for these descriptions which often argue that slaves are the most privileged of the Southern population. Two other slave figures—the returning slave and comic-hero—are also wartime creations that literarily defend the Confederacy. Additional schoolbook genres provide other perspectives on slavery. Geographies and elocution books emphasize crucial differences between whites and blacks. While readers and religious texts encourage young masters to exhibit kindness in their treatment of slaves and assure them that slavery is divinely sanctioned, arithmetic books—with their exercises of figures and sums—most directly acknowledge the commerce at the heart of slavery. As much as authors of Confederate schoolbooks assumed their readership would be children of the master class, what they offered, in totality, was an educational program they believed would ensure (in both propagandistic and pedagogical terms) the continuance of white planter class privilege and accompanying black slavery.

Confederate schoolbooks are, first and foremost, wartime productions. As such, their representations of slavery reveal the intrusion of the war on the plantation system and on slavery itself. Indeed, a striking feature of Confederate schoolbooks is the extent to which they reveal the war's impact. The wartime scarcity of ink and paper is evident in the generally poor production quality of the books themselves. Confederate schoolbooks, as a group, also suffer a lack of varied illustrations: some textbooks reuse and share the same woodcuts, many others go without.[33] At times, the content of Confederate textbooks also reveals the conditions of war. Despite intermittent assertions of bravado—such as in the grammar exercise that asks students to insert conjunctions in the following sentence: "General Lee defeated the Yankees, — his army was much smaller — theirs" (Branson 22)—some descriptions of the war show a South in distress. For example, the essay "The Fine Little Gentleman" in *The Dixie Elementary Spelling Book* (1864) cautions readers about the South's shifting fortunes when it urges them not to behave like the main character, who makes fun of a poor boy: "he should remember how many rich people have been broken up and driven from their homes during the present war" (M. B. Moore 51). Such essays admit that the war has introduced to antebellum Southern literature an apparently irrevocable loss of stability which had been a mainstay—indeed, the core ideological promise—of earlier

Southern children's fiction. In depictions of the war's violence, Confederate schoolbooks show a corresponding social chaos—as made clear in Moore's reference to the incidence of a master class "broken up and driven from their homes."

The wartime intrusion of loss and uncertainty about the future possibilities to command either the plantation or the world at large is perhaps nowhere more evident than in the Confederate edition of *Robert and Harold*, which Goulding published in 1863. There, in a brief addition to the preface, Goulding acknowledges that "since that time [of 1852, when the novel was first published] the magic circle has been broken." The antebellum novel's promise of the expansive, if not limitless, possibilities of the next generation of masters is exchanged by Goulding for a eulogy of Robert and the South:

> At the first call of their country for defenders, the boys, long since grown [. . .], rushed to arms, and proved true to the characters ascribed to them in the story. The battlefield has, time and again, been dyed with their blood; and the manly heart of him who is known as "Robert" sleeps in [. . . a] cemetery, near Richmond, Va. May a merciful Providence spare the others, and bless their still struggling country. (v)

The future of the "still struggling country" was in doubt when Confederate schoolbooks were produced. Nonetheless, they continued the task of teaching young children of the planter class how to master slaves. At times defensive about the privilege of slaves, at other times revealing a repressed anger at the disruption of plantations and the independence of slaves leaving the plantation, authors of Confederate schoolbooks often tried to maintain the plantation myth's veneer. By the time of the war, that veneer showed signs of wear.

As in some of Caroline Gilman's antebellum plantation stories, in some Confederate schoolbooks a reference to slavery appears almost neutrally as a non sequitur amid spelling or reading lessons. In the popular *Chaudron's Spelling Book* (1864),[34] for example, the word "slave" appears in a four-by-six grid of "Words of Five Letters" (Chaudron 27) and in a review exercise listing the following sentences: "The slave found a purse in the ditch. / I was in great haste to catch my horse. / Your niece is a very sweet girl" (29). In such instances, the unrelated and uncontextualized words and sentences do not interrogate the meaning of "slave." Recognition of words, rather than meaning, seems to be the intended learning experience here. Nonetheless, such minimal references to slavery are culturally evocative, for in them slavery is presented as an understood background to Southern life, both expected and unremarkable.

More often in Southern textbooks, when slavery appears, it does so with a more overtly ideological bent.[35] Readers and primers are most likely to present a defense of slavery by shifting attention from the privilege of white masters to the fortunate conditions of slave life, even in scenes depicting slave labor. For example, essays in *The Southern Primer* (1860), published just before the war, and *The First Reader* (Chaudron 1864), mask the enervating work of picking cotton by instead focusing on the aesthetics of cotton. Although field hands "pick, pick, pick" from a "wide field," they only gather "soft down" (*Southern Primer* 27) in a place where "cot-ton is as pret-ty as snow" (Chaudron 49). And in *The Southern Primer*, slaves are privileged workers, for (in what becomes both a reading and counting exercise) students learn that field hands have their own homes: "See! [. . .]. One, two, three, four, five, six. Six nice huts" (27). Here, readers are directed to an accompanying woodcut that shows these "nice huts," along with the master's house. The hierarchy implicit in the disparity in size between the grouped huts and the house is visually bridged, for the huts seem as neat and sturdily built (although not as large) as the Big House. Moreover, the clearing that encloses the structures pictorially unites them, evoking a sense of the sheltered space described in plantation novels.

At the same time, the call for young readers to "take a walk this fine day [. . . . to] go and see the field hands" (as readers literally "see" the laborers in this illustration) invites white students into the scene, as if positioning them as masters (*Southern Primer* 27). The gaze of the unidentified narrator, invited reader/viewer, and pictured overseer—all focused on working slaves—suggests the power of whites who view but do not participate in labor. It also positions the slaves as indistinguishable objects, evoking Ann Kibbey's description of the enforced anonymity of slaves, viewed by masters as "ideally a repetition of identical forms" (173). Racial hierarchy is visually apparent here, for while nothing distinguishes one black laborer from another, they are collectively distinguished by race, as well as by clothing, posture, and action, from the sole white man who watches them. By contrast, although Chaudron describes the aesthetics of cotton, she fractures the pastoral idyll in her essay's

FIGURE 2.2. *"The Cot-ton Field" from* The Southern Primer *(1860). Courtesy of the Rare Book Collection, The University of North Carolina at Charlotte Library.*

final sentence: "cot-ton is as pret-ty as snow, but it is worth a great deal more" (49). In so doing, she acknowledges that whatever cotton's ostensible beauty, it is commerce and the master's financial profit that are important lessons. Underpinning that commerce, however, is the real lesson to be learned: the value of the slave labor that produces cotton.

In some ways, Confederate readers support images of antebellum plantation stories. Slaves are happy, well fed, and although they may work, their labor is not strenuous; slaves are here, as in plantation stories, protected by guardian masters. Yet the Civil War years introduced keener anxieties to slaveholders, and economic problems exacerbated already simmering conflicts between poor whites and the planter class.[36] That change is also evident—and even exploited—in Confederate representations of the plantation where slaves are the envy of poor whites. Here, despite facing shortages, white masters are shown generously providing for slaves who are described as largely insulated from the war's economic effects. Such contrasts both reinstate the quarantine of the plantation idyll (in the protected condition of slaves) and puncture it (in acknowledging the economic problems of the wider Southern society). Defining the ease of slaves' life through contrast with poor Southern whites not only heightens the cultural insularity of the planter class but also inherently contributes to a trope that pits poor whites in racial competition with enslaved blacks for economic survival.

Two essays in Marinda Branson Moore's *The First Dixie Reader* (1864),[37] for example, depict the plantation idyll by contrasting the privileged status of slaves with the near-starvation of poor whites. In a South beset by war, blockades, scarcity of food, and ensuing illness, descriptions in "The Cane Mill," of the "rich juice [that] runs down" while making syrup (49), emphasize the sensuality of food as well as its recuperative qualities, for "it is said that per sons us ing much of it are not apt to have fe vers" (50). The syllabically split lesson assures young readers that the difference in the living conditions of slaves and poor whites is the difference between celebration and misery, health and illness, excess and deprivation: "See them ["ser vants"] with their pots boil ing over [. . .]. Some of them will have four or five gal lons by the time the sea son closes. Well done for the dar kies. Many poor white peo ple would be glad of what they leave for the hogs" (50).[38]

Moore's other essay, "Old Aunt Ann," counters abolitionist descriptions of the treatment of aged slaves, such as Frederick Douglass's description of the "base ingratitude" (*Narrative* 91) shown to his grandmother and Noah Webster's fictionalized slave in "Lamentation of an Old Female Slave" also "cast out to shift for [. . . her] self" (*Little Reader's* 44). Moore here typifies proslavery arguments that slaves, old and unable to work, enjoyed permanent and well-fed retirements, resting upon the largesse of the master class. When young students meet "Old Aunt Ann," they are told "when she was young she did good work, but now she can not work much. But she is not like a poor white wo-man. Aunt Ann [like "maum Nelly" in Caroline Gilman's "The Country Visit"] knows that her young Miss [. . .] will take care of her as long as she lives" (22).

As in "The Cane Mill," Moore uses food in this second essay to show that in a Confederacy where goods are scarce, slaves—even unproductive ones—enjoy good fortune, health, and sustenance through the protection afforded by kindly masters. Moreover, in the plantation ideology that argues the mutual affection and loyalty of master and slave, Aunt Ann, as a retired slave, possesses authority, status, and power even over whites, for "ma-ny poor white folks would be glad to live in her house and eat what Miss Kate sends out for her din-ner" (22). While the intrusion of whites' deprivation reveals the dissolution of the wider Southern society, such essays that focus on the plantation reflect the central ideology of the master class—that "the preservation of the plantation was the *raison d'être* of the Confederacy" (Roark 44). By acknowledging the dangers waiting just outside the plantation's borders, these essays imply that the plantation needs preserving from the war's onslaught and its attendant effects. The central plantation figure who enjoys the beneficence of its protection and plenty is the slave. The assurance of the plantation's viability in a time of war is thus framed as an assurance of the bounty still enjoyed by its slaves. By contrast, poor whites represent the deprivation slaves would face were they free to live beyond the plantation's boundaries. For young white readers of the master class, poor whites also represented their own threatened loss of social and economic status because of the war.

The argument that slaves live better lives in slavery than in freedom was a long-standing one in proslavery literature. The assertion redefined slavery as a higher type of freedom—freedom from want, freedom from responsibility, and (at times in the plantation idyll) freedom from work. Yet the war clearly had an effect on slavery, and Confederate texts for children particularly acknowledge that in two slave figures: the repentant, returning slave who functions as a type of prodigal slave; and the comic-hero who fights to defend slavery. The trope of the repentant, returning slave argues the lack of perspicacity and steadfastness in those slaves who are easily persuaded that life will be better elsewhere. It reveals the context of war and the destabilization of Southern slave-holding society, since it is interfering Yankees who typically lure the slave away from the plantation. The trope critiques Northern abolitionists, for Yankees invariably prove to be unfeeling taskmasters, at the same time that it asserts the unwavering largesse of Southern masters. Although the figure of a slave abandoning the plantation admits a master class losing authority, status, and slaves (in short, losing its identity and raison d'être), in focusing on the slave's voluntary return, the trope also counters the slave owner's tenuous control with a fantasy of the master class' return to power. It assures young readers that while slaves may be disloyal and while the plantation may seem to be disintegrating, master and slave will eventually resume their proper roles, and the plantation be reconstituted.

Uncle Ned, in an essay of the same name, is a quintessential repentant-returning slave figure. When invading Yankee soldiers tell Ned "that he should be free, and live like white folks," Ned, along with his wife and children, leaves the plantation, "but he soon found they had not told him the truth. He did not fare so well as he did at home wtth [*sic*] his mas-ter." Ned then abandons his wife and children, escapes from the Yankees, and returns to his "kind mas-ter," telling him, "'dem Yan-kee no be good to poor nig-ger, can't stay wid um. Ned lib wid you all his life." More loyal to slaves than slaves are to him, the master welcomes Ned back. The slave nonetheless seems divinely punished for his disloyalty, not knowing whether he will ever be reunited with his wife and children. Yet Ned declares that he has reunited with a more important family—his master—and has happily returned to his proper state and place in life (M. B. Moore, *First Dixie Reader* 39).

Another figure used to critique Northern attempts to emancipate slaves is the proslavery faithful negro as heroic slave. Actively loyal to his master, this character takes up arms or in other ways directly engages and thwarts those who would assault the plantation or the institution of slavery. Not a symbol of the free black or meant as a justification for emancipation, the heroic slave in proslavery literature is ultimately diminished so that his agency and independence are contained. He becomes, in the end, a type of fool. A proslavery comic-heroic slave appears in "The Mountain Guide," a story in *Boys and Girls Stories of the War*, one of the few recreational books published for children during the Confederacy.[39] Here, readers meet an "Uncle Ned" quite different from Moore's Ned. This character becomes a military hero as he defends slavery and the South, capturing a Yankee soldier in the process. After Yankees take Ned's master and steal food from his garden, Ned agrees to lead Confederate soldiers over the mountains to facilitate their attack on Union soldiers. During that battle, the Yankees virtually enslave Ned when he is "taken prisoner and forced away with them" (13). Following a later attack by Stonewall's men, Ned escapes and victoriously rides into town "on a little pony with a [captured] Yankee behind him." Ned tells the soldier not to fall off or "I'll blow your head off with dis here pistol. You is de chap dat took my milk and potatoes, and now I'se goin' to carry you to de prison where all de rogues lib" (14).

No Pomp (of Trowbridge's *Cudjo's Cave*) nor Hatchie (of Adams's *Hatchie, the Guardian Slave*), Uncle Ned is ultimately a loyal but comic slave. Although the Yankee prisoner's discomfort—"the Yankee did not like to ride behind Uncle Ned"—exposes Northern racism, the essay ultimately affirms racial hierarchy. It seems to be the publicly acknowledged embarrassment of a white man captured and commanded by a black "Uncle" who rides a "little pony" that provides "great amusement" (14) to the white observers "laughing fit to kill themselves" (13). Conservative abolitionist heroes Pomp and Hatchie, unlike Ned, never become an object of comedy for whites; neither are they described as "Uncles." With that repeated appellation, which in proslavery ideology signals a (not too) familial connection between master and slave, Uncle Ned is rhetorically tamed. Despite his personal and public retribution in triumphing over the Yankee (the point seems to be that *even* a slave can capture a Yankee), Ned's virility is compromised both by him riding on a "little pony" and by being an object of entertainment to white onlookers (a common role for plantation slaves).[40] Illustrations, too, show the contrast in these anti- and proslavery heroic slave figures. While Hatchie's agency is emphasized in the illustration of him threatening to lynch his white enemy (see fig. 1.5), Uncle Ned is shown looking out a window, perhaps nostalgic for his life with his master, perhaps inviting readers into his world, but not (despite the verbal narrative) engaged in battle, wielding a gun, nor capturing a Yankee soldier.

The proslavery comic-heroic slave figure became the fantasy of Confederate authors who were witnessing the collapse of the slave-holding system and the mass exodus of slaves to the North and to Union armies.[41] While some slaves certainly remained on and returned to the plantation, the master's idyll of plantation life (if it ever existed) was shattered. During the war years, the master class was routed, plantations destroyed, slaves emancipated and, in large numbers, the happy "Uncles" and grateful "Aunts" of plantation stories had, in truth, abandoned the plantation for freedom or Union service with no plans to return to slavery. As "The Mountain Guide" and "Uncle Ned" show, in the midst of that upheaval, Confederate authors tried to reconstitute plantation fiction. Yet, the very depiction of slaves escaping the plantation and fighting in the war hinted at a defensiveness to current events and deep-seated fears on the part of the slave-holding class, particularly of plantations without slaves.

Despite the expected propaganda of these essays, "Uncle Ned" is an odd piece to include in a children's schoolbook with the stated purpose of teaching the "first principles of spelling and reading" (M. B. Moore, *First Dixie Reader* u.p.). The heavy inflection of Ned's

FIGURE 2.3. *"The Mountain Guide" from* Boys and Girls Stories of the War *[ca. 1863] by Edward M. Boykin. Courtesy of the Rare Book Collection, Wilson Library, The University of North Carolina at Chapel Hill.*

dialect—"dem Yan-kee no be good to poor nig-ger, can't stay wid um. Ned lib wid you all his life" and his recommendation for "eb ry nig ger to stay at home and mind his work" (40)—would seem to undermine the intent of a reading exercise so rudimentary as to be delivered in a one- and split-syllable presentation. Yet in such books there seems to be a more fundamental lesson being offered by the Confederacy: teaching white students the early principles of racial hierarchy.

Young white Southern readers were frequently taught that "*correct* pronunciation [. . .] is highly important" ("Pronunciation"). That elocution was an important educational concern in a slave-holding society indicates its significance as a sign of racial difference.[42] That difference—indeed, the fear that white slave-holding children would speak in black dialect—is emphasized by Adelaide de Vendel Chaudron in her *Third Reader* (1864), where she cautions students against "some very common colloquial errors, which, for want of a more scientific name, we will call AFRICANISMS. The [. . .] words bear so little resemblance to those for which they are substitutes, that we will treat them as grammatical 'barbarisms.'" Chaudron lists and translates some of those "astounding barbarisms" and argues that they are the "dialect first learned by every Southerner, from that dusky deity of his infantine worship, his 'Mammy.' Many a distinguished Southern orator has had to study hard before he could break himself of 'Mammy's' Africanisms" (26).

In defining a white child's affection and respect of Mammy as "infantine," Chaudron argues—like Caroline Gilman in her description of Clara leaving Nelly—that slaveholders' children must separate themselves from Mammy's influence in order to assume their status as "distinguished [i.e., slave-holding] Southern[ers]." Chaudron never advises that slaves receive elocution lessons; the distinction between white and black fictionalized speech in antebellum Southern literature (as in a significant portion of Northern, even abolitionist, literature) was maintained to signal irrevocable differences between the two races. The more unintelligible is black slave dialect—the wider the chasm between "white" and "black"—the more necessary the defense of white civilization against the influence of the "barbaric" African. In descriptions of slavery for children, Confederate authors, like proslavery authors before them, thus attempted to retain the facade of slavery as a system of attachment while at the same time teaching children that any real attachment to slaves—or erosion of the boundaries between white and black, master and slave—could signal destruction to the master class and race.

This assertion that Africans are essentially different from whites also underpins many geographies. Since geographies speak about generalized groups rather than individuals, and since a main focus of many nineteenth-century geographies is distinguishing between people of different countries and races, they have been a particularly elastic genre for the transmission of ethnocentric and racist ideologies for authors on either side of the Mason-Dixon Line. In *The Geographical Reader for the Dixie Children* (1863), for example, M. B. Moore teaches students that the Caucasian race "is civilized, and is far above all the others" while "the African [. . .] race is [. . . .] slothful and vicious, but possess[es] little cunning" (10). In such assurances of racial hierarchies and white supremacy, Confederate geographies share much with many Northern (even moderate and conservative abolitionist) geographies.[43]

Like Gilman's writing for children, Confederate schoolbooks never debate whether or not one should be a slaveholder, but instead offer instruction on what *kind* of slaveholder one should be. Among the religious lessons in *The First Reader, for Southern Schools* (1864), for example, students are assured that "it is not a sin to own slaves. It is right. God wills that some men should be slaves, and some masters. It is a sin to treat a servant ill. [. . .] It is not best to set him free, but to keep him and be kind to him" (17). Indeed, these lessons often use biblical text to justify slavery and encourage kindly relations between master and slave. One sees this, for example, in the Confederate *Our Own Third Reader* (1862), as authors Sterling and Campbell quote Colossians to young students: "masters, give unto your servants that which is just and equal; knowing that ye also have a Master in heaven" (220).

Yet such assurances that slavery is based on responsibility rather than commerce are undercut in other religious lessons that—like Chaudron's warning against "Africanisms"—position the slave as the noncivilized "other." Elsewhere in *Our Own Third Reader,* Sterling and Campbell cite Leviticus to claim God's irrefutable support of the enslavement of Africans. Although God directs that one shall not rule over "the children of Israel," he does grant that "thy bondmen and thy bond-maids, which thou shalt have, shall be of the heathen that are round about you [. . .]. Moreover, of the children of the strangers [. . .] shall ye buy [. . .] and they shall be your possession [. . . .] for ever" (213). Not needing to type Africans as anything other than "heathen" who are further made "strangers" in white America, religious training promises white students that God has ordained blacks to be their slaves.

Of the varied subject-area Confederate textbooks, it is in the arithmetics that the veneer of the plantation romance utterly disappears. Indeed, Confederate arithmetic books most clearly support the assertions of proslavery's literary nemesis, the slave narrative. Harriet Jacobs's contention that "these God-breathing machines [the enslaved] are no more, in the sight of their masters, than the cotton they plant, or the horses they tend" (8) rings true in Confederate arithmetics, where slavery unambiguously becomes a matter of business. Some problems—such as "Mr. Tillett had eleven slaves, five of whom were women; how many of them were men?" (Lander, *Primary Arithmetic* 15)—acknowledge a slave society without further comment. Others, like this problem in Samuel Lander's *Our Own School Arithmetic* (1863)—"if 5 white men can do as much work as 7 negroes, how many days of 10 hr. each will be required for 25 negroes to do a piece of work which 30 white men can do in

10 days of 9hr. each? [Ans. 15.12 da.]" (171)—not only teach lessons of white superiority but also implicitly justify long work hours for slaves. More tellingly, however, in *Our Own School Arithmetic*, the problems "if 125 slaves sell for $75125, what is their average value?" (136) and "A owns $10475 in real estate, $3850 in slaves, $4095 in good notes, and $1415 in cash; what is the value of his whole estate?" (135) define the attachment of master to slave as a strictly commercial one, marked by a simple mathematical equation. While the lesson in Confederate readers is often to "be kind" to slaves (*First Reader, for Southern Schools* 17), proslavery arithmetics often teach children that their responsibility as slave owners is to be able to figure out the market value of the slaves they buy, sell, and own. No Nellys or Neds here, slaves are not personalized but defined only as overt objects of sale.

Even when slaves are noted by name in arithmetics, it is clear such identifiers signal specific property, not acknowledgment of personhood. In *The Student's Arithmetic* (1861), when authors Caldwell and Everett offer "necessary knowledge to all [future] men of business" (ix), included in this "business" are lessons in the buying and selling of slaves. In an appendix that models legal documents are forms future slaveholders will be expected to understand. Among them is a "Bill of Sale," the italicized sections highlighting information individual slaveholders would supply, depending on the specific sale: "received of *Lewis M. Martin, one thousand* dollars, in full payment for a *negro boy* by the name of *Henry*, about *nineteen* years old, of *yellow* complexion, I warrant said *boy* to be sound, both mentally and physically, I also warrant the right and title, unto the said *Lewis M. Martin* [. . .] against the claim of all other persons whatsoever" (141). Caldwell and Everett further emphasize the importance of understanding the possession and distribution of slaves in the following model of a "Written Will," where four of the six itemized property bequests involve slaves:

> I give and bequeath to my beloved wife [. . .] my negro man, *Harry*, known as my *carriage driver*, my negro man *Sam* about *thirty* years of age. *Sam's* wife *Sallie*, about *twenty-five* years of age; and their *four* children [. . .].
>
> I give, bequeath, and devise to my son *Robt.* [. . .] *Reuben*, a man about *twenty-five* years of age; and his wife, *Phebe* [. . .]; and their four children [. . .] to him forever [. . .]. (142)

As much as Confederate arithmetic books rent the veil of the plantation myth in their depictions of slaves as objects of commerce, they nonetheless propagated the assumption (especially evident in modeling wills) that slavery would not only continue in perpetuity for these slaves, but for the South as well. Although Caldwell and Everett taught young students how to bequeath slaves to their own children, those students, in just a few years, would be the South's first generation of an expectant master class *without* slaves.

• • •

One might argue that the slavery lessons offered in Confederate schoolbooks were ultimately unnecessary for that generation of students—that the depictions were only the last gasp of a soon-vanquished system. But Confederate representations of the privileged, returning, and comic-heroic slave—along with arithmetic lessons that blacks (but not whites) could be measured as finite commodities—did not disappear. They combined with earlier proslavery images from adventure novels and plantation stories that defined the slave as animal-like and utterly dependent upon white noblesse oblige. The fusion of commerce and dependency as themes in these images inspired a raft of racialized character-types that would long survive the incursion of Union soldiers and slavery's legal end.

CHAPTER 3
RECONSTRUCTING SLAVERY
1865–1919

"I won'er what you kinky-head niggers is fur[,"
said Mammy. . . .] And, picking up a cotton-stalk,
she gave each of the little darkies a sound whipping.
—Louise-Clarke Pyrnelle, *Diddie, Dumps and Tot, or, Plantation Child-Life* (1882)

Black is no mark of reproach
to people who do not worship white.
—Edward A. Johnson, *A School History of the Negro Race in America* (1890)

Following the Civil War, three new amendments to the Constitution seemed to promise much: the Thirteenth abolished slavery; the Fourteenth guaranteed citizenship and equal protection under the law; the Fifteenth provided the right to vote (to black males). Despite the goals of postwar Reconstruction—what W. E. B. Du Bois had called "one of the most singular [. . .] attempts [. . .] to grapple with vast problems of race" (*Souls* 55)—in little over a decade, the Freedmen's Bureau and concurrent legal moves toward civil rights collapsed amid an array of challenges, and Reconstruction formally ended in 1877. While white resistance to black enfranchisement underwrote the creation of the Ku Klux Klan in 1866 and the rising number of lynchings throughout the South, following Reconstruction, Southern states also engineered a legal backlash against freedmen in a series of Jim Crow laws which, for all practical purposes, nullified earlier-passed amendments. The U.S. Supreme Court also upheld segregationist policies, declaring the Civil Rights Act of 1875 unconstitutional and, in the *Plessy v. Ferguson* (1896) case, affirming the constitutionality of "separate but equal" in a decision that would protect racial segregationist policies into the mid-twentieth century.

The dangers of emancipation had been long argued; in 1835 Alexis de Tocqueville had prophesized race warfare and "perhaps [. . .] the extirpation of one or the other of the two races" as its probable outcome (245). It was not only the emancipation of over four million slaves that riddled the white imagination; it was what those slaves—particularly because of their color—had come to mean. Because slavery and race were combined in the American imagination, legal emancipation was not sufficient to counter the weight of centuries of race theories that had argued the inferiority of blacks. Indeed, as historian George Fredrickson has argued, this "conjunction of servitude and color [. . .] had planted the seeds of disaster by creating a problem of race more fundamental and difficult to solve than the problem of slavery" (23). Hence, emancipation legally freed the slave in a way it could not free the black man, woman, and child in America.

Children's literature from the end of the Civil War through the turn of the century reveals the ways in which the first generations of authors living in postslavery America re-presented slavery as a way of explaining the past, interpreting the present, and reimagining the nation's racialized future. As such, this literature—including freedmen's schoolbooks, postplantation novels, and antislavery responses—encompasses a range of ideological perspectives. Articulating the South's cult of the Lost Cause, postplantation novels became a popular staple of the time, assuring white readers of the Confederacy's nobility. Antislavery literature contested such depictions to varying degrees, at times offering images of heroic slaves rebelling against enslavement, at other times presenting depictions of faithful slaves, albeit with Union loyalties. In the midst of such literary contestations, new audiences were engaged, as more literature was written specifically for African American children, particularly bureau-sponsored schoolbooks early in the period and African American–authored books later in the century. While both often presented biographies of actual people in their depictions of slavery, each worked in different ways to define the expected roles of African Americans in a postslavery United States.

FREEDMEN EDUCATION AND SCHOOLBOOKS

In 1865, the federal government established the Bureau of Refugees, Freedmen, and Abandoned Lands, better known as the Freedmen's

Bureau. Charged with supporting the civil rights of newly freed slaves, the bureau sought to develop fair labor practices, protect legal rights, and establish schools. Its limited effectiveness in setting up those schools revealed the problems and possibilities of education for freed blacks during the postbellum years. Despite suffering a lack of funds, the Freedmen's Bureau coordinated the efforts and resources of Northern reformers and freedpeople who supplied both funding and teachers for the schools. The results were impressive. Between 1865 and 1870 as many as four thousand schools opened for freedpeople, enrolling over two hundred thousand child and adult students (Gates and McKay 463; Wyatt-Brown 427).[1]

Although in large part destitute, the newly freed black population supported and established freedmen's schools across the South. Some black communities chose to raise taxes; others donated their labor to help build schools or opened their homes to teachers. Despite resistance from planters, some parents refused to sign labor contracts that did not have an "education clause" which stipulated the plantation owner's support of schools. Since some slaves and freed blacks had—secretly or otherwise—already provided for their own education during antebellum times, when agents of the Freedmen's Bureau moved into Southern areas to open schools, they sometimes found black-run schools already in existence (Foner 97). In those and other freedmen's schools, black teachers significantly contributed to the educational enterprise. While, for example, many teachers in freedmen's schools were Northern, middle-class, white women, the number of black teachers increased so much that by 1869 they outnumbered their white colleagues.[2]

Education for slaves had been outlawed for much of the same reason that education for freedmen often met with resistance. As a writer in 1865 noted, for freedmen, "knowledge is power, and [. . .] much of this knowledge must be book knowledge. Whether the suffrage is or is not limited to those who can read and write, it is just as clear that the black man who has those arts is the superior of the clay-eating white who cannot [*sic*]. And this is as clear to the black man as it is to his old master" ("Education of the Freedmen" 536). While this writer imagines the disruption of racial hierarchies limited to the poorest of whites, many believed that an educated class of freed blacks would also upset the previously protected privilege of the now-slaveless white planter class. So, while teachers in freedmen's schools faced the disapprobation of many Southern whites, few resources, and difficult living situations, they did not face unenthusiastic students.

The specific content of freedpeople's education was a matter of debate as well. Although a few Confederate textbooks were reprinted after the war (showing an 1866 publication date), for the most part, Reconstruction-era schools for former slaves used textbooks commonly found in Northern classrooms. Freedpeople could be expected to read such popular series as *Webster* spellers, *McGuffey* readers, and *Peter Parley* histories and geographies. Because few schools could afford new books, most classrooms were stocked with donated used books from the North that would have been published before the war (Morris 187; M. Mitchell 104). Some of those would have been the very books against which Confederate educators had railed. Indeed, in schools across the South, teachers of white students also using these Northern textbooks often did so with "offensive pages pinned together," so that students would not be exposed to abolitionist or pro-Northern perspectives (Elson 8).

Formerly enslaved children often received mixed messages in their education. Some freedmen's schools offered lessons rebellious to the former Confederacy; the song "John Brown's Body," which extolled the (in)famous abolitionist while mocking former Confederate President Jefferson Davis, for example, became highly popular with freedmen students (Morris 178–179). At the same time, many officials of the Freedmen's Bureau sought to placate local planters by advising teachers against partisan politics. One teacher in Arkansas, for example, was urged to teach "as a devoted Christian Minister, [. . .] letting politics alone, and avoiding all participation in the quarrels that blacks may have with whites" (qtd in Morris 182).[3]

In addition to *McGuffey* readers and *Peter Parley* textbooks intended for general (which in the racial politics of the time is to say, "white") students,[4] freedmen's schools were also supplied with the *Freedman's* series of schoolbooks. Published by the American Tract Society (ATS) specifically for newly freed slaves, the series offered a mixed curriculum of conservative social control and a progressive revisioning of the racialized status quo. On the one hand, as several historians have noted, the series patronizingly lectured freedpeople about the importance of piety and the efficacy of the Protestant work ethic. On the other, it presented a series of biographies that showed the significant contributions of slaves and freedpeople.[5]

This series, including *The Freedman's Spelling-Book* (1866) and the *Second* (1865) and *Third* (1865) *Freedman's Readers*, comprised the largest collection of schoolbooks produced for freedmen (Anderson 30). Its publisher, the ATS, claimed as its mission "to diffuse a knowledge of our Lord Jesus Christ [. . .] and to promote [. . .] vital godliness and sound morality" (qtd in Morris 188). An expression of the society's missionary goal, the ATS's publications encouraged readers to godly acts in their acceptance of Christ, their kindness to others, and their industry and temperance. As such, the moral lessons provided throughout the *Freedman's* series—as in the list of sentences,

> It is a sin to sip rum.
> [. . .]
> A la-zy man can not get a job.
> God is ho-ly; he can see if men sin.

—articulated values that the ATS offered to audiences at large, not just to ex-slaves (*Freedman's Spelling-Book* [1866 rpt.] 13).

Nonetheless, in these schoolbooks, those commonly expressed values of religious faith and social responsibility were often refashioned for freed black audiences. One sees this as rhetoric about slavery frames moral lessons, as in the caution that an "idle spirit [. . . can] make you its slave for life" (*Freedman's Second Reader* 93) and "a life of self-renouncing love / Is a life of liberty" (*Freedman's Third Reader* 68). While such lessons did not differ substantially from values touted to white students in ATS publications (or, for that matter, those presented in mainstream children's books at large), the *Freedman's* series responded specifically to debates about the "fitness" of slaves for freedom by lecturing on the expected duties and social interactions of freedmen, as in *The Freedman's Spelling-Book*, where students read that "a freed-man should be prov-i-dent; that is, he should pro-vide for the fu-ture, and not be neg-li-gent" (79). "The Freedman's Home," an essay in *The Freedman's Second Reader*, offers an obvious example of the civilizing objective of the ATS: "Once you had to [. . .] run as fast as you could to the field of work. But not so now. Now you may wash and dress with care and put your room in order. [. . .] When the food is cooked [. . . .] first, you must thank God for it [. . .]. Now you may eat, but not too fast, nor with a noise like the pigs" (36).

Although the evangelical ATS had avoided taking an antislavery stance before the war,[6] these readers share some key precepts and images of radical abolitionist children's literature. As antebellum radical abolitionist texts such as *The Slave's Friend* argued racial equality, for example, so too, does *Freedman's Third Reader* in an essay titled "All Mankind of One Blood": "As God is one, so also the entire race of man, whatever their habits, customs, character, or color, are one. [. . .] We are all created by God, and of one blood; therefore we are brethren" (47). In three significant ways—particularly in visual representation, the redefined role of the black child, and a focus on slave biographies—the *Freedman's* series emphasizes the agency of freedpeople and slaves more directly than did even the radical abolitionist *The Slave's Friend*. Particularly in the biographies, however, agency is circumscribed to reflect the ATS's agenda of socializing newly freed slaves to peaceably incorporate themselves into postslavery life.

In an illustration of "The Good Schoolmaster" (1837), appearing in the antebellum *The Slave's Friend*, black education is visually represented as a white male teacher standing over young black students gathered about him. While the proximity of black students and white teacher suggests their companionability, his height and the fact that he stands reading to them signal his authority. The position and scale of these figures are reminiscent of the abolitionist icon of the supplicant slave pleading for white aid (see fig. 1.2). By contrast, although the benevolent white reformer is reiterated in the cover illustrations of *The Freedman's Second* and *Third Readers*,[7] the fact that these respective teachers are seated, and students are at their height and even above one, diminishes the representation of white authority found in *The Slave's Friend*. Moreover, the cover illustration of *The Freedman's Spelling-Book* emphasizes the engagement and agency of black students as leaders. Perhaps a student because of her age, yet functioning as a model teacher, the young girl visually writes her own story. In the midst of writing herself and others in the classroom into "freedom" without white oversight, she shows the inseparability of literacy and political power.

This figure demonstrates how the *Freedman's* series reshapes antebellum abolitionist discourse in its representation of the black child. Where white children largely function as reformers in antebellum radical abolitionist children's literature, here the black child becomes a reformer. One also sees this in the essay, "How Father Henson Learned to Read," from *Freedman's Third Reader*. When Josiah Henson believes he "can't begin now to learn to read," his

FIGURE 3.1. *"The Good Schoolmaster" from* The Slave's Friend *(1837). Courtesy of American Antiquarian Society.*

FIGURE 3.2. *Illustration from* The Freedman's Spelling-Book. *Boston: American Tract Society, 1866. Courtesy of Special Collections, Monroe C. Gutman Library, Harvard Graduate School of Education.*

son assures him "you are never too old to learn." Henson ultimately relents and "became a scholar to [his . . .] little son" (21–22). Such scenes—of black children gaining literacy and using their talents to teach others—expand the racial expectations of republican childhood to position the black child as one who will reform the nation in the postbellum world. By fostering black literacy, it is the black child who becomes the hope for the newly emancipated generation moving from slavery to freedom.[8]

Freedman's Third Reader, which among the *Freedman's* schoolbooks most references slavery, also offers something new to young readers in its number of biographies of freedmen and former slaves, including Paul Cuffee, Frederick Douglass, Josiah Henson, the Reverend Doctor Pennington, and Phillis Wheatley, along with an account of the *Amistad* captives. In so doing, *Freedman's Third Reader* not only begins to establish a canon of pivotal black leaders in America, but does so by highlighting the achievements of slaves and freedmen (in itself, a radical representation of slavery). Moreover, the *Reader*'s attention to biography and autobiography implicitly reinforces the authority of antebellum slave narratives as an early expression of the slave's emotional depth, intellectual abilities, and personhood. (The story of "How Father Henson Learned to Read," noted above, for example, draws from a passage in Henson's autobiography, even at times verbatim.)[9]

At the same time, however, authors of these *Freedman's* books sculpt excerpted antebellum slave narratives and biographical information in specific ways to further the ATS's objectives. Similar to antebellum radical abolitionists who were influenced by evangelical religion, the *Freedman's* series repeatedly calls for forgiveness on the part of its readers, who are taught that "the Word of God not only teaches us to love all our fellow-beings [. . .], but it also bids us love our enemies" (*Freedman's Third Reader* 50). This advocacy for peace and forgiveness, also found in antebellum radical abolitionist texts, deemphasizes ideologies of dissension in favor of elevating slaves as sacrificial figures. Indeed, representations of slave rebellion generally do not appear in these texts. The biography of Frederick Douglass in *Freedman's Third Reader* is a case in point, particularly as one compares it to the one included in Lydia Maria Child's *The Freedmen's Book* (1865). More specifically geared to adult audiences, *The Freedmen's Book*—like *Freedman's Third Reader*—presents biographies of important slave figures, but its biographies condemn slavery often more passionately than those that appear in the ATS publications.[10]

Both biographies borrow, at times verbatim, from Douglass's own accounts of his life, but while Child includes the famous scene of Douglass's successful battle against Covey (170), *Freedman's Third Reader* instead focuses on Douglass's religious conversion and attendant expression of forgiveness. Drawing from Douglass's later *My Bondage and My Freedom* (1855), the ATS quotes Douglass's declaration that "I loved all mankind, slaveholders not excepted, though I abhorred slavery more than ever. My great concern was now to have the world converted" (*Freedman's Third Reader* 207; Douglass 122–123). While in *My Bondage and My Freedom* Douglass recounts his battle with Covey in detail, *Freedman's Third Reader* not only omits that, but here and in other biographies the ATS consistently avoids descriptions of the frustration and anger felt by slaves in favor of focusing on their religious faith. This censoring of the rebelliousness articulated in antebellum slave narratives reveals the focus on social control in the education of the newly freed population. Fearing the anger of a people recently enslaved, many post–Civil War writers would encourage racial cooperation and forgiveness, specifically on the part of former slaves. In its *Freedman's* schoolbooks, the ATS found a convenient means of directing that message to those formerly enslaved.

As the *Freedman's* books rewrite antebellum depictions of slavery, they also recast representations of slavery's violence, at times censoring it, at other times sublimating it in favor of assuring readers of the reward for hard work. *Freedman's Third Reader* acknowledges the violence of slavery, particularly the forced separations of families and the kidnapping of people from Africa. In these biographies, for example, one learns of Paul Cuffee's father "dragged from his home in Africa [. . .] and sold into slavery" (51) and of the "brutal treatment" endured by those enslaved aboard the *Amistad* (105). In an essay titled "Africa," also in *Freedman's Third Reader*, freedpeople would read of the slave trade that "sometimes [. . .] the captains of the vessels would rob the people of their children, or they would go on shore with a body of armed men, and carry away the inhabitants of a whole village. [*] It was by this cruel trade that slavery was introduced into various parts of America and the West Indies" (227). The passage obviously criticizes slavery.

What is important in understanding the ATS's representation of slavery lies in the contrast of this passage to its originating source. In compiling the *Freedman's* readers, the ATS at times took material from other books; the above passage on the slave trade, for example, is taken from a passage of Peter Parley's *Universal History on the Basis of Geography* (1837). As part of Samuel Goodrich's popular "Peter Parley" schoolbook franchise, the textbook appeared in repeated printings, and while new sections were added to subsequent editions, much of the original information remained the same.[11] Although the passage in *Freedman's Third Reader* about the slave trade was otherwise extracted verbatim from Peter Parley's *Universal History*, what was excised (and appears in the *Freedman's* text where the asterisk is placed, above) is an intervening passage describing how

> the poor negroes thus taken from their homes, and separated for ever from all they held dear, were crowded into vessels, where they were half-starved, and suffered so much from disease, and the most barbarous treatment, that they frequently threw themselves into the sea to escape from their miseries. (Goodrich 1837, 122; 1860, 124)

The 1860 edition continues with:

> [. . .] Or beat out their own brains in despair. Millions of these poor negroes have been taken from their homes; and probably more than half of those who entered the ships, from the beginning of the trade to this day, perished before they reached the countries to which they were bound. (1860, 125; 1875, 167)

What the ATS does in redacting these descriptions is to remove sensory details, leaving the remaining passage emotionally sterile by comparison. While still denouncing the slave trade, the ATS version ultimately ignores the genocidal results of enslavement. Although the postbellum editions of the Parley text retain more explicit descriptions of slavery (see, for example, the 1875 edition), the ATS's censoring of those passages reflects the racial politics of the *Freedman's* schoolbooks as part of the federally sanctioned project to socialize newly freed slaves. Diminishing representations of slavery's violence made it easier for the ATS to argue one of their central objectives: forgiveness on the part of former slaves. It also anticipated the further retellings of slavery that would occur throughout the postbellum years.

In one sense, that the ATS offered biographies that do not emphasize the victimization of slaves redirects focus to one's agency despite enslavement. Yet the scope of agency condoned in the ATS schoolbooks is significantly narrowed from representations in antebellum slave narratives which include physical rebellion and creative dissension. In the *Freedman's* series, slave agency is typically confined to hard work which was then rewarded. One sees this, for example, in the account of Paul Cuffee's father: although "dragged from his home in Africa," once in the United States, he was able to improve his plight because "being of good behavior and industrious habits, [he] was favored by his master [. . .] and allowed to work for his freedom" (*Freedman's Third Reader* 52). The commendations of hard work and positive attitude in these biographies did not merely offer models to the newly freed slaves whom the Freedmen's Bureau hoped would peaceably transition into a free society. They also implicitly repositioned the responsibility for the ill treatment of slaves (and in some sense, for slavery itself) onto the slave.

Thus, while acknowledging slavery as a "cruel and wicked system of oppression" (32), *Freedman's Third Reader* moves past depictions of violence to focus on the success slaves and freedpeople enjoy as rewards for diligence and talent. It is the assured success of what would later be termed the Protestant work ethic, for example, which stands as the central lesson in Phillis Wheatley's biography in *Freedman's Third Reader*. Both Child's *The Freedmen's Book* and the ATS's *Freedman's Third Reader* use Margaretta Matilda Odell's *Memoir and Poems of Phillis Wheatley* (1834) as the common originating text for their respective biographies of the poet, and both liberally borrow (in content and often in specific phrasing) from Odell. Nonetheless, which narrative moments each chooses to include as they sculpt their respective versions of Wheatley's life, reflects significantly different ideologies.

The two highlight similar incidents and developments in Odell's account, particularly that Wheatley was kidnapped from Africa, arrived in the colonies weakened, was bought by Mrs. Wheatley, soon after learned to read and write, and became well known as a talented poet. Both versions also emphasize (as did Odell) the poet's humility, offering Wheatley as a model of one who lived through slavery with an "amiable, affectionate disposition" (Child 88). Where the two biographies most dramatically differ, however, is in their recounting of Wheatley's later life. Child's account echoes Odell's

Memoir in describing the poet's painful marriage, impoverishment, and ultimate death "alone, in a cold, dirty, comfortless room. It was a mournful reverse of fortune" (92–93, cf. Odell 23).

By contrast, the ATS avoids any acknowledgment of Wheatley's problems in later life. Noting briefly that Wheatley died "in her twenty-sixth year," *Freedman's Third Reader* concludes: "the life of Phillis Wheatley gives most interesting proof of the power of talents and virtues, crowned with 'the pearl of great price,'—the love of Christ,—to raise one from the lowest position to the notice and esteem of the wise and the good" (77). Although a rendition of Odell's introduction in *Memoir and Poems of Phillis Wheatley* (5), the ATS version excises Odell's account of Wheatley's trials to turn the poet's life story into a lesson that assures readers that God will reward industry and the wise use of talent. By contrast, while Odell's *Memoir* acknowledges Wheatley's renown, she never argues that it protected her from the vagaries of life's suffering. In Child's account to freedpeople, there is also no assurance that God will reward labor and talent with continued earthly success and accolades. Rather, Child acknowledges that one may be "gentle and modest" (86), "possess [. . .] uncommon intelligence" (87), and be recognized as a poet "wonder" (89), yet none of that guarantees protection from financial or personal misery. By denying the efficacy of the Protestant work ethic, Child not only more realistically reflects the lives freedpeople would face, but also provides a clearer critique of slavery to contradict the ATS's assertions that hard work and an even temperament on the part of slaves had improved their conditions.

Freedman's Third Reader thus demonstrates the ideological conflict of postbellum reformers. Its biographies offer as heroic models black leaders and abolitionists: Frederick Douglass, who "speak[s . . .] in behalf of the slave" (208); Paul Cuffee, whose petition "granting to free negroes [. . . in] Massachusetts all the privileges of white citizens" is passed by the state legislature (53); and the Reverend Doctor Pennington, who "preach[ed . . .] the gospel of Christ to his own people" (118). At the same time, these biographies refashion originating texts to socialize freedpeople to amicable racial interactions, encouraging them to work "faithfully [. . . and be] contented, obedient, and industrious" (*Freedman's Third Reader* 86). In an attempt to offer forgiving, content, and pious role models to newly freed slaves, the *Freedman's* series rewrites the power structure of slavery. Not ultimately a matter of racial oppression, slavery becomes at times a testing ground for character and the virtues of hard work. As the ATS literally rewrote narratives, they thus rewrote slavery itself. Although the freed men, women, and children who filled the schoolrooms would know better, idyllic images of slavery and transferring responsibility for its hardships to those who had been enslaved would not be altogether fleeting.

POSTPLANTATION NOVELS

In *Diddie, Dumps and Tot, or, Plantation Child-Life* (1882), Louise-Clarke Pyrnelle has her "Mammy" character rail against the punishment a white teacher has imposed upon one of her white charges. Mammy and fellow slave Aunt Milly both believe that "the lowest class of persons in the world were 'po' white folks' and 'free niggers.'" Mammy knows the teacher must fall into the first category, for "efn she's so mighty rich, whar's her niggers?" (129). While the white child later reconciles with the teacher, Mammy's assertions are never contradicted. In Mammy's view, whites who do not own "niggers" and "niggers" without masters are unfortunate creatures of a fallen society.

Published in the post-Reconstruction years, *Diddie, Dumps and Tot*—along with other then-popular children's texts such as Thomas Nelson Page's *Two Little Confederates* (1888) and Joel Chandler Harris's "Daddy Jake, the Runaway" (1889)[12]—offer fictional worlds that attempt to counter the loss of the Southern slave-holding class. As creators of these consolatory realms, the first generation of postslavery white authors both acknowledge slavery's demise and describe the plantation with a sense of wistful nostalgia. Literary historian Francis Gaines has argued that plantation novels of the 1870s and 1880s written for adults elaborate on this tendency, exceeding their antebellum counterparts in "romantic [. . .] attitude" (62): "estates swelled in size and mansions grew proportionately great," while slave quarters are "cozy" and slave voices more "melodious and tender" than ever (64). Yet postplantation literature for children, as the term implies, acknowledges a world that has lasted beyond the time of Southern slave-holding plantations and, as such, it admits the dissolution of the plantation idyll and the scripted white hegemony that had been staples of antebellum proslavery novels. Page's popular *Two Little Confederates*, for example, tells the story of young slave-holding brothers who live on what "passed in old times as one of the best plantations" (1). The fictional time of the novel is no longer those "old times," and although the boys' adventures include outwitting Yankee soldiers, *Two Little Confederates* ultimately admits of "a funeral—the Confederacy was dead" (143). Throughout the novel, readers witness the rapid dissolution of what the boys had once believed to be "the greatest place in the world" (1); void of its master, raided by Yankee soldiers, suffering the onslaught of war and deprivation, and abandoned by slaves, the plantation is finally left in "ruins" (155).[13]

This and other postplantation works for children, such as Pyrnelle's *Diddie, Dumps and Tot* or Harris's "Daddy Jake, the Runaway," sculpt the genre (wittingly or not) to reveal the racial anxieties of a former master class in a postbellum world. Whether or not the intranarrative setting is postbellum (Harris's "Daddy Jake, the Runaway," for example, is set in antebellum times), the acknowledgment of an extratextual postbellum world most often lies in narrative tensions that admit the loss of the antebellum plantation novel's insularity, leisure, financial security, and racial amity, while at the same time assuring readers that antebellum plantation life had been "a jolly time for both white and black" (Pyrnelle 22). Although postplantation novelists attempt to replicate the antebellum plantation novel, their narratives nonetheless more explicitly reveal the dissatisfaction and dissension of slaves as well as the anxieties of the master class, particularly its fears of losing political and racial control.

One especially sees this in the sometimes conflicted representation of slave figures. Chief among these is the "Mammy," who lingered in the imaginations of many post-Reconstruction novelists as a maternal caretaker of unvarying devotion to young white children. Both Pyrnelle and Page had been born into slave-holding families; both remembered with fondness childhoods ensconced in white privilege and the care of black slaves. Born in 1850, raised on a plantation, then dispossessed of family fortune by the Civil War, Pyrnelle[14] acknowledged that her motivation for writing *Diddie, Dumps and Tot* was her nostalgia for the Old South and her determination "to tell of the pleasant and happy relations that existed between master and slave" (vi). In her novel's preface, Pyrnelle eulogizes plantation life, regretting that "there are now no more dear old 'Mammies' and 'Aunties' in our nurseries, no more good old 'Uncles' [. . .]. The child-life that I have portrayed is over now; for no hireling can ever be to the children what their Mammies were, and the strong tie between the negroes and 'master's chil'en' is bro-

FIGURE 3.3. *Illustration from* Daddy Jake the Runaway and Short Stories Told after Dark *(1889) by Joel Chandler Harris. Courtesy of Mark West, private collection.*

ken forever" (v, viii). Page echoes a similar sense of loss when he writes longingly of the "old-time Negroes" of his plantation childhood (*Negro* 165): of "Uncle Balla" the carriage driver, "guide, philosopher, and friend of my boyhood"; and "mammy" of whom "only those can apprehend [. . .] who were rocked on her generous bosom, slept on her bed, fed at her table [. . . and] watched by her unsleeping eye" (*Negro* 171, 176).

Particularly in white-authored postbellum children's literature, the Mammy figure signals for white readers an idyllic time of racial and childhood comfort. In Pyrnelle's and Page's literary (and apparently literal) imaginations, “Mammies,” “Aunties,” and “Uncles” provide solace to young white children, principally assuring them of their racial superiority and importance in the world. These white slave-holding children find in the “Mammy” and her male counterpart, the “Uncle,” figures who not only answer their needs, but all their various desires, from entertainment to comfort. In their descriptions of young, white slaveholders, postplantation authors equate the happy childhood of whites with the slave system, hence heightening the authors’ sense of nostalgia for the lost days of their youth and of the plantation system. The effect of a seeming recount of childhood memories—particularly in novels by Page and Pyrnelle—suggests a claimed veracity to their descriptions of benevolent slavery at the same time that it further sentimentalizes slavery and slave figures.

Proslavery fiction for children published during the Reconstruction and post-Reconstruction years thus retains the racial ideology of antebellum plantation fiction in assertions of the beneficence of a slave system typified by kind white masters and loving slaves. In some ways revealing postbellum anxieties of formerly slave-holding whites, this literature almost ubiquitously insists on the affection of black “Mammies” and “Uncles” for the master’s children. A central problem for postbellum slave-holding society was, of course, what masters would be without slaves. Unwillingly emancipated from a slave-holding society, members of the slave-holding class faced an existentialist dilemma in terms of their social, political, cultural, economic, and racial identities. If the possession of slaves defined who they *were*, a master class without slaves could only be defined by what they were *not*. Similarly, if “white” power and authority meant something only within an oppositional paradigm of conscripted “black” powerlessness and slavery, what would the “master” class be without those markers?[15] In postplantation stories, the “Mammy” and “Uncle” function as significant markers of white centrality and power.

Postplantation novels for children often echo antebellum plantation stories, such as Caroline Gilman’s “The Country Visit,” by following the daily activities of young, white slaveholders as a way to evoke the more confident expression of white supremacy found in antebellum proslavery literature. Pyrnelle’s novel, set in 1853–1854, describes the often small events of childhood experienced by three slave-holding daughters on a Mississippi plantation. While the birth names of the girls, aged nine, five, and three years old, are Madeleine, Elinor, and Eugenia, respectively, those names have long since been replaced by the "pet names" of "Diddie," "Dumps," and "Tot" given them by their Mammy. Seemingly powerful in her naming of the children, the actual authority of this Mammy over her white charges is nonetheless contained by the girls' sense of their racial power.

Mammy becomes a perfect mother figure for these girls, who want to have playful adventures without the interference of adult figures. Particularly for child readers, the image of a loving mother is deeply comforting. In racial terms, the image of a black woman who loves the white child above any of her own becomes a fantasy of emotional and racial security for whites. Despite Confederate author Chaudron's earlier assertion that the "Mammy" is a "deity" of the master child's "infantine worship" (*Third Reader* 26), in Pyrnelle's novel, the white children's racial security is compounded by Mammy's ultimate powerlessness. Although Mammy is a seeming surrogate mother figure for the white girls, they understand and even script her limitations. Dumps, for example, points out that "tain't none of her business not to be lettin' us play" (51), and later informs Mammy (and young readers) that the woman's insignificance is racially derived: "You ain't none o' my mother [. . .]. You're mos' black ez my shoes" (94). When Mammy tries to manage the girls, they upstage her—either by ignoring her or by turning to their parents, who easily countermand Mammy's directives.

Generally impotent in directing the master's children and careful not to discipline them herself, Mammy is nonetheless relentless in her physical punishment of slave children. Diddie, Dumps, and Tot have "three little negroes, who belonged to the little girls and played with them, and were in training to be their maids by-and-by" (14). These children, Riar, Chris, and Dilsey (readers are never told their ages), accompany their young white mistresses in their daily play. When events end badly, the white children repeatedly avoid punishment while their slaves suffer it. After an escapade initiated by Dumps goes awry, for example, the white children promise Mammy "we won't never run away any more." Mammy leaves their punishment to their mother, but, "picking up a cotton-stalk, she gave each of the little darkies a sound whipping" (65). By contrast, the white girls' mother only "lectured [her daughters . . .] on the sin of running away from Mammy [. . .] and kissed all of the dirty little faces."

Although "disgust[ed]" by their mother's "leniency," Mammy does not—or cannot—intervene (66).

In another instance, when Mammy begins to tell the children a story, Diddie interrupts, then contradicts Mammy "contemptuously." The slave child Dilsey comes to Mammy's defense. In return, Mammy chastises Dilsey, saying "look er hyear, yer kinky-head nigger, whar's yer manners [. . .] 'ruptin uv eld'ly pussons" then returns to her story, addressing "Miss Diddie, honey" (45). Mammy's frequent and often stunningly cruel punishment of the slave children—as she "boxed [. . . one young slave] soundly" (120) or later "slapped the little darkies" (154)—is often placed in close juxtaposition to a moment when the white children get in trouble, contradict, or—as above—interrupt Mammy, in some way or another questioning, deflating, or denying her authority. In short, black children are repeatedly punished by Mammy when the white children are the ones who do something wrong. In such incidents, unjustly punishing slave children provides a moment when Mammy's rarely articulated anger against her white charges and her own impotence in a white-commandeered world can be displaced onto black children whom—by the rules of slavery—she is forbidden to love. The cruel Mammy character-type thus both capitulates to slavery's dictates (in her dismissal of young black personhood and value) and shows her frustration with masters (as black slave children who are owned by these girls become scapegoats for white children's arrogance).

The literary violence of Mammies toward black children[16] reinforces proslavery justifications that black women do not care for their own children as much as white women do theirs (which is ironic, since white mothers in postplantation novels frequently reside off-page rather than engaged in their children's daily care). It also suggests that black children require much less affection than white children—even that they are ultimately disposable. These child-slave figures are thus objectified by white children as live-doll playmates to be ordered about at their whim[17] and by otherwise impotent black adults as scapegoats for their own frustrations. Ultimately, they function as doppelgängers of the master's white children—reflective opposites in power, position, value, and, of course, race. In postplantation novels, such representations of cathartic violence against child slaves metaphorically comment on the anxieties of white authors who realized that the young generation of freed blacks would become economic and political competitors of the white masterless class in a postslavery world.

The violent Mammy figure of children's books also reflects, as Donnarae MacCann points out, "a toned-down facet of the brute image" (*White Supremacy* 95). The black "brute" figure (such as Cudjo in the antebellum *Cudjo's Cave*) signals the primitivism of Africans as defined by nineteenth-century race theories,[18] a bias that provided further justification for slavery in its presumed civilizing effect. The character trope also spoke to the (not only subconscious) anxieties of the Southern antebellum master class, particularly following Nat Turner's insurrection in 1831. For the former master class in the postbellum era, the emancipation of nearly four million slaves compounded their fears of black anger and retribution.

Pyrnelle implies that the "brute"—a slave prone to violence—lies in wait, even in slave children. For example, on an ostensibly idyllic day when "all the children, white and black" are playing together (188) and their play goes awry, in frustration one slave girl tells another "wat you doin', you nigger you? [. . .]. I'll beat de life out'n yer." Although white Tot stops the ensuing "rough-and-tumble fight" of the two slave girls (189), slave violence directed against other slaves (even if as a displaced expression of their frustration with white oppression) becomes, in children's postplantation stories, a site of safety for white characters. Slave-on-slave violence assures white readers that blacks will not turn their anger on them (even if it originates in white oppression). These scenes also reveal the racial self-loathing of slave characters, particularly as racial epithets accompany expressions of hatred. Moreover, despite Tot's intervention in the slave girls' fight, slave-on-slave insults and violence have an entertainment value for white characters and presumably the white audiences that made postplantation novels so successful.[19]

In *Diddie, Dumps and Tot* (as in other plantation and postplantation novels), slaves are provided as the source and object of entertainment for young slaveholders and readers alike. Adult and child slaves also serve as white children's guardians and playmates; here, Aunt Edy "was never too busy to amuse them" and Uncle Snake-bit Bob "always had a story ready for the children" (13–14). For Diddie, Dumps, and Tot, simply watching slaves is amusing, "for there was nothing the children enjoyed so much as going to the quarters to see the little negroes play" (41). Literary and theatrical minstrelsy of black characters posits its humor in the disjunction between the attempt and ability of black (slave) characters to mimic white civilization. In plantation novels, mispronunciations resulting from slaves' mangled imitations of their masters' vocabulary are often italicized to emphasize their failure; slaves' attempts to dress and act as whites become a humorous diversion for masters, as when Diddie, Dumps, and Tot watch slaves walk in "the funniest sort of a procession" and other "little nigs [. . .] make a comical little 'bob-down' courtesy" (31, 32). While the slave's inability to be "white" is a site of humor (and at least subconscious relief to white readers assured of their racial preeminence), the desire of the black slave characters to imitate whites provides fictional confirmation of the desirability of whiteness.[20] The comical representation of slaves, like the impotence of Mammy, dichotomizes "whites" and "blacks" as competent or foolish, intelligent or stupid—ultimately free or slave.

What is less safe for white readers and characters are narrative moments that hint at or at times directly acknowledge slave resistance to white authority. One sees this in a scene of a Christmas Day play in *Diddie, Dumps and Tot*, when the white children ask their mother if they "can't [. . .] have some of the little quarter niggers to [. . .] play Injuns with us?" Typically, "the little girls were not allowed to play with the quarter children" (35), but the mother relents and "each of the children were told that they might select one of the little negroes to play with them" (36). The white children then script the scene, determining what role each is to play: the white children and their house slaves will be settlers, while the slaves from the quarters will play attacking Indians.

That black slaves pretend to be Indians here retains racialized hierarchies of lower, savage races, at the same time that it redefines character-types. Nineteenth-century race theories cast Indians as less docile and more dangerous than Africans, characteristics that defined them as poor candidates for slavery.[21] In this scene, the quarter slaves find freedom in their play. Enacting their roles with gusto, "the fierce savages dragged out Chris [Dumps's house slave], and she was soon tied hand and foot." The white children are then caught and the "little captives were laid on their backs, and Polly [one of the quarter slaves] scalped them with a clothes-brush for a tomahawk. As soon as they were all scalped they started over again, and kept up the fun" (38). Implicit in this scene is the vicarious pleasure the quarter slaves have in being allowed into the master's house to play "Injun," particularly, in hunting and attacking both their master's children and the more privileged house slaves. This role playing provides a liminal space where the master's children acknowledge the hatred racialized others have for them as they enact their own loss of racial power. Although the quarter slaves act the role of obedient slaves as they follow the white children's directives, in these fantasies of play there is an embedded narrative conflict in their exuberant violence as the quarter-slaves-playing-attacking-Indians are allowed an outlet to be "Nat" figures, overwhelming both masters and their attendant house slaves.

Later in the novel, Pyrnelle's Daddy Jake seems to have fully inculcated his subservient role as slave, offering the master's children (and the novel's presumed young, white readers) a creation story that assures them of their racial supremacy. In Jake's story, after God creates people, the "nigger" falls asleep while God "finishes" up the "wite man." Once "de nigger he waked up [. . .] he wuz bu'nt black, an' his hyar wuz all swuv'llt up right kinky. De Lord, seein' he wuz spilte, [. . .] wuz des 'bout'n ter thow 'im 'way, wen de wite man axt fur 'im" (206–207). Defining black skin color and hair texture as signs of a "spoiled" creation, Daddy Jake describes slavery as black people's salvation. The hero is the white man—the "finished" creation—who agrees to take the "nigger" (who, in Jake's story, exists as a type of preform and not fully realized "man") to save him from certain destruction. The racial self-ablation on Jake's part is obvious. Yet, immediately following this story, the slave children reveal that "ole Daddy [Jake] wuz er *trick* nigger. [. . .]. Hit's pow'ful wicked ter be trick niggers" (210). That this revelation occurs as the children travel the space between Daddy Jake's house and the master's house suggests the unrecognized presence of black rebellion and power on the plantation. Although seemingly domesticated as "Daddy" Jake, the character counterpoints the ineffective Mammy figure of the Big House. Jake represents an implicit dangerousness in slaves who may appear to be content and domesticated by slavery, but in truth are capable of a feared, "wicked" control over others.[22]

The most well-known fictional representation of racial accommodation and resistance is perhaps found in Uncle Remus, a creation of Joel Chandler Harris who is—by Harris's own description—"an old negro [. . .] who has nothing but pleasant memories of the discipline of slavery" (*Uncle Remus* 46–47). Literally a postplantation story in that its setting is postbellum and Remus is a former slave, *Uncle Remus: His Songs and His Sayings* (1880) is the first in a series of books in which the titled character tells stories to the plantation owner's young, white son. While Remus evinces power as a storyteller and in some of his critiques of whites, he is essentially the kind "Uncle," the loving male Mammy figure to the white man's child who eagerly listens to his tales. As such, Uncle Remus provided a salve to white angst after Reconstruction. As critic Robert Hemenway has pointed out: Remus was "a figure who could contribute to the country's reunification. [He . . .] reassured Southern whites [that . . .] free black people would love, not demand retribution. At the same time he assured Northern whites that abandoning black people was not a failure of moral responsibility. Uncle Remus, immensely popular, witnessed that black people would turn the other cheek, would continue to love, despite all the broken promises of American history" (20). Essentially an idealized depiction of the "faithful slave" figure of plantation stories, Uncle Remus presents the move from slavery to emancipation as seamless precisely because in the collection's narrative frame he remains the "faithful negro" regardless of the time period and his legal status.[23]

The core tales of the collection, however, tell a very different racialized story. Unlike the self-deprecating tale Pyrnelle's Daddy Jake tells, Remus's stories interrogate the presumed superiority of the master class. Representing "the largest single collection of Afro-American folktales ever collected and published" (Lester, Foreword xiii), the core stories offer a radical voice that contests hegemonic order. Through the texture of coded language, rich in metaphor and double signification, such tales as these had formed a cornerstone of slave culture. They offer catharsis and psychological space from an oppressive white culture, teaching children and adults how to survive in a dangerous world where enemies often feign friendship and a "mere look, word, or motion,—a mistake" can mean punishment or even death (Douglass, *Narrative* 118). In the context of the slave community, these tales reflect a world of conflict and rebellion.

Deemed personally insignificant by the system of slavery, the enslaved would have told stories of small crawfishes that unite, "bo'd inter de groun'" (Harris, *Uncle Remus* 66), and release a flood which drowns the bigger animals who had indifferently trampled upon them. Against the backdrop of a world where gossip could mean a costly betrayal of secret plans, one heard stories of Mr. Jack Sparrow, who sets out to tattle on Brer Rabbit and only succeeds in getting himself eaten. One also meets here the preeminent trickster, Brer Rabbit, who variously feigns friendship, obsequiousness, and officiousness in order to obfuscate his real intentions to thwart, humiliate, and exploit the array of predators, competitors, and sometimes even allies that surround him. Indeed, the tales are metanarratively trickster tales, at times told to the children of masters unable to fully appreciate their revolutionary import.[24] The nuanced coding and cultural resistance indicative of these tales stand in awkward juxtaposition to Harris's happy "old darkey," Uncle Remus (62). The result is a conflicted collection in which the rebellious core text remains in uneasy tension with the reconciliatory figure of the narrative frame. Embedded one within the other, this contrasting racialized discourse about slavery reflects the tension of postplantation literature, particularly its impulse to re-create the antebellum plantation novel against the framework of a postbellum society.

In contrast to the implicit rebelliousness embedded in postplantation novels, explicit rebellion is most consistently depicted as slaves leaving the plantation. Although in the Confederate *First Dixie Reader*, the slave "Uncle Ned" claims he was enticed away by Yankees, in postplantation novels for children, when slaves leave the plantation they typically choose to do so. Some flee cruel masters or overseers, as do characters in Pyrnelle's *Diddie, Dumps and Tot* and Harris's "Daddy Jake, the Runaway." Others leave, particularly en masse, when freedom comes, as in Page's *Two Little Confederates*. In both cases, the primary narrative fantasy of the postplantation novel is the reconciliation between master and slave, with its attendant reestablishment of racialized hierarchies.

In her antebellum "The Country Visit," Caroline Gilman's child characters are purveyors of the status quo, lauded when they reiterate the lessons of their wise slave-holding parents. Reconstituted as social agents for an ideal lost to (and by) their parents, young white protagonists of postplantation novels often reunite slaves and masters, but in so doing they lecture masters of their parents' generation about how they have erred in losing slaves. While acknowledging the loss of the master class, the racialized fantasy in such scenes is of the younger white generation mending those losses, retrieving slavery, and effecting the return of the slave to the plantation.

In short, these characters implicitly attempt to fix what the adult generation has gotten wrong—principally their loss of control over slaves and the plantation.

When the slave Daddy Jake, of Harris's "Daddy Jake, the Runaway," reluctantly flees the plantation after striking and fearing he has killed a violent overseer, the master's two young children set out on their own to bring Jake the news that the overseer was not killed, and that their father is not angry with him. When Pyrnelle's Diddie and Dumps find a runaway who fled his master because he feared he would receive a whipping, the children go about converting the cruel-hearted master and reuniting reformed master and repentant slave. The ensuing reunions between black slave and white master are sentimentalized, especially in depictions of the grateful, returning slave. When Jake returns to the plantation, "nobody was any happier than Daddy Jake" (82), and the slave in Pyrnelle's novel profusely thanks the children for reuniting him with his master, telling them, "I gwine pray fur yer bof ev'y night" (181). In each case, the cruelty suffered by the slave is defined as an aberration and respectively attributed to an overseer who is not a gentleman and a master not of the true planter class.[25]

While such classist paradigms were meant to present the planter class as honorable, the assertion that violent treatment is rare is even less convincing in "Daddy Jake, the Runaway" when readers meet "Crazy Sue," whose infants died when her master prevented her from caring for them. Since their deaths, Crazy Sue says, "I kin year dem babies cryin' yit, an' dat de reason folks call me Crazy Sue." When the master's young son, Lucien, "indignantly" asks why Crazy Sue did not tell his father about her treatment (65), Sue tells them, "yo' pa is a mighty good man [. . .] but he ain't got no medicine wa't could 'a' kyored me an' my marster" (66). Unlike the assurance of a master's protection in Pyrnelle's novel, here, Lucien's belief that his father can aid slaves is revealed as the foolish arrogance of privileged white children who know little about the realities of slavery. While Crazy Sue mothers white Lucien and his sister during their stay in the woods, she is no Mammy willing to relinquish or punish her own children. Rather, her assurance that there can be no reconciliation between slave and master disrupts the narrative closure and benevolence of slavery in the counterpointing story of Jake's joyful return to the plantation.

The loss of the plantation idyll underlies postplantation novels, for even under "good" masters, depicted loyal slaves *do* flee the plantation, some never to return. Although acknowledging the loss of a slave-holding society, postplantation novels attempt to re-create plantation life by arguing for reconciliation between masters and slaves inasmuch as reconciliation reestablishes a pseudoslavery paradigm. One sees this in *Two Little Confederates.* When the white boys' mother learns that the Yankees are coming and offers her slaves their freedom, they refuse. The trusted Uncle Balla tells his mistress: "Whar is I got to go? I wuz born on dis place an' I 'spec' to die here [. . .]. Y' all sticks by us, and we'll stick by you" (49–50). Later, however, once they hear that General Lee has surrendered, "every negro on the plantation left, excepting lame old Sukey Brown," whom one assumes cannot leave (142). Page ultimately depicts a reconciliation between mistress and slave, telling readers that a "number of the old servants, including Uncle Balla [. . .] had one by one come back to their old home" (152). This reunion scene is pictorially emphasized in a sketch of three returning former slaves, each waiting to be received by the mistress. Standing one step above them, the mistress holds the hand of a former slave woman in both of her own. That gesture, and the lowered head of the former slave, signals a scene of apology on the part of the returning woman and forgiveness as an expression of the mistress' noblesse oblige to the repentant slave-now-servant. Loyalty and compassion have been exchanged, mistress and slave reconciled. In typical postplantation style, former slaves have found the plantation a better home than freedom.

The cultural strength of this reconciling master-slave trope is evident as well in the way it is grafted onto antislavery texts such as Grace Duffie Boylan's adaptation, *Young Folks' "Uncle Tom's Cabin"* (1901). Unlike in Stowe's version, Boylan's Uncle Tom is not killed but instead rescued by "Mas'r" George and returned to the Shelby plantation, where he and the other slaves remain as hired laborers. In a postbellum world where most plantations lie in ruins, the Shelby plantation remains "as productive as ever," largely because of the "wise judgment" of Tom, who becomes its manager (155). Including developments such as these, along with a final scene where Uncle Tom offers a "benediction" of sorts to characters and readers alike as he "waved [. . .] 'Good-night' from the rose-covered doorway

FIGURE 3.4. *Illustration from* Two Little Confederates *(1888) by Thomas Nelson Page. New York: C. Scribner's Sons. Courtesy of the Rare Book Collection, Wilson Library, The University of North Carolina at Chapel Hill.*

of his own home" (166), Boylan argues that a post-emancipation refashioning of slavery is mutually beneficial to former masters and slaves alike.[26]

In the postbellum years, Mark Twain's Jim replaced Harriet Beecher Stowe's Uncle Tom as the most contentiously debated literary slave figure. A central figure in a novel that "implies that [. . .] the United States has not made good on its promises of freedom and equality for all men" (Trites 42), Jim's character is made all the more problematic because the overall racial politics of Twain's *The Adventures of Huckleberry Finn* (1884) have been so difficult to define.[27] In this novel adopted by young readers, one finds Huck's fluctuating responses to slavery and societal expectations—whether he decides to suffer the pains of hell for not turning in Jim or to capitulate to Tom Sawyer's views on slavery—beg the question of where the ethical core of the novel stands. Moreover, as Gail Schmunk Murray points out, although Twain's "position on race relations and the abilities of African-Americans seems ambivalent at best, his novel is so shot through with irony that the reader cannot always discern his narrative intent" (129).

While *Uncle Remus: His Songs and His Sayings* textually separates the conciliatory Remus character and the rebellious core slave tales, ambiguity infuses Twain's novel. That ambiguity is perhaps nowhere more apparent than in the character of Jim. He is the necessary adult black male slave companion of the young white free boy. Yet Jim at times breaks free of the trope's requirements. In scenes juxtaposed in often dizzying proximity, Jim is, variously, the clever Sambo, manipulating Huck's sense of guilt; an ostensible Sambo (who may still be masking); a male Mammy; a rebel demanding respect from a white boy; an abolitionist planning to steal his family out of slavery; and a minstrel in drag acceding to Tom Sawyer's outlandish direction. The fool who is not a fool, the supplicant who manipulates whites, the manipulator who is a fool—Jim continually eludes a cohesive racial frame. At the close of the novel, readers discover that Jim had been legally free the entire journey, although always in danger of capture and enslavement. He is, ultimately, slave and not-slave. Shifting roles as he both evades and is scripted by a slave-holding society, Jim serves as a composite of antebellum and postbellum literary slave tropes. In the end, the riddle of his character lies in the way it reveals both the tensions and alliances between proslavery and antislavery racial ideologies.

POSTBELLUM ANTISLAVERY RESPONSES

Antebellum abolitionist views had never been cohesively homogeneous; postbellum views were similarly varied. More than that, federal legislation during Reconstruction gave the illusion that freedmen's civil rights would be protected, and many reformers who had once supported abolition turned their attention elsewhere.[28] Formerly abolitionist sentiment also soon fractured after the war, particularly in the case of female abolitionists. As leaders in the movement decided to support calls for black male suffrage and return at a later time to argue for female suffrage, Susan B. Anthony and Elizabeth Cady Stanton not only dissented, but did so with increasingly racist rhetoric. In her address to the National Woman Suffrage Convention in 1869, for example, Stanton asked: "shall American statesmen [. . .] so amend their constitutions as to make their wives and mothers the political inferiors of unlettered and unwashed ditch-diggers, boot-blacks, butchers, and barbers, fresh from the slave plantations of the South?" (Stanton 255).[29] Racism such as Stanton's, along with a resurgence of proslavery ideology, antiblack legislation, and racially focused violence, made the years after emancipation ones in which those once enslaved experienced precious little of the liberty that had been legally promised to them.

Called the "Decades of Disappointment" and "the Nadir of Black Experience" (Gates and McKay 464), the end of the nineteenth century and beginning of the twentieth engendered what theorist Ron Eyerman has termed a "trauma of rejection" for African Americans: "it was not so much the direct experience of slavery that would prove traumatic, but its aftermath as the hopes and promise of equality and acceptance were crushed finally and formally in the 1880–90s" (39). While slavery—as the root of racist exploitation against blacks in America—has been culturally traumatic for African Americans,[30] the inability of "white" America to reimagine the country postslavery in new paradigms of race, citizenship, and full enfranchisement meant that although slavery was legally ended, the full potential of the radical abolitionist agenda, which included an acknowledgment of racial equality and citizenship, had not been reached.

The question one faces in examining postbellum literature for children is how writers represented abolitionism when the primary abolitionist impulse—to end slavery—seemed resolved, although racial equality remained nonetheless unrealized. Especially in the final year and those closely following the end of the Civil War, the antebellum radical abolitionist perspective—condemning the violence of slavery and particularly its forced separation of families—was still evident in children's literature.[31] Yet it shared space, as had antebellum radical abolitionism, with more conservative antislavery views, particularly as white-authored literature argued for a vision of racial amity that obfuscated racial oppression. By the closing decade of the century, African American authors, writing specifically for African American children, offered counternarratives to prevailing postplantation tropes of "Mammies" and "Uncles." Evoking images of the agency, courage, and determination of slaves from antebellum slave narratives, these authors provided African American children a vision of postbellum success. Writers of the half century following the war who might be classified as abolitionist to one extent or another, thus presented several main slave figures that reflected divergent visions of race and racial hierarchy in a postslavery world. The war and postwar years provided writers a landscape upon which to draw opposing definitions of heroism: the rebel, who echoed many antebellum slave narratives, and the faithful slave, who reflected the plantation myth. In the midst of this, writers continued the exploration of what race meant and how it might be identified.

Unlike "Uncle Ned" who fought Yankees and defended slavery in the Confederate *Boys and Girls Stories of the War* (ca. 1863), some slaves or former slaves in radical antislavery war stories are heroic figures that fight slavery consistently, whether it is represented by the Confederate army or slaveholders. Although they may aid whites, that aid does not compromise their allegiance to their own families. The serialization of Edmund Kirke's "The Little Prisoner" (1865) and Carleton's "Winning His Way" (1865) in *Our Young Folks*, for example, bridged the end of the war and early postbellum months to demand recognition of black agency.[32] Both tell of young white, Northern soldiers saved by slaves. In "The Little Prisoner," when twelve-year-old James is wounded on the battlefield, he is rescued by Aunt Katy, an old slave woman from a nearby plantation, and in "Winning His Way," when young Paul is imprisoned at the notorious Andersonville, he is "comforted and reassured by Uncle Peter, an old gray-headed negro, who had been a slave all his life" (Carleton 735). These representations may seem, at first glance, to hearken back to other images of black slaves caring for whites—of Uncle Tom's rescue of Little Eva in *Uncle Tom's Cabin* or *Hatchie, the Guardian Slave*'s eponymous hero who saves his mistress. Yet when Aunt Katy and Uncle Peter rescue white Northern children, it becomes a way for them to strike *against* slaveholders, not *for* them.

In the Northern imagination, black aid typically signaled requisite gratitude to Northern troops. However, although Aunt Katy tends to a white Northern soldier, she never forsakes her own family's well-being for his. When Katy's grandson unexpectedly returns to the plantation, she chooses to save him, rather than James, from pursuing troops. These former slaves are not nostalgic for the governance of masters. No happy slaves of plantation fiction, both Uncle Peter and Aunt Katy describe the painful loss of family members. Peter, for example, tells how his wife and children died "after cruel whippings and scourgings by their master" (Carleton 735). Katy describes how her children "were gone,—[. . .] stolen, sold away [. . . .] because her master owed gambling debts, and her mistress loved [. . .] diamond things" (Kirke, Part II 243).

Unlike Stowe's Uncle Tom, whose religiosity motivates him to forgive his master even in the midst of his own murder, Uncle Peter and Aunt Katy want retribution, not reconciliation. They are certain, as Uncle Peter declares, "de Lord is coming to judge de earth with righteousness, and den I reckon de Rebs will catch it" (Carleton 736; compare Kirke, Part II 243). Not waiting for divine intervention, both work against the Confederacy, particularly as they rescue Union soldiers. Stories like these thus refigure black Mammy and Uncle tropes, politicizing representations of black aid as rebellion. Ultimately, these stories reorganize popular racial paradigms to present whites as the weaker race and to argue that slaves evinced tremendous strength to survive brutality that whites, such as Paul and James, could not have endured. The antislavery perspective is further expressed in implicit representations of the "fitness" of slaves for freedom. Having survived slavery's brutality, independent-minded and strong, these former slaves will not be dependent on whites when free, since, by implication here, they had never been dependent upon either masters or Yankee soldiers in the first place.

The simultaneous expression and containment of black agency is often shown in the representation of a slave or former slave joining the Union fight against the Confederacy. Most typically presented as a "contraband," this figure often reveals irreconcilable tensions in the escaped slave as both hero and possession. As defined by the Federal Confiscation Act of 1861, Confederate property, including slaves, that was seized by Union troops did not have to be returned to prior owners. The legal designation of escaped slaves as "contraband," while providing a political strategy to thwart the Confederacy, also reinstated escaped slaves as property. Indeed, as Alice Fahs argues, "there is every indication that the term 'contraband' caught on rapidly precisely because it provided a means for Northerners to continue thinking of escaped slaves as property, without disturbing antebellum racist preconceptions" (152).[33]

In *The Three Scouts*, published during the transition year of 1865, John Townsend Trowbridge explores such issues of racial power and containment through the figure of Pomp, earlier introduced to readers in *Cudjo's Cave*. Here, Pomp has become a spy and scout for the Union army. That he works outside a more structured military authority shows his independence and resourcefulness. Moreover, that Trowbridge never refers to Pomp as a "contraband"—even though the term was commonly used to refer to any free black working for the Union army—shows how the author works against the "contraband" stereotype to present a self-possessed hero. When readers meet Pomp in this novel, he has been kidnapped by Confederates who plan to sell him. Pomp's predicament suggests a common white-abolitionist scenario: the helpless slave requiring the aid of a white intercessor (here, a young, white Northern soldier). Once released, however, Pomp takes command of the situation and retains it throughout the novel. Overturning the reader's initial impression of Pomp in the fairly predictable role of needy slave, Trowbridge uses Pomp to explore cultural expectations and literary depictions of race and slavery.

Through performative mastery, Pomp enacts varied roles of slave and freedman. Adopting what readers would recognize as typically rendered slave dialect, as well as "a lazy and slouching pace" (108), and "the air of a menial proud of rendering service" (143), Pomp transforms himself in language, physicality, and overt attitude. Unlike Twain's Jim who appears in drag at the behest of Tom Sawyer, Pomp remains in performative command of the situation. When Pomp tells whites who try to sell him, "I do jes' what you say [. . .]. Tank ye, massa: s'pose ye know best" (159), he is merely biding his time. He has already obtained information about a planned Confederate attack and will soon master those who believe they have bought and sold him. Pomp is the insightful Sambo, able to switch masks to obtain his objectives. When he reveals that "Pomp" is only "one of my names" (99), he signals not only the roles he must play as a spy, but also the roles slaves and freedmen adopted in order to navigate a slave-holding system in which feigning acceptance was a means of survival. Pomp here as well navigates a war in which a free man could be instantly converted to property.

A natural leader with "innate power and sagacity" (156), and evincing "singularly calm, intelligent, proud features" (78), Pomp uses performative shifts to confuse those who expect slaves and black men to be fools. Self-controlled and needing no master, Pomp becomes a figure of divine retribution against the Confederacy and slaveholders alike, for as the slaver "had done unto him, so now he did unto" the slaver (173). He works for the Union army, but it depends upon him for the intelligence that will win battles. No brute, no servant, no fool, no "Uncle," Pomp is heroic in personal, racial, and national contexts. Although there are two other scouts in the novel, a white immigrant and an abolitionist Southerner, Trowbridge retains Pomp as the preeminent hero even in the novel's final lines, which describe that "where services [. . .] involving greatest danger and hardship, are to be performed, there the fearless and sagacious black scout [Pomp] is to be found" (383). Through Pomp, one of the most heroic of fictionalized slaves in the postbellum literary repertoire, Trowbridge examines issues of black identity, both interrogating white society's racialized stereotypes of the "slave" and imagining free blacks as perfectly capable of assuming heroic roles in American society.

By contrast, the ostensible antislavery perspective of racially conservative literature—like Dolly Dixie's "The Colored Mammy and Her White Foster-Child" (1868) and Elizabeth Kilham's "Tobe's Monument" (1872), both published in the popular children's magazine, *Our Young Folks*[34]—simply imagines the role of former slaves in a postbellum world by reframing proslavery antebellum slave tropes. In essence, they keep proslavery racial hierarchies intact while transferring the object of slave loyalty to emancipators. This vision is antislavery inasmuch as it acknowledges a postslavery world, yet its narrow racial vision is evident in the way black agency remains clearly circumscribed. The premise of each story is, at first glance, antislavery: in "Tobe's Monument," the young slave Tobe flees his cruel master to work for the Union army, and in Dixie's story, a child slaveholder disavows slavery and frees her slaves when she comes of age. Yet in each, arguments about the fitness of slaves for freedom depend upon the representation of the slave as unremittingly loyal—to the point that one sacrifices his life, another her child, for the love of a white patron.

In "Tobe's Monument," when Tobe meets Union soldiers, he offers his services to a captain who directs Tobe to "take particular care" of the officer's boots (86). When Tobe is later found by Confederate soldiers who demand the boots or his life, Tobe's loyalty to the Union captain is literally self-annihilating, and in his dying breath, Tobe tells the Union officer, "Mass Cap'n, I done de bes' I knowed. I kep' de boots" (87). That Tobe's raison d'être is not merely service to the captain, but more specifically to his *boots*, would seem to provide fertile ground for critiques of Northern hypocrisy; Tobe's death could be seen as a parody of Tom's death in *Uncle Tom's Cabin*. Yet, Tobe's loyalty and self-sacrificing death are treated with solemnity by Kilham: at the story's close, the captain places the blood-stained boots as "Tobe's monument" in a glass case with the inscription, "In Memory of Tobe, Faithful unto Death" (87).

"Tobe's Monument" validates Northern white supremacy in Tobe's ultimate commendation of Union soldiers. This revision of the supplicant slave/white savior image posits a postbellum world where slaves are freed but, figuratively or not, remain on their knees to laud whites.[35] Indeed, other than the obvious reassignment of allegiance, Tobe's character remains indistinguishable from proslavery representations of loyal slaves grateful for the oversight of kind masters. If anything, Kilham argues former slaves will be *more* self-effacing, offering their willing martyrdom as a sign of gratitude to Northern troops. By presenting fealty unto death as the most honorable service former slaves can perform, she envisions that the memory of their existence—not their actual presence—informs white postbellum society.

In Dolly Dixie's story, that the conversion of the young slaveholder, Mary, is predicated upon Mammy's care for her defines abolitionism as a type of reciprocal response of the master class to loyal slaves. One could argue that Mary's declaration, "my good old Mammy [. . .] has been the most faithful friend I ever had [. . .] and I love her" (140), and her horror that Mammy's husband, "black Pappy," will be sold by a neighboring master, are transgressive moments. Yet the interracial familial relationship of "The Colored Mammy and Her White Foster-Child" depends upon Mammy's rejection of her own family in favor of this white child. As the story begins, one reads of a master who "had several slaves, and one of them had a healthy baby. He told her to wean her own little one, and give his sickly little child [Mary] all her milk." Mammy then "willingly put away her own dark baby, and nursed the little white one with the tenderest care," promising her that "you sha'n't cry for anything. I'll watch over you, and wait on you, and love you always" (137).

In Lydia Maria Child's antebellum "Mary French and Susan Easton," the final disappearance of the black child reflects the irreparable destruction slavery wrought on black families, as when Susan's family "wept without hope" at the loss of their daughter (202). Unlike Susan Easton, Mammy's child has no name and is only defined in terms of skin color. Not even referenced by a gendered pronoun, the black slave child becomes a commodity who narratively disappears after it has served its purpose, presumably to have its mother's milk come in for the benefit of the white child. In a story ultimately critiquing the possession and exchange of people (as when "black Pappy" is sold to cover his master's debts), Dixie nonetheless lauds the commodification of this largely anonymous "dark baby" "willingly" relinquished by its mother for her master's child. In contrast to Child's story, the exchange and subsequent disappearance of the slave child renders narratively irrelevant the black child's response to abandonment, regardless of whether the child is left grief-stricken or malnourished. In a postbellum world, where many white authors would continue to assert the dispensability of the youngest generation of freed blacks in favor of white preeminence, Dolly Dixie's ostensibly abolitionist message is fully infiltrated by a proslavery ideology in which a slave's devotion to her young mistress represents the pinnacle of racial amity, for "it was a pretty picture to see that small fair face cuddled close to the brown neck, and the little white hands patting the dark cheeks" (137).

As the title "The Colored Mammy and Her White Foster-Child" indicates, skin color signals an essential marker of identity. Whether a sign of unassailable difference or of distinctions that could be bridged by a sense of shared humanity, the reiteration of "black" and "white" as descriptors evokes a sense of opposition. By contrast, the presentation of "colored" and "mulatto" characters begins to erode those distinguishing barriers by diminishing the oppositional framework of "black" and "white." Lighter skin color is then constructed within a racialized hierarchy to signal one who is imagined to be more easily incorporated into a free America. In Dixie's story, for example, while Mammy's "dark child" and her "black" husband narratively disappear ("black Pappy" presumably living as a slave on an unknown plantation), it is Mammy, a "mulatto woman" (137), who is given her freedom. Such a racialized schema, which determines who is allowed freedom, was also not uncommon in antebellum abolitionist texts; in *Uncle Tom's Cabin*, for example, the light-complexioned Eliza, George, and Harry survive while the "full glossy black" Uncle Tom does not (68).[36] The hierarchy thus uses skin color to define slavery as a contrastive construction of whiteness, and freedom only as the purview of those light-skinned or white.

More than "colored" slaves, depictions of "perfectly white" slaves who are "to all appearance[s] of unmixed white race" (Leigh) had become a source of fascination for white audiences who bought mass-produced photographs of freed "white slave" children. Objects of "speculation, voyeurism, and moral outrage" (M. Mitchell 55), white-complexioned slaves engendered sympathy, likely because the transgressions of slavery appeared more pressing to whites when imagining themselves as the enslaved. The focus on skin color also reveals how ante- and postbellum abolitionism explored the construction of whiteness in relation to the slave figure.

As Mary Niall Mitchell points out, one sees the visual reconstruction of race in a photograph from the adult magazine *Harper's Weekly*, titled "Emancipated Slaves, White and Colored" (1864), which was recast in *The Youth's Companion* as "White Slaves" (1865), just a month before Lee's surrender (Mitchell 52–55). The children's magazine not only visually edited the original photograph to four figures (presumably to focus on the children), but more significantly, racially refigured the image by replacing the head of the "black boy" Isaac with that of the "very fair" Charles (Leigh) in order to provide an exclusively white visual representation of child slavery.[37]

This (mis)representation of race underpins the argument of *Companion*'s accompanying editorial, that white enslavement is "the great wickedness of slavery." The writer's racial outrage and insulation seem evident as he addresses what he assumes is an exclusively white audience: white slave and free children of masters "are all as fair to look upon as you or I, and in the sight of God there is no reason why there should be any difference between one and another" ("White Slaves" 38). In its erasure of blackness, the revised portrait not only urges an imaginative transference to heighten viewers' sympathy by seeing themselves as the enslaved, but it also denies equality between the earlier "black" Isaac and the "perfectly white" girls Rebecca and Rosina (38). Although in *Harper's Weekly*, C. C. Leigh describes Isaac as "a black boy [. . .] but none the less intelligent than his whiter companions" (71), in *The Youth's Companion*, Isaac is visually valuable (and a figure of sympathy) only when

FIGURE 3.5. *"Emancipated Slaves, White and Colored" from* Harper's Weekly *(1864). Courtesy of Special Collections General, Martha Blakeney Hodges Special Collections and University Archives, University Libraries, The University of North Carolina at Greensboro.*

he is racially erased to become a boy "of light complexion" ("White Slaves" 38).

Representations of white slaves were probably of particular interest (and concern) to white audiences because they threatened to destabilize notions of white identity. For the most part, whites expected the "slave" to be a sign of essential difference marked by distinguishing physical features, which in turn implied a host of character traits as defined by race theorists. Mary Niall Mitchell, for example, argues that whites who viewed images of white redeemed slave figures were "doing their utmost to read [the figures' . . .] race. We can imagine that viewers studied the portraits carefully, searching each photograph for the curve of the nose or the shape of the head that might indicate the child's African ancestry" (64–65).[38]

That slavery, like blackness, is better made invisible is an underlying argument in Augusta Moore's "Turn About, Fair Play" (1865), which appeared in *The Youth's Companion* just after the war's end. Here, Regina, an apparently white girl, enjoys torturing her young slave and declares that "I'll treat my stupid nigger as I see fit." Upon

FIGURE 3.6. *"White Slaves" from* The Youth's Companion *38.10 (9 March 1865): 37. Courtesy of American Antiquarian Society.*

her father's death, Regina learns she "was the child of a slave; her mother had never been a wife [. . .]. *Regina was a slave*," and she is sold for debts. Regina's plight follows the expected route of a cautionary tale as she experiences the treatment she had once meted out to others. Eventually rescued by Union soldiers, Regina repents of her earlier cruelty, but will also keep "secret [. . .] having in her veins the negro blood, or with having been a slave" (57). Moore's abolitionist perspective both disrupts notions of who is "white" and "black" and also posits that, in a postbellum society, slavery and "negro" race are best kept as a secret of American society. Unlike the more radical representation in *The Three Scouts*, where Pomp's visible race is used by him as a means of power, the racial secrets that Regina will keep define blackness as shame. Such representations of the "white slave" reflect conflicting racial agendas. Regina's racial obfuscation and secrecy imply a postslavery world where race becomes indeterminate. At the same time, it argues white discomfort and fascination with the parameters of race and the safety race had once seemed to promise whites in a racially based slave society.

• • •

At the turn of the century and into the early twentieth century, when African American writers came to write about slavery specifically for African American children, unlike many white authors, they would not turn to fiction. Instead, they anticipated both the focus and form of African American–authored stories about slavery that would find fuller expression in the 1920s by reframing representations of slave narratives and presenting heroic black figures to inspire young African Americans. Edward Johnson's textbook, *A School History of the Negro Race in America, from 1619 to 1890* (1890), is a case in point. Johnson sought to redress "the sin of omission and commission on the part of white authors, most of whom seem to have written exclusively for white children [. . .]. The Negro is hardly given a passing notice in many of the histories taught in the schools; he is credited with no heritage of valor; he is mentioned only as a slave" (E. Johnson 3–4).[39]

This ubiquitous depiction, according to Johnson, has defined the slave as without bravery, initiative, resource, or as having made any contribution to the nation. Through biography and "true historical records" (E. Johnson 4), Johnson reclaims an otherwise lost history to redefine the "slave." His *School History of the Negro Race in America* thus details both America's long involvement in slavery and the distinguished history of enslaved Africans and freedpeople despite continued oppression. From disproving the biblical "curse theory" (12–13) and describing how, during the Middle Passage, kidnapped Africans "would jump overboard rather than be taken from their homes" (15), as well as detailing the history and abuses of slavery in the colonies (14–50), Johnson's textbook is unwaveringly antislavery.

While some white-authored textbooks that remained popular throughout the century, such as Peter Parley's *Universal History on the Basis of Geography* (Goodrich), include passages that condemn slavery, they rarely give any attention to the contributions of slaves or freedmen.[40] By contrast, Johnson's schoolbook comprises nearly two hundred pages of Negro history and accomplishments. What Johnson primarily adds to postbellum nonfictional representations of slavery for children is this focus on black heroism. Rather than the more popular trope of grateful slave and white savior, Johnson highlights black agency, describing how the slave in the New England colonies "by valor, patriotism and industry, began to loosen the chains of his own bondage" (24) by enlisting against the British during the Revolutionary War, service for which slaves were promised their freedom. While acknowledging the efforts of whites who fought against slavery, Johnson establishes the contributions of black abolitionists and points out racial discrimination perpetrated even by white abolitionists, as when blacks were "shut [. . .] out" of white abolitionist organizations (79). Such readiness to examine racial hypocrisy, even of whites who gave support to the cause, shows how Johnson echoes the focus and tone of many antebellum slave narratives to reclaim the importance of black authority and activism.

Throughout this textbook, Johnson lauds individual slaves for their strength, rebellion, and intelligence, from Crispus Attucks during the Revolutionary War to mathematical genius Thomas Fuller. Johnson acknowledges, as well, an unnamed many, such as the "Negro troops" who showed "unrivalled daring and heroic courage" during the Civil War (109); and he redefines the often undifferentiated people subsumed under the term "slaves" as talented individuals despite the trials of enslavement. Rather than slavery being a necessary reliance upon white masters, Johnson defines it as white dependence, pointing out that the labor of slaves was the "basis of Southern prosperity" (99).

What also distinguishes Johnson's text from earlier white-authored slave biographies, such as those offered in *Freedman's Third Reader*, is his acknowledgment of slaves' anger and resistance. The focus on religiosity and forgiveness in *Freedman's Third Reader*, for example, is evident in its description of the religious conversion of the *Amistad* captives who were tried and acquitted after overtaking the ship on which they were forcibly held. *Freedman's Third Reader* quotes one former slave who affirms, "we owe every thing to God. He keeps us alive, and makes us free. When we get home to Mendi we tell our brethren about God, Jesus Christ, and heaven" (106). By contrast, although Johnson recounts the same quote verbatim, his profile of the captives continues: "One was [also] asked, if he was again captured and about to be sold into slavery, [. . .] if he wouldn't pray for rather than kill [the enslavers . . .]? Cinquez [the leader] heard it and replied, shaking his head, 'Yes; I would pray for 'em and kill 'em too'" (94). Whether lauding slaves who escaped to the Florida everglades, where they would rather "die in the swamps with liberty [. . . than] feast as a bondman and a slave" (45), or the "immense courage" (89) of Nat Turner, who "in order to arouse his brethren [. . .] believed it necessary to kill such of the whites as would be most likely to give them trouble" (88), *A School History of the Negro Race in America*, unlike the biographies in *Freedman's Third Reader*, argues (as did many antebellum slave narratives) the rebellious resolve of the enslaved and the sometimes necessary role of violence.

In answer to debates about fitness for freedom—"can the Negro learn anything?" (E. Johnson 153)—Johnson responds with over forty profiles of successful African Americans. Finishing his history with accounts of "Progress Since Freedom," including "Religious Progress," "Educational Progress," and "Financial Progress" (140–164), Johnson argues "how well [Negroes . . .] deserved to be citizens" (99). In this discussion of the transition from slavery to freedom, Johnson reflects most directly on postbellum life, and in this way shapes representations of slavery to reflect contemporaneous racial politics.

Called the "emancipation generation" to signal the unique position of this generation that witnessed the move from enslavement to legal freedom (Eyerman 44), African Americans at the turn of the century had experienced the failure of Reconstruction's promise of full citizenship. African American authors for children, such as Edward Johnson and Silas Floyd, knew that failed world was what African American children faced. In his conduct book for African American children, *Floyd's Flowers: Or, Duty and Beauty for Colored Children* (1905),[41] Silas Floyd describes how "the sufferings which are inflicted upon the colored people in this country are many and grievous. I know that we are discriminated against in many ways [. . .]. The right to vote is being taken away from us in nearly all Southern states. Lynchings are on the increase. Not only our men but our women are also being burned at the stake" (321).

When Floyd poses the rhetorical question to children, "what shall we do?," his answer is both pragmatic and philosophical:

> There are those who say that we must strike back—use fire and torch and sword and shotgun ourselves. But I tell you plainly that we cannot afford to do that. The white people have all the courts, [. . .] all the newspapers, [. . .] all the arms and ammunition and double the men that we have. In every race riot the negro would get the worst of it finally. But there is a higher reason than that. [. . .] We cannot afford to lose our decency, our self-respect, our character. [. . .] no race is superior to the race it tramples upon, robs, maltreats, and murders. In spite of prejudice [. . .] we cannot as a race, afford to do wrong. But we can afford to be patient. [. . .] It is ordained of God that races, as well as individuals, shall rise through tribulations. (321–322)

Arguing for optimism, hard work, and determination in the face of violence and race-targeting lynching, this paradigm of "ris[ing] through tribulation" underwrote the literary reevaluation of slavery by African American post-Reconstruction authors.

As a part of this literary rehabilitation, both Floyd and Johnson promote incidences of exemplary behavior. Floyd gives little attention to slavery, instead warning against bad habits such as smoking, and encouraging hard work, "self-help," and personal development. Floyd and Johnson also seek to model black heroes for young readers. Johnson, for example, hoped his book would engender race pride in young African Americans and "inspire in them a new self-respect and confidence" (4). In a chapter titled "Negro Heroes," Floyd notes the role "brave negro men have played on the field of battle in the defense of liberty"—including Negro soldiers of the Civil War—and hopes that his recounting of it will provide the reader with guidance into and "inspiration for the future" (315).

Of any slave figure, it was (and in many respects, remains) Frederick Douglass who has become "a conspicuous representative of the talents and capabilities possessed by the colored race" (E. Johnson 83). What Eyerman calls the "progressive narrative" (26) and what Gates and McKay call "progress report autobiographies" (468), postbellum and post-Reconstruction narratives focus on the success of former slaves.[42] In their respective texts, Johnson and Floyd show that narrative trajectory in the life of Douglass: of his "rise" from the dispossession of enslavement to providing a role model for young African American children who faced continued race violence and who desperately needed black heroes.

Without the religious impress of the *Freedman's* series, both Floyd and Johnson describe incidents of Douglass's youth (while excising accounts of his battle with Covey), before quickly moving on to discuss those involving his freedom. With an accompanying portrait that presents Douglass as dignified and financially successful in a formal suit and tie, Johnson describes that Douglass was "born a slave on a plantation [. . . but that] he has gradually, by industry and patient labor, worked himself to the highest rank of honor" (83). Floyd's description is similar: "This man, born so lowly and surrounded by such circumstances, turned out to be in the course of time by hard work and self-application one of the most influential American citizens and one of the greatest orators that this country has ever known. [. . .] Every boy and girl in America should read the life of this pre-eminent negro and strive to emulate his virtues" (135–136).

As "conspicuously representative of the talents and capabilities possessed by the colored race" (E. Johnson 83), Frederick Douglass is presented as a different kind of hero, a "New Negro" to contrast "Old Negro" figures like Uncle Remus that ubiquitously populated postplantation novels. This figure of the New Negro became a way to rewrite racist discourse and tropes, principally by refiguring slave stereotypes of the "Sambo" and "Uncle." Rewriting representations of slavery was central in this refiguring of black identity. As Gates argues, the term "New Negro" signals a "sort of self-willed beginning [in which . . .] its 'success' depends fundamentally upon self-negation, a turning away from the 'Old Negro' and the labyrinthine memory of black enslavement and toward the register of a 'New Negro'" ("Trope" 132).[43] In biographies, Douglass becomes the preeminent representation of this New Negro figure.

With it no longer necessary to argue the end of legal slavery, these authors recontextualize and reframe slavery as a lens through which to explore contemporaneous racial oppression. In so doing, they recover former slaves—particularly Douglass—and, in emulative biographies, use slavery as a way to reconfigure the future. Edward Johnson's call to young Negro readers—that "much has been done [. . .] to raise the race in the estimation of the world, but much more remains to be done. [. . .] to inspire new zeal and fresh courage, that each one of you may add something more to what has already been accomplished" (164)—articulates the focus of African American literature for children at the turn of the century and during the forthcoming Harlem Renaissance. Indeed, African American authors would use representations of successful slaves to call for no less than the revisioning of American racial politics.

• • •

From the end of the Civil War to the beginning of the twentieth century, children's literature refashioned antebellum tropes as a way to imagine racial identity in a newly postslavery America. While some sought to resuscitate slavery through literary re-creations of plantation myths with their assertions of the amiability of race relations based on a faithful black slave/kind white master paradigm, others drew upon images of the heroic slave from antebellum slave narratives to envision a new racialized future for America. Debates about the "fitness" of slaves and tensions between expectations for and experiences of former slaves in a "free" America informed these representations. For these first generations of postslavery writers, defining what slavery meant—and, particularly, what the "slave" meant as a signifier of race—became a way to both explain the past and make sense of their present.

CHAPTER 4

CONFLICTING VOICES DURING THE HARLEM RENAISSANCE ERA

1920-1950

> The leader of this band was Crispus Attucks. [. . .]
> He knew only too well how precious a thing is freedom
> and how no sacrifice is too much for its purchase.
> —"America's First Martyr-Patriot," *The Brownies' Book* (1920)

> In his untamed state it would not be well to give
> [freedom to . . .] him too soon. [. . .] He is part animal now.
> What would he do but run wild?
> —Elizabeth Yates, *Amos Fortune, Free Man* (1950)

Despite some forays into representations of diversity—such as Lorraine and Jerrold Beim's picture book *Two Is a Team* (1945), which shows a friendship between an apparently African American and Anglo-American boy[1]—children's literature booklists of mainstream publishers remained firmly entrenched in notions of white superiority during the first half of the twentieth century. When African American characters did appear, they generally maintained the role, as does Dinah in the *Bobbsey Twins*, of "cook, maid and mammy" (Deane 163); of comic relief, as in the *Tom Swift* series (which began in 1910); or of shiftless workers, as in the first book of the Nancy Drew Mystery Stories series, *The Secret of the Old Clock* (1930).[2] Picture books generally offered no different vision of race, from U.S. reprints of *The Story of Little Black Sambo* (1899) to the racialized caricatures of Ida Chubb's *Little Pickaninnies* (1929).[3] The fact that the pickaninny, the fool, the loyal servant, the cheat, and the sluggard were the racial lexicon of black characters in much of popular children's literature during the first half of the twentieth century reflected racial stereotypes embedded in American culture at large, from D. W. Griffith's film, *The Birth of a Nation* (1915), which praised the Ku Klux Klan as "the organization that saved the South from the anarchy of black rule," to Margaret Mitchell's *Gone with the Wind* (1936) with its loyal Mammy, foolish Prissy, and nostalgia for the slave South.

The absence of independent African American characters in some ways reflected eugenics studies and pseudoscientific race work of the early twentieth century that not only continued to tout the intellectual, physical, and moral superiority of Europeans, but even theorized the eventual extinction of African Americans altogether. Jim Crow segregationist policies were compounded by that threat of annihilation, and the battle for literal survival by African Americans was particularly evident during the "Red Summer of 1919," when race riots in cities across the country left hundreds of African Americans dead. Lynchings continued, particularly in the South, and the Ku Klux Klan, buoyed by Griffith's movie, enjoyed a major resurgence in the early 1920s, its members numbering over three million nationwide (Trelease 626).

Yet during the 1920s, the cultural movement termed the "Harlem Renaissance" because of the concentration of work produced in New York, or the "New Negro Movement" to acknowledge its wider influence, inspired a period of exuberant creation for African Americans. Supported in their efforts by African American publishers, many African American writers shared a focus on racial pride as they explored black identity, recovered black heroes, and debated the nature of art, race, and politics. With the creation of the National Association for the Advancement of Colored People (NAACP) in 1909, and its monthly magazine, *The Crisis*, a year later, African Americans had established important political and literary forums through which to debate and lobby issues of race, politics, and social justice. The struggle between the hopes and realities of full enfranchisement was heightened, particularly following World War II, when African Americans who had fought to defend democracy and freedom abroad returned to an America that guaranteed them neither. Legal gains were made, but they often went hand in hand with realized failures: Supreme Court decisions for black enfranchisement and against segregation on interstate buses, for example, did not readily translate to guaranteed rights which African Americans could freely exercise. Yet in debates about democracy and civil rights, and through the work of early protestors who would test racially prescribed social and legal barriers, these years provided important grounding for the civil rights movement of the mid-twentieth century.

Children's literature about slavery during these years reflected the nation's contested racial politics. Proslavery perspectives continued in plantation stories of historical fiction and also found new life in neoplantation novels that placed proslavery characters and scenarios within twentieth-century settings. While those novels approximated the ideology of their literary predecessor, white-authored pseudo-abolitionist adventure novels argued an antislavery position that was ultimately undermined by both character tropes and narrative stance. The genre responsively reflected issues of antebellum abolitionist literature while denying the possibilities of emancipation, and hence it wrote against the grounding points of antebellum radical abolition. In the midst of this, the 1920s ushered in a new era of contesting voices in children's literature with the emergence of strong African American authorship writing to a specifically African American readership. Using nonfictional accounts and biography reminiscent of portrayals in slave narratives, these authors recovered African American heroes otherwise lost amid the din of racist tropes more common to children's literature. In the case of each of these forms, authors borrowed from antebellum literature in their translation of current issues of race, enfranchisement, and citizenship. In so doing, they shaped the historical memory of slavery through often vying twentieth-century perspectives.

TWENTIETH-CENTURY PLANTATION AND NEOPLANTATION NOVELS

The plantation story in traditional form still continued to find interested audiences among American children, particularly in historical fiction that re-created antebellum plantation literature by using an antebellum setting. Lucy Fitch Perkins's *The Colonial Twins of Virginia* (1924), for example, uses a "great" plantation (iii) of the late 1600s as the setting for a story about young white slaveholders defending their home from pirates. Other than Mammy, who interacts with the children largely by preparing them food, Perkins depicts slaves as a group of undifferentiated members that serve two narrative functions: silent background characters to define the story's milieu and contrasting racial markers to white superiority.

Perkins's white protagonists quickly determine that the slaves would be useless in catching the pirates; they may be "faithful" (99), but they are also "chicken-hearted" (74). Unenviable in the "weary round of their lives" (30), these slaves seem nonetheless content as they sing and laugh while working. They are as easily dispensed with by the white protagonists as they are in the story at large; one of the white children, for example, remarks, "one has to love people, and there aren't any other people here to love except the slaves, and of course they don't count" (20). That the slaves "don't count" evinces an antebellum proslavery sentiment without any inflection of a postslavery sensibility. Although *The Colonial Twins of Virginia* was written sixty years after the legal end of U.S. slavery, it exemplifies how traditional plantation stories continued into the twentieth century through historical fiction. Indeed, Perkins re-creates the setting and characters of antebellum plantation stories and her narrative stance remains solidly and uncritically proslavery.[4]

By the early twentieth century, the traditional plantation story also metamorphosed into the neoplantation novel. While the late nineteenth-century postplantation novel represented the end of slavery as a loss of an idyll and a civilization only tentatively recouped as masters and freed slaves recommitted themselves to a recovered plantation hierarchy, the neoplantation story explores the next generation of race relations. These are "neoplantation" novels because they re-create the earlier genre in a twentieth-century context where the plantation and slavery are given "new" life. They thus provide a subtextual commentary on U.S. slavery while also arguing for a continuance of its racial hierarchies in the twentieth century. In neoplantation novels, the unironic use of racist tropes drawn from antebellum plantation novels can influence a reader's perception of the fluidity of time. The contemporary setting is infiltrated by proslavery perspectives so that the fictional time period becomes confusingly kaleidoscoped with the antebellum era, and the ostensible modernity of the twentieth century is often submerged in nostalgic representations of the old South. Clarifying the fictional time period, and whether black characters are "slaves" or "servants," can be a sometimes confusing task, particularly, one would suspect, for young readers. Indeed, neoplantation novels seem to dissolve the boundaries of ante- and postbellum time periods. Were one to take away technological markers such as automobiles, telephones, and radios, neoplantation novels would often seem to be set in antebellum times.

A series which epitomizes the neoplantation genre is the once-popular *Miss Minerva* series (1909–1939), described by one historian as "Southern stories for Southern boys and girls" (J. Wilson 69).[5] Presented as humorous stories about the "spinster" Miss Minerva who marries a Confederate veteran and takes care of her adventurous nephew Billy, the series offers a plethora of well-worn racist tropes. One here meets the "amazingly fat" cook and Mammy, Aunt Cindy, who is unvaryingly kind to her white charges while also a "dictator" to the black boy in her care (Sampson, *Miss Minerva Broadcasts Billy* 14, 62). Young readers also meet "the shiftless nigger" as well as "little pickaninnies" and "little darkies" who are "happy indeed at being invited to a white folks' party" (Sampson, *Miss Minerva on the Old Plantation* 91, 122). Reflecting antebellum plantation stories like Caroline Gilman's "The Country Visit" with its description of slaves as "monkeys" ("Arrival"), here Aunt Cindy's husband, the lazy Uncle Jimmy-jawed Jupiter, has "sad monkey eyes" and Aunt Cindy even describes him as looking "mo' like a baboon than ever" (*Miss Minerva on the Old Plantation* 268, 92). As in antebellum plantation stories, the physical alignment of black characters with animals signals their status as not fully human; white characters, by contrast, are never described in animal terms. Further, having Aunt Cindy make this comparison fictively absolves the white author and compliant reader of its racism and asserts a type of insider authority on race hierarchy—even black Cindy recognizes a man/baboon when she sees one. From heavy dialect—described as being "niggerfied in [. . .] talk" (*Miss Minerva on the Old Plantation* 229)—to such exaggerated names as "Admiral Farragut Moses the Prophet Esquire," hyperbole and the inability to grasp standard grammar narratively ridicules black characters who ineffectively try to "ape" white civilization.

In *Miss Minerva on the Old Plantation* (1923), the characters return to Billy's boyhood home to enjoy "the delights of plantation life" (73). Like antebellum stories where a "large number of the slaves were awaiting [the white family's . . .] arrival" (Gilman, "Country Visit, Arrival"), when Billy and the others reach the plantation, "all of the colored children who could get there were waiting at the landing to receive the travelers" (299). A centerpiece of the plantation's racial ambience, these greetings—like those of slaves in antebellum plantation stories—suggest that black residents live in an anticipation only fulfilled by the arrival of white masters.

In neoplantation stories, the space of white adulation represented by the plantation extends beyond its antebellum borders in both time and geography. In *Miss Minerva Broadcasts Billy* (1925), for example, Deci, a young black girl, leaves the plantation to fulfill her heart's desire by "going up to live with the white folks" (179). The plantation site is not so much lost here as exchanged as a necessary acknowledgment of modernity, its reach extending far beyond the quarantined space of its antebellum representation. If the white master class has left the rural plantation for a more modern, technological world, black servants hope to follow, and here a proslavery ideology of race relations infuses Miss Minerva's home so that it becomes a type of pseudoplantation.

For Deci, it is "Heaben": "Said I's gonter go live with [. . .] white folks. Lawdy! Lawdy! Done got to Heaben!" (215). Yet the fulfillment of Deci's desires is not simply living in the white family's home, but serving in it:

> Deci belonged to Josephine [Miss Minerva's daughter] as much as though the war between the states had never been fought and the proclamation freeing the slaves had never been made.
>
> "I done come up here to b'long to you an' I b'longs to you jes' as much as Flumpy or Brownie or yo' doll baby. My gran'-mammy done tol' us time an' agin how she uster b'long to Billy's pappy's mammy's sister, an' that's the way I'm gonter b'long to you. What you tell me to do I does, an' what you tell me to stop, I leaves off." (236–237)

Happily positioning herself as Josephine's dog (Flumpy), pony (Brownie), or toy, Deci willingly objectifies herself, claiming to be the rightful inheritor of her grandmother's slavery. This image of a free black child claiming slavery as her birthright posits a white audience's fantasy of slavery as a site of amiable black servitude and benevolent white superiority.[6]

More than only arguing the benevolence of nineteenth-century American slavery, neoplantation novels also present a contemporary world where freed blacks are indistinguishable from antebellum proslavery representations of slaves in their relationship to paternal (or maternal) whites. Half a century after the end of legal slavery in the United States, neoplantation novels such as these in the *Miss Minerva* series promised new generations of children that the future of race relations in the United States would replicate the idyllically depicted slavery of antebellum plantation novels. They offered white readers the narrative illusion that racial equality (or even legal freedom) was not something desired by the Aunt Cindys or Decis of the world.

Giving black children exaggerated, if not preposterous, names as a type of minstrelized humor also provides further racial commentary. For example, in *Miss Minerva on the Old Plantation*, black children's names—such as "Bibble & Brothers Mercantile Company" and "Alice Ann Maria Dan Step-an'-Go-Fetch-It" (88)—are a source of amusement to young white Josephine. That one child is named "Iovory" because her Granny hoped the whiteness of the product would rub off on the child and that "she mought be smart like white folks an' clean like soap" (87) also reveals the implicit racial desire of these black characters. Yet, the misspelling of the product's name (which also signals the inability of the child to ever attain whiteness) is central in the racist humor.[7] Yet in the case of the protagonist's black companion, Wilkes Booth Lincoln (his name is always cited in full), the use of a seemingly ridiculous name provides a commentary on slavery. That his name is composed of those of both Lincoln and his assassin presents a pointedly mixed message. Described as a pacifist, the boy is in no real danger of becoming an assassin, and thus is no Nat figure who might trouble the imaginations of white readers. Yet, the child has little affinity for Lincoln, since "as for Wilkes Booth Lincoln, the emancipation of the negro was nothing to him. He boldly declared he 'b'longed to little Missy'" (Sampson, *Miss Minerva's Baby* 169). Like his sister, Deci, who wishes "the proclamation freeing the slaves had never been made," Wilkes Booth Lincoln represents the neoplantation novel's new hero: a black child born legally free who fantasizes about being a slave.[8]

PSEUDOABOLITIONIST ADVENTURE NOVELS

While proslavery texts of the early twentieth century fully embraced the racial tropes of their antebellum predecessors, contemporaneous abolitionist novels were more ideologically conflicted. In their attempts to encourage activism, white antebellum radical abolitionists had created an almost indelible image of black powerlessness and white agency. Three novels that received early Newbery Honor recognition illustrate the longevity of this image while refashioning it as suspicious of abolition itself. Each of these novels is set in antebellum times with plots that revolve around issues of abolition. In Charles Boardman Hawes's *The Great Quest* (1921), when the protagonist's uncle is tricked into buying a ship that may be used to transport slaves, young Joe leaves the safety of his small New England town to sail to Africa and to defend his uncle from slavers. In Agnes Danforth Hewes's *Glory of the Seas* (1933), John Seagrave and his Uncle Asa flout the newly passed Fugitive Slave Law of 1850 by hiding an escaped slave. And Elsie Singmaster's *Swords of Steel* (1933) is set against the coming Civil War, as John Deane's friend, Nicholas, is kidnapped into slavery. Historical fiction garnered a large portion of Newbery attention in the award's first several decades, and that white protagonists in these three books take stands against slavery would seem to bespeak a concern for racial awareness, perhaps even inclusion and equal rights on behalf of its authors and the Newbery committees that commended them. Yet as much as these novels purport to be about abolition, they are, instead, pseudoabolitionist in that each retains a strong counternarrative which ultimately argues against both emancipation and racial equality.

The novels share a common thematic trajectory of young, white male protagonists who come of age by participating in abolitionist activities. In some ways, that plotline extends depictions of the white reformer child of antebellum radical abolitionist literature: aiding a slave becomes a sign of the white protagonist's heroism, his readiness to thwart society's pressures, and his transition from a protected childhood to young adulthood. In the midst of the white protagonist's personal and public rite of passage, slave characters serve as coins of exchange. This commodification of the slave is evident, for example, in *Swords of Steel*, when the white protagonist fantasizes about how "thrilling" it would be to come upon a runaway slave and "save him!" (16). The scene reveals the banality of white protagonists to whom the slave is a vicarious object for their own romanticized adventures. Unlike Twain's more complex *Adventures of Huckleberry Finn*, in these novels there is no narrative critique of that objectification.

Antebellum slave narratives had sought to humanize the often objectified "slave," not only by showing the suffering each endured, but also by encouraging in white audiences a sympathetic understanding of the slave's plight. The radical argument for the abolition of slavery depended upon what Harriet Jacobs, in her autobiography of her years as a slave, referred to as a "realizing sense" (1). This sought-after "realizing sense" was more than intellectual awareness; it was an emotionally sympathetic understanding based on the imaginative extension of empathy to traverse otherness. It would have white readers understand their racial privilege as an undeserved protection in a society which determined that one's condition in life depended on skin color alone.

In an almost perverse recasting of this "realizing sense," in these ostensibly abolitionist novels of the early twentieth century, readers are asked to appreciate the suffering of *white* protagonist-abolitionists, not that of those enslaved. While antebellum abolitionist children's texts, like J. Elizabeth Jones's *The Young Abolitionists* or Matilda Thompson's "Aunt Judy's Story," present white characters who function as amanuenses to tell the stories of slaves, pseudoabolitionist adventure novels further co-opt the slave experience by transferring a reader's sense of sympathy for suffering to white characters. Thus, runaway Jasper, the only black character in *Glory of the Seas*, appears only briefly, and the principal narrative tension is not whether Jasper will be caught by authorities but whether white characters will be arrested for aiding him. When Jasper promises that he would never betray John, the white protagonist "heaved a sigh of relief" saying, "good for you. [. . .] You know it goes pretty hard with those who help you people" (221). Indeed, what is remarkable is that these books contain so few black characters, either slave or free; their presence is marginalized to prevent diverting attention away from white protagonists.

This shift of focus to the endangerment and agency of white characters is generally proportional to the depicted narrative invisibility and foolishness of slaves. Antebellum abolitionists called upon white readers to "try to put yourself in [the slave's . . .] place" ("Cart-Whip" 5–6) as a way to recognize the slave's essential humanity. By contrast, the authors of these adventure novels repeatedly distance white and black figures, with black characters (slave and free) serving as a type of "other" figure to provide for a contrasting exploration of whiteness. In *Glory of the Seas*, the distance between whites and what John describes as "you people" is further shown when Jasper ignores John's orders, crashes over a fence, and is discovered by authorities. Unable to be measured, to be rational, or to listen to the apparently more intelligent white boy, Jasper is arrested and returned to the South. Such contrasted pairings of the effective, intelligent, powerful young, white male with powerless adult, black male slaves hearken back to antebellum proslavery novels, such as Goulding's *Robert and Harold*. In an unintentionally ironic contrast to the young slaveholders of *Robert and Harold*, in *Glory of the Seas*, the response of the supposedly abolitionist white characters is strikingly unsympathetic. When John learns that Jasper will be returned to slavery, he resentfully responds, "it was his own fault. If he'd done as I told him—" (227–228).

In these adventure tales, black characters who are not foolish commonly occupy one of two opposite tropes: the passive, grateful slave or the vicious, unreasoned savage.[9] The dichotomy leaves little room for a representation of thoughtful black independence and implies the threat of blacks not compliant to white authority. When the novels admit black heroes, they do so within clearly circumscribed roles. *Swords of Steel* and *The Great Quest*, for example, each present a physically strong black male whose power is domesticated by a young, white female whom he serves and protects.

Jo-Ann Morgan argues that in the pairing of Uncle Tom and Eva, "readers could flirt with the couple and what their mingling might suggest, only to contain these errant fantasies by emasculating Tom and eulogizing Eva" (39).[10] The antebellum *Hatchie, the Guardian Slave*, for example, "flirts" with culturally prescribed racial/sexual boundaries: Hatchie's emotional response to his young, white mistress suggests the possibility of a sexually charged relationship that remains unconsummated, its sexual energy played out in his unswerving dedication and heroic protection of the young woman. A similar scenario is played out in *Swords of Steel* and *The Great Quest*, where physically strong black males serve as companions and protectors of white females who are on the cusp of their sexual adulthood. Thus, in *Swords of Steel*, Nicholas "of heroic proportions" (1) is paired with the white daughter of his master/employer, Maggie, "a beautiful little girl with a delicate figure [who. . . .] was devoted to Nicholas and Nicholas to her" (3). Similarly, in *The Great Quest*, the white missionary's daughter, Faith, who "appeared so slender, so frail" (299), is protected by a "great black Fantee servant" (294) whom she commands as one would a dog. In this trope, the slave/servant's physical size is contrasted with the small frame of the young girl; his virility with her virginity; his blackness with her whiteness.

The possibility of a fully realized heterosexual relationship between a black man and white woman in these adventure novels transgresses socially and legally prescribed codes of the time. The eroticism of their relationship lies in the tension between the possibilities of such a transgression and the fact that, within these novels, those transgressions will never occur. Moreover, the racist fear of black men raping white women[11] is dispelled, for the black male is Christianized and ultimately a fictive eunuch who never marries or becomes sexually active. Although Stowe's Eva dies, *Hatchie, the Guardian Slave*'s Emily, *Swords of Steel*'s Maggie, and *The Great Quest*'s Faith either marry or become betrothed by the close of their respective novels, in each case to the white protagonist. The betrothal assures readers of a white protagonist's manhood and racial superiority, as well as the continuance of the white race. The white protagonist (and not a black man) will marry and have children, creating the next generation and shaping the future of the country.

While these pairings of a black male guardian and white female mistress might "flirt" with the possibilities of transgressing racial and class boundaries, boundaries remain firmly in place between the black slave and white male protagonist. In gendered, cultural, and racial terms, the adventure genre is one often laden with prescriptive depictions of heroism. As John Rowe Townsend has pointed out, nineteenth-century adventure novels for boys encapsulate "man's dream, to build a nation or empire, win wars, pioneer newly-won territories, or develop [. . .] wealth. [. . . In novels for] boys there was the life of action on land and at sea" (39). Although Townsend does not specify here, the implication is that these are "white" men's dreams translated—by extension—to "white" boys' fictional adventures. From Daniel Defoe's *Robinson Crusoe* (1719) to H. Rider Haggard's *King Solomon's Mines* (1885), adventure stories have often been the purview of "white" heroes who command or battle a racialized "other" to garner territory or treasure, and, especially in the colonizing impetus of traditional adventure novels, racial dominance. These novels do not draw upon the black hero of the slave narrative; rather, they write against him.

In *Playing in the Dark*, Toni Morrison argues that

> autonomy, authority, newness and difference, absolute power—not only become the major themes and presumptions of American literature, but [. . .] each one is made possible by, shaped by, activated by a complex awareness and employment of a consti-

> tuted Africanism. It was this Africanism, deployed as rawness and savagery, that provided the staging ground and arena for the elaboration of the quintessential American identity. (44)

This is perhaps nowhere truer than in American literature about slavery, particularly in representations of the rebellious Nat figure who metes out vengeance upon whites (Blassingame 235).[12] Such a fear of the Africanist presence as "rawness and savagery" underpins *The Great Quest*'s ultimate rejection of abolition.

The contrast between hero and villain in *The Great Quest* initially revolves around issues of slavery. The antislavery position of Joe, the white protagonist, seems unequivocal when he describes the Middle Passage as a site of "horrors such as all human history elsewhere can scarcely equal" (313). The immorality of Gleazen, however, is highlighted by the fact that he is a slave trader who repeatedly uses the epithet "nigger." Yet, in their views on race, the hero and villain are of like mind, and when the two travel to the "heart of Africa" (215), friends and enemies become redefined strictly in terms of race. Joe finds Africa to be a "terrible nightmare" (308) as the group is surrounded by "hundreds of blacks, if not thousands" (242), all "alive with rage and vindictiveness" (269). This "nightmare" of whites surrounded by "horde[s]" (268) of uncontrollable black Africans bent on their death is white America's racial nightmare of Nat Turner, a reincarnation of antebellum racial fears still evidenced in twentieth-century culture.

In their crazed state, these Africans—variously described as "wolves" (285), "enraged maniacs" (284), and "ungodly" (292) "creatures ten thousand times worse than any crawling son of the serpent of Eden" (264)—enact violence motivated by race hatred. The author's contention that raging blacks will kill any and all white people is obvious; this is unvarnished race warfare. Against this group, Joe, too, grasps identity only in terms of race. Trapped in a hut by attacking Africans, he suddenly sees his white nemesis in a different light. Survival against blacks requires a commitment of white unity; as Joe describes it, "we were six men [. . .] three of us arrant desperadoes, but all of us at least white of skin, surrounded by a black horde" (265). *The Great Quest* assures young readers of the inviolability of race: against the onslaught of that "black horde," all white men—murderer and potential victim, slaver and abolitionist alike—become "brothers" (266). Battling "blacks behind us and blacks before us" (296), Joe experiences a cultural and racial coming-of-age, sealing his status as a man (specifically as a white man) when he "killed a negro in his tracks" (297).

Unlike the antebellum proslavery *Robert and Harold*, in *The Great Quest* readers learn that journeying outside white-dominated spheres of influence invites a chaos that cannot be controlled by white imperialism. While in *Robert and Harold*, Goulding envisioned worlds of white surety because he never imagined black power, Hawes's description of black power introduces a sense of horror on behalf of white characters who cannot contain black vengeance, but, if fortunate, may escape it. This depiction of race warfare argues that blacks and whites cannot coexist: black power means white extermination.

That in each of these novels the white male protagonists shed their abolitionism as they come of age thus defines abolitionism as the uninformed sentiment of children, including the reformer child. The black slave has fulfilled his function in the white male's rise, and is no longer necessary to the plot or protagonist. The genre is thus pseudoabolitionist because it adopts a pose of abolition to further the central story of a white boy's coming-of-age, then shows the white protagonist's racial coming-of-age in his ultimate disaffection with abolition. Similar to Dorothy Broderick's argument about the insidious effect of black characters that offer the most antiblack statements (116), pseudoabolitionist adventure novels offer ostensibly abolitionist characters who express antiabolitionist views.

In these novels, the abolitionist perspective is ultimately disillusioning or dangerous to white characters. Indeed, in *The Great Quest* active abolitionism is a threat to white civilization. The "raging black horde" (268) is, after all, abolitionist in that they are fighting against white slavers. Those Africans are, in that way, the true abolitionists, the incarnation of Nat Turner's revolt. Yet in Hawes's depiction of them as inhuman and satanic, he reveals whites' fears of the chaos black emancipation will inflict on white society. In *Swords of Steel*, when the protagonist's father cautions against the coming Civil War because "the question is, what to do with the slaves if they are freed," John enthusiastically responds, "they could earn their living! Nicholas could!" Yet John's father, who works on the Underground Railroad and whose judgment readers are meant to trust, assures his son and young readers that "there aren't many like Nicholas" (26). The conclusion of *Glory of the Seas* also acknowledges the failure of abolition. Although he had aided fugitive slaves, the protagonist's uncle announces that "I gave up my part with Abolition," and determines to head to California to work on keeping the Union together rather than continue as an abolitionist (305).

It is not only the determination of abolitionist characters to "give up their part with Abolition" that marks its rejection in these novels. That the movement of the white male to adulthood is defined against that which is not-blackness is also played out in the conclusions of these pseudoabolitionist novels which depict a world largely absent of black characters. Neither *Glory of the Seas* nor *Swords of Steel* can envision a world of emancipated slaves. At the close of *Glory of the Seas*, Jasper, presumably enslaved on a Southern plantation, has ceased to be even a point of discussion, and at the close of *Swords of Steel*, Nicholas is dead, and another black man, Caesar, has fled, searching for freedom elsewhere. The martyr-slave may be lauded as a "man" upon his death (259), but the general invisibility of slaves in these novels transforms into utter absence by their conclusion. Nonetheless, the central white male figures have come of age and look forward to socially and politically significant futures.

The fact that only white characters have the stage at the end of these novels posits more than an affirmation of white hegemony. It posits an exclusively white world which frighteningly evokes contemporary eugenics debates of the early twentieth century that prophesied the extinction of the black race. Evinced in 1920s anti-immigration legislation and so-called scientific studies that mapped racial hierarchies, eugenics studies betrayed a racially defensive fear of the "other," that is, of those not narrowly defined as Anglo-Saxon.[13] In terms of white angst about African Americans, that fear had strong roots in slavery and was grounded in fears of race warfare and anxieties of white racial extinction. These adventure novels reflect those fears in that, ultimately, abolitionist sentiment collapses. Being an abolitionist marks the protagonist's humanity; abandoning abolitionism marks his maturity. The novels thus finally write against abolition, particularly in their conclusions, where previously abolitionist characters admit its failure or doubt the ability of slaves to incorporate themselves into society as free people. Moreover, the absence of black characters in the conclusions of these novels suggests an inability on the part of these Newbery-lauded authors to imagine those formerly enslaved as having any role in American society as emancipated citizens.[14] To the extent that these are "American" adventures that seek to define what is American through the protagonist's experiences, these stories show that there is no place in America for the black "other." Rather, they declare that emancipation was a well-intentioned but failed experiment, and that the only good "African" was a loyal slave or dead freedman.

SLAVE BIOGRAPHY

When W. E. B. Du Bois proclaimed that he would publish *The Brownies' Book* (1920–1921) "for all children, but especially for ours, 'the Children of the Sun'" ("True Brownies" 286), the central authorship and audience of this magazine—by and for African Americans—marked a critical landmark in American, African American, and children's literatures by providing a range of literature to a wider young African American reading audience than ever before.[15] Expressing a not uncommon view that children carry the hope of the adult generation, Du Bois racially refigured representations of republican childhood by arguing the centrality of African American children in changing American racial politics, for it is, he wrote, "the children of the darker world who hold in their little hands so vast a destiny" ("Immortal Children" 267). *The Brownies' Book* furthered the vision of earlier African American texts for children—of, for example, Edward Johnson's *A School History of the Negro Race in America* and Silas Floyd's *Floyd's Flowers*—in its call for a recovery of African American heroes and its determination to engender race pride in young African Americans.[16] To Du Bois and others, reframing the racial education of children could reorder an American society that Du Bois believed suffered from a "failure in human education: That failure is due to the fact that [. . .] the world regards [. . .] education first as a means of buttressing the established order of things rather than improving it" ("Immortal Child" 206–207). *The Brownies' Book*, in many ways, restructured "the established order" of racial representations to demonstrate the intersections of Du Bois's ideologies about education, children, race, and citizenship.

Providing coverage of current events and discussions about racial violence,[17] the magazine both confronted and countered popular representations of racial stereotypes. In contrast to stereotypes of black intellectual inferiority, *The Brownies' Book* offered list upon list of school graduates. In visual contradiction to ubiquitously caricatured images of African Americans, the magazine showed the beauty of African American children by publishing photographs of its young readers. And in contrast to Eurocentric fairy tales, *The Brownies' Book* published an array of stories foregrounding African and African American cultures.

It also retrieved the cultural authorship of folktales that Joel Chandler Harris had contained within a narrative frame of black servant and white auditor in his *Uncle Remus* collection. Especially in stories by Julian Elihu Bagley, the narrative frame and auditor/focus of the *Uncle Remus* tales are drastically revisioned: Harris's plantation South is replaced by Harlem; the plantation owner's son as intratextual audience is replaced by a young African American boy, Cless; and the happy former slave Uncle Remus is replaced by Cless's Granny, who tells stories that strengthen her grandson's self-esteem and racial pride. By moving folktales out of Harris's pro-plantation ideology and repositioning them within the African American community, Bagley writes responsively, exemplifying what, in an African American context, Henry Louis Gates Jr. has termed "signifyin'." As Gates explains, entailing "formal revision and an intertextual relation," when "one text Signifies upon another text, by tropological revision or repetition and difference, the double-voiced utterance allows us to chart discrete formal relationships in Afro-American literary history" (*Signifying* 51, 88). In these tales, Bagley signifies on oppression and cultural appropriation by the hegemonic culture at the same time that he returns the folktales more closely to the purposes they had held within slave communities.[18]

In the hands of African American authors, biography, too, became a means to attack racialized hierarchies. Answering the question of "didn't colored folks do anything?" (Seymour), *The Brownies' Book* became a recovery project, offering young readers biographies of African Americans, many of whom overcame seemingly insurmountable obstacles to make major contributions to American society. One meets, here, among others, Crispus Attucks, "America's First Martyr-Patriot" of the Revolutionary War; Katy Ferguson, who founded New York City's first Sunday school; Blanche Bruce, elected senator of Mississippi; and Sojourner Truth, who agitated for Woman Suffrage. Against the ubiquitous onslaught of racial stereotypes populating literature and the culture at large, the magazine assured young readers that African American heroes were no mere fiction. Indeed, nearly each of the magazine's twenty-four issues includes a biography; moreover, most of them feature people who had once been enslaved. More complex than the brief accounts in either Silas Floyd's *Floyd's Flowers* or Edward Johnson's earlier *A School History of the Negro Race in America*, the biographies in *The Brownies' Book* develop a sense of story and express a more nuanced ideology[19] to offer paradigms of resistance and success. They also expand the canon of slave biographies, for they include a number of female subjects.

In *The Brownies' Book*, biography also allowed ways of reflecting on slave narratives, if not always by borrowing specific scenes then certainly by entering the debate about authority and authenticity that had marked antebellum discourse about slavery. As antebellum authors on all sides of the ideological divide had written about slavery, they had done so amid contentious arguments about *who* had a right to describe slavery—and which arguments were trustworthy. Autobiographies of former slaves were often received with skepticism, particularly from those who argued that such accounts outstripped the literacy or reasoning abilities of former slaves. Yet time and again, former slaves testified to the veracity of their accounts, and in so doing, argued against racialized prescriptions that denigrated black ability and identity.

As much as authors of slave narratives distinguished themselves from the fiction of pro- and antislavery novelists by asserting their accounts were "strictly true" (Jacobs 1), early twentieth-century African American authors would use biography as a way to reauthorize the slave narrative and claim their own authority to write about black history.[20] To discredit the accumulation of proslavery and racist stereotypes, these authors would argue "strictly true" racial representations by recounting the lives of actual people, and—at the same time—argue the cultural authority of African American writers to tell these stories. This was particularly the case about slavery. That in its two-year run, *The Brownies' Book* included no fictional stories about U.S. slavery argued the truth of slavery as a historical atrocity. Slavery, these biographies would repeatedly assert, was historical fact, not fiction.[21]

Yet slavery was nonetheless a problematic issue for African Americans writing for young African American readers in whom they hoped to inspire race pride. Situated between a painful past and the hope of an optimistic future, African American authors of the early twentieth century presented, as Deborah McDowell argues, "a complex view of history, one that necessitated looking simultaneously toward the future and the past" (151). These biographies for children show the struggle to make meaning of slavery in an early twentieth-century context, particularly in ways that could inform children without, as Du Bois feared, presenting explicit accounts of violence that would "educate them in human hatred" ("True Brownies" 285). These authors also worked against the accumulation of long-standing representations of slavery in fiction, histories, and supposedly scientific studies that declared slaves to have been foolish, passive, intellectually vacuous, and grateful for their servitude. In the face of those often overwhelming cultural voices, the slave narrative, with its representation of the rebellious, intelligent black individual, had been virtually silenced in children's literature. Under the weight of such cultural representations, these authors at times revealed, as Katharine Capshaw Smith has noted, that the "sense of shame surrounding enslavement was tangible" (188).[22]

In a time of continued lynchings, race riots, and the resurgence of the Ku Klux Klan, the retrieval of antebellum slave narratives allowed an examination of continued race conflict in the early twentieth century to place contemporaneous events within a historical context of black racial oppression in the United States. As much as the figure of the slave and its attendant racist stereotypes persisted as the root of racialized representations of African Americans, slavery served as the primary event of black exploitation in America, the defining moment that shaped the racial culture of the nation. To both contextualize and counter contemporary racism, many African American authors sought to reclaim and redefine the root image of the slave figure for young audiences. Shaping the story of slavery for African American children of the early twentieth century who were generations away from slavery itself meant refiguring the objectives of abolition; as McDowell argues of post-Reconstruction and Harlem Renaissance literature for adults authored by African Americans, it meant "confront[ing] the challenges of representing slavery in 'freedom's' time. How could they treat the subject of slavery when the urgencies of abolitionism had passed?" (150–151). What had not passed, however, was racial oppression in America, its urgency made all the more evident during the "Red Summer" of race riots just months before the release of *The Brownies' Book*'s inaugural edition.[23]

The biographies in *The Brownies' Book* were also intended to engender a sense of responsibility in young African Americans and an appreciation of those who came before them. In a story appearing in *The Brownies' Book* titled "The Heritage," when a young girl complains about her studies, arguing that "two years more of slaving is more than I can stand," an older woman reproves her: "two years ain't nothin' in comparison with three hundred years that yo'r fo'parents spent in endless drudg'ry without no hope of reward." When the young girl argues, "but that is all over," the woman interrupts her, saying, "no it ain't all over [. . .]. You owe it to them never to quit till you have showed that you can use the opportunities you have. [. . .] The only reward that yo'r unhappy fo'fathers ever will get is through you, an' if you fail, you disappoint yo'r whole race" (Patterson 250). The attention to current events, race pride, student achievement, and African American culture in *The Brownies' Book* demonstrates how Du Bois reconfigures the meaning and popular representations of "race" for young readers. This revisioning disempowers the racist binaries of white supremacy and black insufficiency, and argues that for African Americans "belonging to a race [. . .] involves mission and duty, giving a message to the world, producing the 'greatness' that a great race is capable of" (Eyerman 62). Although designations of race had been used to oppress African Americans, its reconstructed use by Du Bois and as a cornerstone of the New Negro Movement became a sign of cultural pride and power. As theorist Ron Eyerman argues, "from the perspective of cultural trauma, race was a conceptual weapon, a trope and an instrument in the struggle to transform negative into positive, lifting a distinctiveness out of a distinction" (62). That redefinition depended upon reclamation of the heroic slave and patriot.

Descriptions of slavery in *The Brownies' Book* often hearken back to the representations of violence and resilience found in slave narratives. Unlike the biographies of Frederick Douglass in the earlier *A School History of the Negro Race in America* and *Floyd's Flowers*, for example, in *The Brownies' Book*, Douglass's biography is more nuanced and more representative of his antebellum slave narrative, describing both the violence he endured and his own rebellions. In biographies published in *The Brownies' Book*, readers learn about the violence faced by those enslaved: that the slave breaker Covey "starved and beat [Frederick Douglass . . .] unmercifully" (Wilkes 267–268), and that when six-year-old Harriet Tubman tried to escape her mistress' whipping for taking a cube of sugar, she hid for several days, "fighting with [. . .] pigs for the potato peelings and scraps that would come down in the trough" (Bird 84). Unlike popularized depictions of Mammy figures who love white children above their own, these biographies retrieve the representation of enslaved women found in slave narratives to show "one of the chief horrors of slavery,—that of the separation of slave parents from children." A mother's irreconcilable grief over the loss of her children is a focus of Sojourner Truth's biography where Truth recalls how "my old mammy would [. . .] look up at the stars and groan, [saying . . .] 'I [. . .] think of my poor children: they do not know where I be and I don't know where they be. I look up at the stars and they look at the stars!'" ("Pioneer Suffragette" 120).

While antebellum radical abolitionists had called upon readers to "pity the poor slave" ("Collection Box [1836] 3) as a means of engendering abolitionist support, Frederick Douglass had denounced such sentiment as ultimately demeaning. "Human nature," he wrote, "is so constituted that it cannot *honor* a helpless man, although it can *pity* him; and even this it cannot do long, if the signs of power do not arise" (*My Bondage* 180). Unlike some antebellum radical abolitionists, biographers in *The Brownies' Book* encourage readers to "stop and think" about slavery as a way to appreciate the suffering of those enslaved, not as a way to pity slaves ("Katy Ferguson"). Rather than affirm common tropes of the passive sufferer and supplicant slave, these biographies echo slave narratives by showing myriad ways in which enslaved men and women rebelled against slavery. One reads how Douglass "beat[. . .] and badly hurt" the sadistic Covey (Wilkes 268); how Blanche Bruce secretly learned how to read (Fauset 95); and how Denmark Vesey, a man of "wonderful courage," planned a slave rebellion in Charleston (Allison 58). Indeed, even when biographies acknowledge that slaves received aid, that remains marginal to the central story of the subject's determination.

The focus on agency is evident even in seemingly small details, as one sees in single mirroring sentences from biographies of Paul Cuffee in both the postbellum *Freedman's Third Reader* used to educate newly freed slaves and *The Brownies' Book*. The self-determination evinced in *The Brownies' Book*'s description of Paul Cuffee's father, John, as "a slave, who had, through great and unswerving persistence, bought his freedom" ("Great Sailor" 38), envisions a markedly different figure than in *Freedman's Third Reader*, which had commended how John, "being of *good behavior* and industrious habits, was *favored* by his master [. . .] and *allowed* to work for his freedom" (52, emphasis added).

Biographies in *The Brownies' Book* also argue against a range of racist stereotypes. They counter assertions that "black and ugly" were synonymous (Goulding, *Robert and Harold* [1852] 35), presenting instead figures who are "black [. . .] and handsome" (Allison 58). As Dianne Johnson has pointed out, the prose and illustrations of biographical subjects in *The Brownies' Book* emphasize positive descriptions of the subject's physical features—that physicality evokes more than superficial appearance, and also "grows out of their actions and their talents" (26). One reads that Sojourner Truth is "an impressive figure [, . . .] very tall and dark, with a keen, unflinching eye" ("Pioneer Suffragette" 121); Crispus Attucks is "a tall, splendidly-built fellow, and must have been very impressive" ("America's First Martyr-Patriot" 216); and Frederick Douglass is "of noble bearing and possessed a physique of handsome proportions" (Wilkes 270). Also in contradiction to images of slaves as "decidedly stupid" (Goulding, *Marooner's Island* 20), the biographies in *The Brownies' Book* emphasize the intellectual acuity of their subjects. Thus, Phillis Wheatley is presented as "the first Negro in America to win prestige for purely intellectual attainments" ("Story of Phillis Wheatley" 253); Sojourner Truth is described as having "a mind [. . .] keen and broad" ("Pioneer Suffragette" 121); and the revolutionary Denmark Vesey is marked with "beauty, intelligence, and alertness" (Allison 57). To counter the racialized stereotype that the "African" was not heroic in the American imagination,[24] *The Brownies' Book* not only presents images of intelligent, independent, and rebellious slaves, but, like Edward Johnson and Silas Floyd, also places their resistance within a specifically patriotic paradigm. Thus, young readers learn of Crispus Attucks as "America's First Martyr-Patriot" of the Revolutionary War; of Phillis Wheatley, who "proved that the sympathies of the Negroes are always enlisted in the fight for freedom" ("Story of Phillis Wheatley" 253); and of Denmark Vesey and his compatriots who were "hanged for the cause of freedom" (Allison 58).

While authors of these biographies sought to reclaim the figure of the slave from the accumulated racist imagery in popular culture, their representations also reflect specific expectations and hopes for

African American children. Du Bois's concern that children not be educated in human hatred is evident, particularly in the way depictions of violence are contained. Although slavery's violence is condemned, those descriptions are given brief narrative space, often only comprising two paragraphs in a typical two-page biography. While these brief depictions serve as a reminder of historical atrocities, they mitigate representations of victimization and move the reader *through* slavery to the ways in which individuals overcame seemingly insurmountable oppression with optimism and determination.

Unlike many antebellum slave narratives, these biographies do not focus on the racism the formerly enslaved faced when they arrived in the North. Instead, most follow a similar trajectory, as the individual moves from enslavement to freedom, then finally to public service and success. An excerpt from Toussaint L'Ouverture's biography explicitly states this underlying ideology: "What sort of story do you like best? I confess my favorite is the one where the poor or unknown boy or girl, man or woman, struggles up, up, up until he becomes rich or famous or useful, or the leader of his people [. . .]. And when the stories are of real people who have passed through real suffering and have achieved real triumph, my admiration goes beyond all bounds. [. . . And] some day some man realizing what one before his time has accomplished, will do all that and more" ("Toussaint L'Ouverture" 149).

This movement "up, up, up" is not lauded as an isolated rise, and the heroic ideal is more than individual success. Here, one's personal success is inextricably linked to the success of the African American community at large. In this way, the biographies in *The Brownies' Book* model the "racial uplift" ideology of the post-Reconstruction and Harlem Renaissance eras, calling for the educational, economic, and social rise of African Americans who would then assume positions of leadership, particularly to aid other African Americans. Echoing the expressed ideology of post-Reconstruction biographical sketches of slaves authored by African Americans—such as one finds in *Floyd's Flowers*—*The Brownies' Book* focuses on the movement of the slave to post-emancipation success. Indeed, as people who had been so utterly deprived as to have been without legal ownership of themselves, the formerly enslaved provided the most dramatic example of social rise, and hence of uplift ideology.[25]

The Brownies' Book repositions former slaves onto a national landscape as heroes and heroines, particularly by modeling their service on behalf of both black and white communities. As Katy Ferguson sets up Sunday schools, for example, she aids "many neglected children, both white and colored" ("Katy Ferguson"); and although Sojourner Truth found "the needs of her own people were so pressing, she felt that it was also her business to help the cause of all woamnkind [*sic*]" ("Pioneer Suffragette" 121). Focusing on the significant ways in which those formerly enslaved contributed to the development of the nation at large articulates a national identity for African Americans as important political and social figures influencing U.S. society. Presenting "American" heroes, these biographies reinforce calls for true enfranchisement as well as racial integration and cooperation. They also call for the reeducation of all children to recognize the full breadth of their national heroes. The conclusion to Betsy Blakesley's biography, for example, asserts that "every white child and every colored child in this country should be proud because she was an American girl" (Wyman 339).

As they engage antebellum and postbellum debates about the "fitness" of slaves for freedom, these biographies also redefine representations of one's service to another. Reclaiming the contributions that former slaves made to American culture at large, these biographies stress the importance of crossing the color line, of seeing oneself within both African American and larger American communities. Interracial cooperation is a cornerstone of Du Bois's ideology, predicated on moving past lingering anger about slavery. As he writes in *The Souls of Black Folk*, "I insist that the question of the future is how best to keep these millions ["of Negroes"] from brooding over the wrongs of the past [. . .] so that all their energies may be bent toward a cheerful striving and cooperation with their white neighbors toward a larger, juster, and fuller future" (137). A central objective of *The Brownies' Book* is "to teach Universal Love and Brotherhood for all little folk—black and brown and yellow and white" (Du Bois, "True Brownies" 286).

In some measure, *The Brownies' Book* calls for interracial accord based on mutual respect and responsibility. Yet the magazine's biographies do not frequently demonstrate a reciprocal relationship on behalf of whites. Repeatedly here, regardless of how painful the conditions of slavery or how dedicated one's abolitionism, those once enslaved are shown to hold no animosity for slaveholders. In "The Story of Harriet Tubman," for example, even though Tubman is described as spending her life fighting slavery, her biography ends with assurance of racial harmony since Tubman's "charity embraced the whole human race, the slaveholders as well as the fugitives" (Bird 86). That former slaves having survived unimaginable suffering at the hands of whites then argue for racial cooperation provides irrefutable models for young readers to "turn their little hurts and resentments into emulation, ambition and love" (Du Bois, "True Brownies" 286). It also could serve to quell white readers' fears of race violence.

The Brownies' Book's subordination of the violence of slavery to the assurance of one's ability to gain success and overcome adversity through determination and hard work offered images of individual strength and a reaffirmation of the Protestant work ethic. Modeling figures who met (and exceeded) expectations of white America while simultaneously asserting a sense of pride in a uniquely African American cultural identity bespeaks the "double-consciousness" which Du Bois described as a "sense of always looking at one's self through the eyes of others [. . .]. One ever feels his two-ness,—an American, a Negro; two souls, two thoughts, two unreconciled strivings; two warring ideals in one dark body" (*Souls* 45). These biographies often reveal a sense of this "double-consciousness" in their repeated portrayal of an unreciprocated racial amiability marked by African American cooperation and service to white America as a means of overcoming racial oppression. Yet they posit a keenly powerful African American identity in their presentation of heroic African Americans who effect changes in the American political system and who overcome slavery so that not enslavement, but the successes following slavery, come to define them.

The rise from slavery to publicly acknowledged success functioned as a prototype of uplift ideology, but representations of slavery—with its violence, racial exploitation, and victimization—remained problematic. One sees this, as well, in other biographies for children where African American authors use a range of narrative strategies to balance representations of racial oppression with their objective to "inspire" young readers.[26] Some texts avoid discussions of slavery altogether, as in Charles Dawson's self-published *ABC's of Great Negroes* (1933), a collection that demonstrates the significant influence of African Americans in a variety of fields. Each double-page spread contains a brief description and accompanying portrait, interconnecting the verbal with the visual in each biography. Alone on the page, the portraits—as in the case of Frederick Douglass—evince a sense of the subject's strength and seriousness of purpose; they are visual models of heroism, power, and success. That an alphabet book uses as its subject "Great Negroes" defines basic literacy as requiring an understanding of Negro history and accomplishments.[27] Yet, in Dawson's focus on post-emancipation success, *ABC's of Great Negroes* excises nearly every mention of slavery. Of Douglass, for example, readers learn, "he was an outstanding American orator, abolitionist and journalist and very prominent politically. Among the more important positions held by him were, Marshal of the District of Columbia, Recorder of Deeds of the District and Minister to Haiti" (u.p.). As much as "slave" had been a term which legally and literarily restrained blacks in America, Dawson breaks that confinement to define the multiplicity of Douglass's talents, unencumbered by enslavement.

Understanding the context of slavery or even fully appreciating the successes of people who had overcome enslavement here solely depends upon the reader's extratextual knowledge. With a young audience over half a century removed from legalized slavery and during a time when most contemporary histories minimized the traumas of slavery, Dawson could not be assured his young readers would have that knowledge. Thus, although in *ABC's of Great Negroes* Dawson focuses on contributions of free people as a way to inculcate race pride in his young readers, the strategy of avoiding discussion of slavery could contribute to the overall sanitizing and minimization of slavery found in many contemporary children's books. To write *beyond* slavery, in this case, ultimately ran the risk of ignoring slavery and aiding its cultural erasure.

Some biographies mitigated the extent of slavery's oppression by a sometimes confusing omission of certain biographical details. One sees different narrative techniques that accomplish this in biographies of Booker T. Washington in Elizabeth Ross Haynes's *Unsung Heroes* (1921) and Jane Dabney Shackelford's *The Child's Story of the Negro* (1938).[28] Although Washington began his postbellum autobiography, *Up From Slavery* (1901),[29] with the unqualified "I was born a slave on a plantation" (1), in her biography of him, Haynes avoids stating that Washington had been enslaved. Indeed, her final reference to Washington's autobiography—in "'Up from Slavery' [. . .] he told how poor he himself was once" (81–82)—implies that the title was more metaphoric than literal. Despite that, Haynes emphasizes

FIGURE 4.1. *Illustration from* ABC's of Great Negroes *(1933) by Charles C. Dawson. Courtesy of Special Collections and Archives, Z. Smith Reynolds Library, Wake Forest University.*

the painful living conditions of Washington's childhood by developing a sense of story for her young audience based on strong sensory images of pain. From Washington's autobiography, she borrows the description of his having to wear a flax shirt that feels like "chestnut burrs, or a hundred small pin-points, in contact with his flesh" (Washington 11), then makes the image even more vivid:

> Early one winter morning, about sixty years ago, a big rooster began flapping his wings and crowing—flap, flap, flap—cock-a-doodle-doo, cock-a-doodle-doo [. . .]. In the midst of this flapping and crowing, young Booker awoke [and . . .] jumped out of bed, his feet striking the earthen floor and his teeth chattering [. . . . with] the wind, whistling through the cracks in the sides [. . .] of the cabin [. . .]. He dressed quickly, [. . . putting on] a flax shirt [that. . . .] felt so much like pin points or chestnut burrs against his flesh, that he cried 'Ouch, Ouch!' (63–64)

By contrast, in *The Child's Story of the Negro*, Shackelford explicitly states that "Booker T. Washington [. . . .] began his life as a little slave boy on a large plantation in Virginia" (171), but then minimizes painful details from Washington's autobiography. In contrast to Haynes's use of scene-setting story, onomatopoeia, and sensory descriptions to give a sense of immediacy to child readers, Shackelford offers a matter-of-fact account without narrative embellishment. She echoes Washington's description by noting: "There were no glass windows in this cabin. The light came in through square holes cut in the walls. There was no floor except the hard, cold earth" (171),[30] but then avoids scenes—such as Washington having to wear the flax shirt—that acknowledge pain. She also censors Washington's account of the "cold, chilly air" and the room being "very uncomfortable" (3), both of which would heighten the reader's sense of imaginative association. By removing the more oppressive representation of slavery in Washington's autobiography, and avoiding the more sensory-related descriptions of Haynes's biography, Shackelford presents the conditions of Washington's early life as largely unremarkable and indistinguishable from those one would expect of any poor person. Haynes and Shackelford thus come to the same problem—how to represent slavery—in different ways, yet perhaps to the same end. Haynes describes the pain of Washington's childhood, but never acknowledges that he was a slave. Shackelford tells readers that Washington was born a slave, but censors details from

Washington's autobiography to mitigate the painful conditions of his life. Neither chooses to describe Washington as *both* a slave and painfully oppressed, and in so doing they both move away from the more direct representations of antebellum slave narratives.

Even within the same collection, the representation of slavery is at times a conflicted one. This is true of *The Child's Story of the Negro*, one of the more problematic African American–authored histories in this regard. Shackelford evokes images from slave narratives and radical abolitionists when she describes slaves "so unhappy that they wished they could be taken from this earth to a heavenly home" (139). Yet elsewhere in the collection her positive representations of plantation life exceed those of many antebellum plantation novels, as when she describes how "slaves soon learned to love the children of their master and the children loved them in return. Often you could see the master's children and the children of the slaves playing together" (103–104). This insistence that slavery is a site of idyllic interracial accord is supported in the accompanying illustration, titled "On the Plantation," where three children are shown playing amiably together, with no apparent leader.[31] Even more than antebellum plantation stories (such as Kennedy's *Swallow Barn* and Gilman's "The Country Visit") or postplantation novels (such as Pyrnelle's *Diddie, Dumps and Tot*), this image argues slavery is a state of play and racial equality.

At the same time, it would be misleading to suggest that all African American–authored biographies of the time sought to erase or minimize the hardships of slavery. The biography of Frederick Douglass in Derricotte, Turner, and Roy's *Word Pictures of the Great* (1941), for example, heightens images of assault presented in original sources. By focusing much of his biography on Douglass's time as a child, author Jessie Roy shows Douglass at his most vulnerable. He builds upon Douglass's account in *Life and Times of Frederick Douglass* (1881), where Douglass recounts that as a child he had "often been so pinched with hunger, as to dispute with old 'Nep,' the dog, for the crumbs which fell from the kitchen table" (22). Roy emphasizes Douglass's vulnerability by describing his "starved little body" (128). Engendering the reader's camaraderie by referring to Douglass as "Fred," Roy also adds a fictional description of how "Fred's" "thin left hand [. . .] had been painfully scratched while he and Nep, the house dog, had fought together over the crumbs thrown from the master's table" (258).

FIGURE 4.2. *"On the Plantation" from* The Child's Story of the Negro *(1938) by Jane Dabney Shackelford. Used with the permission of the Association for the Study of African American Life and History, http://www.asalh.org. Image courtesy of Social Science and History Department, Free Library of Philadelphia.*

Defining their subjects' model characteristics "as courage in taking hard knocks, ability to overcome obstacles, and persistence in plodding ahead for success" (viii), Derricotte, Turner, and Roy sculpt their biographies to show people not rebelling, but rather "taking hard knocks" and surviving. In pursuit of that objective, they often downplay representations of slave revolt. In his biography of Douglass, for example, Roy intensifies the emotional impact of Douglass's vulnerability (adding the "thin" hand that is "painfully scratched" to Douglass's own account), but then excludes other details from *Life and Times* (such as Douglass stealing corn from Aunt Katy) that show his initiative and rebellion. Moreover, after "the overseer beat him unmercifully" (270), Roy's Douglass is "more determined than ever" (270) to escape slavery, but never physically resists his enslavers. His rebelliousness is instead shown in his determination to learn how to read, as he trades with white boys his cookies for their reading lessons.

When Roy recounts the incident where the unnamed Covey beats Douglass, he pointedly shifts attention to victimhood rather than legitimize the possibilities of violent retribution by Douglass. Indeed, Douglass's original account of his battling Covey may have spoken, perhaps too directly, of contemporary race conflicts. Particularly because of concerns for racial cooperation—Derricotte, Turner, and Roy define, as one of their objectives, "to bring about a better understanding between the races" (viii)[32]—African American histories of the time often censor the slave narrative's acknowledgment of racial conflict and minimize images of physical rebellion.[33] As in *The Brownies' Book* and *Floyd's Flowers* before it, the promise to young African American readers is that if they respond to race oppression with optimism and hard work, they will ultimately succeed and gain the respect of white America.

• • •

The hopes of African Americans to integrate into American life through "persistence in plodding ahead for success" (Derricotte et al. viii) received another cumulative assault in the post–World War II years, for although nearly a million African Americans had held active duty and three million had registered for service during the war (Eyerman 163), African Americans had been kept in segregated units. After the war, they returned to an America whose white population thought little of their service and less of their civil rights. The disparity was striking, and while facing myriad discriminations during the postwar years, African Americans also engaged in legal and social protests that anticipated the coming civil rights movement.[34] By the end of the decade, two children's books about slavery articulated starkly contrasting racial views that seemed to reflect the disparate visions of the time: Arna Bontemp's *Story of the Negro* (1948) and Elizabeth Yates's *Amos Fortune, Free Man* (1950), both of which received Newbery notice.

African American–authored books for children could not match the publication numbers of many white-authored texts, and the listings of large publishing houses remained Anglocentric. The Newbery and Caldecott Awards, too, remained almost exclusively within the purview of Anglo-American authors. Arna Bontemps's *Story of the Negro*, which was published by New York's mainstream Alfred A. Knopf and became the first African American–authored book to receive a Newbery Honor, was a notable exception. The most widely known and read African American–authored history for children to that time,[35] *Story of the Negro* was less conciliatory than most earlier African American–authored slave biographies of the Harlem Renaissance. More closely reiterating the tone and focus of antebellum slave narratives, it would anticipate the neo-slave narrative of the second half of the twentieth century.

A collection of nonfiction essays on Africa, slavery, and individual African Americans, *Story of the Negro* articulates the ideology of the New Negro Movement and *The Brownies' Book* in its description of the handsome appearance of black people, here of David Walker, Frederick Douglass, and William Wells Brown. Like *The Brownies' Book*, Bontemps also focuses on the intelligence, agency, and patriotism of the enslaved, as well as on their varied talents and courage, from Phillis Wheatley's poetry to Crispus Attucks's sacrifice. When Bontemps describes the Middle Passage, he details its violence, describing how those kidnapped and enslaved were "near-dead [, . . .] tortured by chains and gasping for food and drink" (4); of others, "confused and hopeless [. . . who] jumped overboard and drowned themselves" (55); of captives in "dark and filthy holds, lying week after week in the same positions, without sunlight or sanitation, with no decent food and not enough water" (57); and of how ophthalmia struck those in slave ships "like the wrath of an angry God" (58).

Story of the Negro is particularly significant in the way that it departs from earlier descriptions of slavery for children, especially as Bontemps eschews the racial accommodation that typified many African American–authored slave biographies for children written during the early decades of the century. To Bontemps, "slavery was a state of war" based on racial conflict (150). As such, *Story of the Negro* does not echo the more reconciliatory tone of *The Brownies' Book* where, for example, Du Bois hoped his readers would learn to "turn their little hurts and resentments into emulation, ambition and love" ("True Brownies" 286). While biographies in *The Brownies' Book* moved fairly quickly through descriptions of slavery, Bontemps accords more than half of his book to issues of enslavement—including discussions of Africa, the history of slavery, "Man-Hunters," the Middle Passage, conditions on plantations, black abolitionism, individual biographies, and racial exploitation. More than that, it is the type of detail and focus of Bontemps's presentation that distinguishes it from most earlier biographies and nonfictional accounts of slavery for children.

Far from the account of the *Amistad* captives in the American Tract Society's *Freedman's Third Reader* published at the close of the Civil War, Bontemps recounts the story of the *Amistad* rebellion. *Freedman's Third Reader* had begun its account after the uprising, when the ship was found off the New York coast; of that revolt, it notes only that the slaves had "risen upon the crew, and taken possession of the vessel" (105). In line with the ATS's ideological objectives, the essay's focus is on education and Christianity, and the slaves are commended for spending their incarceration making "good progress in reading, writing, singing, and arithmetic" and being converted to Christianity (106). By contrast, Bontemps describes the rebellion at length, situating it within the context of slavery as "a state of war" (150), and acknowledging that crew members were killed. Since enslavement is here an act of aggression, retributive acts of aggression are justified, and presented without apology or obfuscation. Bontemps describes how the leader, Cinqué, killed the ship's captain—his "cane knife struck him dead"—and another rebel killed the captain's "personal slave." Both bodies are summarily thrown overboard (150–151). In *Story of the Negro*, the *Amistad* event is one of resistance and survival, not capitulation to the supposed civilizing effects of white education or religion.[36]

Bontemps presents resisting narratives inasmuch as his presentation of slavery counters prevalent expectations of white hegemony and black accommodation in stories about slavery. Earlier biographies, such as those in *The Brownies' Book*, often conclude with conciliatory statements or representations of racial accord. For example, in contrast to *The Brownies' Book*'s assurance that Harriet Tubman's "charity embraced the whole human race, the slaveholders as well as the fugitives" (Bird 86), Bontemps describes how by leading slaves to freedom, Tubman took "her revenge on the slave system" (141). In Bontemps's biographies, the subjects' responses to exploitation engender a sense of passion that has little to do with striving for racial amity. Even when rebellious slaves are captured, as in the case of Nat Turner, they are described as never relinquishing the fight against slavery. When Bontemps recounts Nat Turner's imminent death, he describes how "even then there was a gleam in his eye [. . . . showing] that his longing for freedom was still as strong as ever. That was a thing that wouldn't die, no matter how many rebellions were crushed or how many slaves perished" (115). In scenes such as these, Bontemps modifies the promise of efficacious agency that had underpinned many earlier African American biographies. He also shows that agency is just as frequently evidenced in rebellion to white authority as in service to the nation.

Bontemps's racial critiques often match the tone that Frederick Douglass had called for in addressing slavery—"scorching irony [. . .] biting ridicule, blasting reproach, withering sarcasm and stern rebuke" ("What to the Slave" 126). He captures the banality of slavery justifications and the commodification of people in his description of how the man who was "perhaps" the "first modern slaver" "may have intended only to take [an African . . .] home as a sort of souvenir" (48). His comment that the "things slave-catchers said to themselves to put their consciences at rest would make a book of marvels" (48) evokes, as well, the sense of sarcasm authors of slave narratives often used in denouncing slavery supporters.

By defining slavery as an act of war and presenting the response of slaves in rebellion, Bontemps puts aside images of the supplicant and passive slave, and rejects any cultural shame on behalf of slaves or their descendants. Like many antebellum slave narratives, *Story of the Negro* investigates the intersections of race and slavery, particularly how race served as a convenient rationalization for slavers: "They ended by deciding that slaves were not people at all. They were just property. And since all the slaves they knew at that time were black, they concluded that Negroes were not human beings and hence did not have to be treated according to the golden rule" (51). Here, slavery is fully made the responsibility of enslavers; it is their assault, their racism, that lies at its core. From the attacks on African villages, the disruption and destruction of African civilizations, and the horrors of the Middle Passage, to assaults and oppression within the United States, the enslaved are shown battling slavery. Such battles against overwhelming odds define slavery as an exploitative social, economic, and political system clearly based on race conflict.

Unlike books that assured children of the value of the Protestant work ethic and that freedom was to be had by those who were sufficiently determined to overcome their oppression, Bontemps acknowledges the many people who were unable to escape slavery through no fault of their own. From those who died or committed suicide during the Middle Passage to those "beaten and brutalized and sometimes murdered" (Bontemps 135), many never escaped slavery and they are described as no less honorable because of that. The declaration that "what every slave wanted, of course, was freedom" (108) denies any bifurcation of value between those who became free and those who did not. It also removes the implied condemnation often literarily placed on those anonymous slaves who did not gain freedom.

Modeled in some measure on the perspective of antebellum slave narratives, Bontemps's text mediates representations of slavery between the individual and group. Each of his biographies of former slaves—including Phillis Wheatley, Frederick Douglass, Josiah Henson, William Wells Brown, and pianist Thomas Green Bethune—functions as a type of subnarrative contributing to the overall *Story of the Negro*. Bontemps is careful to avoid presenting only well-known figures, making sure that their success stories do not invalidate the experiences of unknown slaves. Slaves' anonymity becomes part of Bontemps's exploration of slavery, as he points out that "it is so hard to piece together the things one likes to know about interesting and gifted people, when they happen to have been slaves" (41). His acknowledgment of those otherwise lost to slavery evokes a sense of contemporaneous debates about democracy and enfranchisement; it also comments—as does his representation of slavery as race warfare—on postwar realities and disappointments.

Elizabeth Yates's fictionalized biography, *Amos Fortune, Free Man* (1950), published two years later, would receive the Newbery Award (as opposed to the "Honor" or "runner-up" recognition accorded *Story of the Negro*). Different from African American–authored slave biographies in that it moves more fully into a storied genre, Yates's *Amos Fortune* contrasts dramatically with *Story of the Negro*. In it readers meet a protagonist-slave who serves as a proslavery spokesman. Far from Bontemps's depiction of slavery as "a state of war," Yates describes slavery as an enviable apprenticeship for Africans, thus essentially arguing against an acknowledgment of racial equality or the necessity of emancipation and enfranchisement.

Based on the life of an actual man who was kidnapped from Africa in the early eighteenth century and brought to New England, *Amos Fortune, Free Man* valorizes its titled character for his years as a loyal, hardworking slave. Yates depicts her protagonist as one who sees his master as "someone older and wiser [. . .]. The white man [. . .] had become such a protector to Amos. Amos looked to him with reverence and loyalty" (46).[37] In such scenes, Yates evokes the ideology shared by antebellum conservative abolitionists and proslavery plantation novelists, such as Kennedy's argument in *Swallow Barn*, that slavery is an expression of white noblesse oblige to less civilized Africans, a system of apprenticeship that allows slaves an opportunity for evolutionary development by mimicking civilized white society.

The Middle Passage is typically the site of the most virulent denunciations of slavery in children's literature. While Yates describes the hunger and pain of young Amos when he is kidnapped from Africa, Yates's protagonist nonetheless feels a sense of expansive appreciation for the possibilities of slavery. The abduction becomes a heroic journey to a new world, for "he who had known nothing but the jungle now found wonder stirring in him that there was a world beyond" (18). In Yates's literary construction, slavery may be cruel in its disruption of African villages and in the treatment of slaves as they cross the ocean, but the prospect of leaving Africa—even in a slave ship—evinces the "wonder" of adventure in the main character.

Once on U.S. soil, slavery becomes in Yates's description personally ennobling. There are some slaves who are "ill-treated, beaten, forced to marry against their will or kept from marrying those they loved" (44), but such conditions are noted only briefly and those characters who suffer are never shown firsthand. Amos pities not only their plight, but more often their bitterness and attempts at escape. Although referred to as a "free man" in the book's subtitle, Fortune repeatedly refuses his own freedom, accepting it only as an old man (long past the time when racist stereotypes would have deemed him physically or socially threatening), and even then he is grateful that his years as a slave taught him both Christian values and a trade. An accolade to the Protestant work ethic as a justification for slavery, *Amos Fortune, Free Man* not only applauds white supremacy, but ultimately denies black community or slavery's oppression. If slaves had only worked harder, learned trades, and saved more money, Yates implies, they could have not only bought themselves out of slavery, but also enjoyed a comfortable lifestyle as reward for a "life well lived" (149). Coming so soon after *Story of the Negro, Amos Fortune* reveals the clash of biographical viewpoints, in its most racially essential terms, between African American and Anglo-American perspectives on slavery.[38]

• • •

On the cusp of the civil rights movement, the American Library Association had given its highest honor in American children's literature to a text that assured young readers that slavery provided a good grounding in moral values, skills, and thriftiness, and conflated being a slave (at least for an African) with achieving the American Dream. Following decades in which African American biographies of heroic slaves contested representations of contented, foolish, or dangerous slaves in neoplantation and pseudoabolitionist novels, the Newbery committee's validation of a slave biography with the ideology of a re-created plantation novel begged for a world of black submission and white supremacy. What resulted instead, as the nation entered the 1950s, was the civil rights movement.

CHAPTER 5

THE CIVIL RIGHTS MOVEMENT AND NEW NARRATIVES 1951–2010

I can't get this out of my thoughts: /
If we slipped into a black skin /
like a tight coat, /
everything would change.
—Ann Turner, *Nettie's Trip South* (1987)

Slavery did its best to make me wretched;
I feel no particular obligation to it,
but nature, or the blessed God of youth and joy,
was mightier than slavery.
—Josiah Henson in Julius Lester's *To Be a Slave* (1968)

With its decision in the *Brown v. Board of Education* case (1954), the U.S. Supreme Court unanimously overturned its earlier accommodation to "separate but equal" segregation, yet a decade later only little over two percent of African American children attended desegregated schools in the South (R. Kennedy 899). Because disparities between civil rights laws and practices were entrenched in American society, civil rights protestors fought for enfranchisement on all fronts. Their efforts were frequently met with violent resistance, and membership in the Ku Klux Klan reached its "peak" during the 1960s (Trelease 626). Throughout the 1950s and 1960s, social activism often prompted and provided for the protection of civil rights. Ranging from the Montgomery bus boycotts following Rosa Parks's 1955 arrest to the over two hundred thousand people who joined the March on Washington in 1963, civil rights activists demonstrated a resolve to change the nation's racial politics.[1]

Perspectives about race eventually underwent significant revision in academic circles. In his landmark study, *The Slave Community* (1972), John Blassingame pointed out the necessity of a fresh look at the history of slavery, arguing that proslavery stereotypes had permeated not only the American consciousness in general, but historical analysis in particular, for "twentieth-century historians have often uncritically accepted the most popular literary stereotype as an accurate description of slave personality" (224). Since the most popular literary stereotype of slaves was often some version of the uncomplicated Sambo, histories had most commonly presented slaves as unvoiced objects, and often foolish, contented ones at that. The late 1960s through the 1970s thus offered a renaissance in slave studies, particularly in a new focus on slave culture itself. The slave narrative, too, enjoyed a resurgence, as slave experience was reclaimed as the authoritative voice about American slavery.[2]

Children's literature showed the effect of these changes. In 1970, the Coretta Scott King Award was created to recognize African American authors and illustrators of children's literature who "promote understanding and appreciation of the culture of all peoples and their contribution to the realization of the American Dream of a pluralist society" (American). While in 1975 Virginia Hamilton became the first African American to receive the Newbery Award (rather than Newbery Honor), the Coretta Scott King Award has continued to redress the underrepresentation of African Americans in Newbery and Caldecott Awards, while also recognizing a lauded canon of African American children's literature.[3]

Although racial stereotypes persisted, by the late twentieth century the overt presence of proslavery plantation stories in children's literature was rare. One does, however, sometimes find proslavery tropes embedded in texts that might otherwise seem critical of slavery. One such problematic text is the picture book, *Jumping the Broom* (1994). Told from the point of view of Lettie, a young female slave who describes her sister's wedding celebration, *Jumping the Broom* may ostensibly argue the strength of a slave community, yet its verbal and visual narratives, by author Courtni Wright and illustrator Gershom Griffith, dilute representations of slavery's oppression. Wright acknowledges difficult conditions—cabins are sometimes cold in the winter and Lettie and her family "don't usually have much free time for fun with all the long hours and hard work" (u.p.). Yet these conditions are not exclusive to slavery. Moreover, the slave women easily adjust, sewing beautiful quilts both to fend off the cold and to create opportunities to get together and to celebrate. Wright and Griffith thus often focus on pleasant scenes, from descriptions of a quilting bee to lush depictions of tables abundantly loaded with food.

In the end, the overriding image of smiling, happy slaves presents people largely unencumbered by enslavement. Indeed, Lettie's sadness—as she describes it, feeling "lonely knowing that [sister] Tillie will never sleep next to me again" (u.p.)—suggests that loss through a sister's marriage is more heartfelt (and more a possibility) for slaves than being forcibly separated by masters. In fact, slave marriages were not legally recognized and enslaved husbands and wives were often sold apart—as were their children. Other than one mention of a brother who is not present because "Master sold him away last year," Wright and Griffith's landscape of slavery ultimately ignores historical reality and instead reflects proslavery antebellum and Confederate assertions of generally happy, well-cared-for slaves. Even if the author's intent might be to show the resilience of slave communities, her depiction of slavery ultimately suggests there is little reason, because slavery is not oppressive. As I have argued elsewhere, at the book's end, when Lettie lies awake wondering when the next jumping the broom will occur, Wright describes the wedding celebration and slavery itself "in continuous and even hopeful terms" (Connolly, "Narrative" 109).

A more common example of proslavery representation appears in *When Will This Cruel War Be Over?* (1996), published as part of Scholastic's Dear America series. Author Barry Denenberg presents a fictional Civil War diary of Emma, a slave owner's child who defends slavery and lauds faithful slaves. The central point of the novel, however, is the disruption of proslavery tropes; by the end of the book, war-torn plantations lie in ruins, most of Emma's slaves have left the plantation, and she learns that some slaves have even killed a neighboring master. Unlike Pyrnelle's postplantation *Diddie, Dumps and Tot*, Denenberg's depiction of destroyed plantations leaves little sense of nostalgia for the Lost Cause. Instead, particularly against the narrative backdrop of slave independence, readers are led to read against, not with, the insularity of the protagonist's proslavery sentiment, as when she describes slaves' "ingratitude" for wanting freedom (67).

Despite the persistence of texts that evoke proslavery images, like *Jumping the Broom*, the critical examination of slavery more often than not typifies children's literature from the middle of the twentieth into the beginning of the twenty-first century. Three genres in particular—neoabolitionist stories, diachronous texts, and neo-slave narratives—reframe antebellum antislavery discourse for this period's generations of readers. Neoabolitionist stories explore long-standing tropes and tenets of abolitionism, especially calls for testimony on slavery's violence, for racial equality, and for white agency in response to black need. Diachronous texts about slavery include narrative movements between the present and the past, some as realistic fiction where storytellers relay accounts about slavery, others as fantastic representations of time-traveling protagonists. Neo-slave narratives, which may also be fictionalized, re-create the tone and representations of antebellum slave narratives. Although neoabolitionist literature may feature black protagonists, that narrative perspective is more typical of diachronous literature, and a central feature of neo-slave narratives. The narrative predominance of black protagonists not merely acknowledges but also welcomes a young African American readership in ways that generations of texts with white hero-protagonists and black background-characters had not. Indeed, this change is perhaps what is most "new" about these stories of slavery for children.

NEOABOLITIONIST STORIES

Neoabolitionist stories are historical fiction set in antebellum times that re-create antebellum abolitionist paradigms while also refiguring racial representations to reflect a late twentieth- and early twenty-first-century sensibility. Unlike antebellum conservative abolitionism, neoabolitionist children's literature does not argue beneficent effects of slavery; and unlike antebellum moderate abolition, neoabolitionist condemnations of slavery do not minimize U.S. involvement. Yet in its evocation of antebellum radical abolitionist images, neoabolitionist texts often interrogate abolitionism itself—not in terms of the viability of emancipation (as had earlier pseudoabolitionist texts), but rather in terms of antebellum representations of race. Three central paradigms of neoabolitionism—of the eyewitness, racial pair, and activist-rescuer—provide different ways of exploring similar issues, particularly the possibilities and limits of outsider understanding.

Neoabolitionist texts explore the role of free characters in a culture that allows slavery. These stories typically show free protagonists moving from an insular childhood to a more comprehensive understanding of the world and a more sympathetic appreciation of others' needs, particularly in terms of what author Paula Fox has called "the fact of our union with all others" ("Newbery" 346). At the same time, neoabolitionist stories with white protagonists struggle with understanding, appropriating, or rejecting black slave experience. As Benjamin DeMott argues in another context, the "friendship orthodoxy"—"to see blacks and whites as 'all in the same boat'" (29–30)—encourages "flights into sentimentality" (40) rather than more rigorous explorations of racial oppression. Replicating some of the racial representations and white positioning of antebellum radical abolitionism, these neoabolitionist texts variously reflect and reject such "flights into sentimentality."

Many late twentieth-century neoabolitionist writers with a racially aware consciousness of the civil rights movement implicitly acknowledge America's failure to respond to slavery and race oppression. Neoabolitionist texts (unlike pseudoabolitionist novels of the early twentieth century) thus support emancipation but often explore the failure of enfranchisement and evoke a sense of white culpability and guilt in the face of race oppression. Often far removed from the antebellum trope of heroic white abolitionists, for example, neoabolitionist eyewitness protagonists evince a sense of white culpability and horror at the enormity of slavery. Neoabolitionist racial-pairing texts explore antebellum calls of racial equality, at times exploring its absence in American history. Of the three paradigms, the activist-rescuer model most often replicates racial hierarchies implicit in the iconic abolitionist trope of white savior and supplicant slave. Yet even in traditional rescuer novels when white protagonists help slaves gain their freedom, neoabolitionist authors often provide a more textured depiction of black victimization, which often leads them to investigate representations of white heroism. Taken as a group, these paradigms show authors a century away from slavery still grappling with the continued influence of antebellum racial prescriptions and the legacy of slavery.

In neoabolitionist literature with an eyewitness paradigm, the central narrative motif—of a free (usually white) protagonist who bears witness to slavery—echoes antebellum children's literature in its testimony to slavery's violence. Yet the effect of testimony on current white protagonists differs from stated objectives of antebellum radical abolitionist literature where testimony was meant to encourage the reader's active abolitionism.[4] For antebellum radical abolitionists writing for children, sympathy was a prelude to action, and white readers were often asked to imagine themselves undergoing the conditions slaves suffered on a daily basis. It was a strategy meant to encourage racially privileged and insulated middle-class white readers to appreciate slavery's horrors and to humanize the often anonymous slave figure.

Neoabolitionist literature for children with an eyewitness paradigm offers protagonists who provide testimony about slavery, but to a different end. As historical fiction set in antebellum times, neoabolitionist eyewitness stories often show none of the engaged optimism and belief in abolitionist reform evinced in antebellum radical literature. Instead, these stories often suggest the failure, even the inability, of individual intervention. Neoabolitionist eyewitness texts argue against the trope of the white hero that was a staple of antebellum radical abolitionist literature and later pseudoabolitionist texts to bespeak a paralysis of white action and to explore the limits of reform. In this way, they are books more of reflection than action, and in the process of bearing witness, protagonists move from testimony about slavery to a more conscious exploration of the slave "object" they view and how that racialized other affects white self-perception. Neoabolitionist eyewitness texts thus critique slavery while interrogating the relationship between black slave and free white identity.

In Ann Turner's *Nettie's Trip South* (1987), for example, when white Nettie journeys to the South, the insularity of her outsider's perspective is compounded by her youth and race. When her sister tells her that "slaves are thought to be three-fifths of a person," Nettie admits, "I looked and looked at black people, but I could not see what was missing." This "look[ing] and look[ing]" at slaves is a central focus of eyewitness texts and serves three principal functions: as a way for the protagonist to testify against slavery, as a representation of white power and the slave's commodification, and as an interrogation of racial difference. Commodification is obvious in *Nettie's Trip South* as Nettie and her siblings travel to a slave auction where, as depicted by illustrator Ronald Himler, slaves stand on an auction block surrounded by a crowd of white spectators and possible buyers. The scene presents a passive object (to be gazed upon is prelude to literally being bought), and also its counterpart, a powerful initiator/definer and literal possessor. In this way, to have the power of "looking and looking" is the power of white mastery, of oversight, control, and violence.

It is this objectification that stands at the heart of criticism surrounding Paula Fox's earlier controversial and Newbery Award–winning *The Slave Dancer* (1973), a book that tells the fictional story of young, white Jessie, who is kidnapped, brought aboard a slave ship, and made to play his fife while enslaved Africans are forced to "dance" to exercise their limbs. Fox's descriptions of the horrifying conditions aboard the ship—of the "foul stench that came from the holds" (79); of Africans "half-conscious from the press of the bodies of their fellow captives" (65); of "a woman's scream, hair-raising, heart-squeezing" (78)—evoke descriptions from antebellum slave narratives.[5]

Yet in Jessie, Fox has created a problematic protagonist who often emotionally colludes with the crew in their objectification of Africans.[6] Throughout the journey, his feelings toward the slaves vacillate from sympathy to disgust, and, in the novel's most well-known scene, to hate: "I hated the slaves! I hated their shuffling, their howling, their very suffering! [. . .] I wished them all dead! Not to hear them! Not to smell them! Not to know of their existence!" (79). Although after being whipped himself, his hatred dissipates, Jessie is, in the end, an observer of slaves, not one himself, and his fluctuating feelings reflect an underlying tension of white captivity narratives in which protagonists believe they have experienced the full effects of slavery even though they are returned home to a waiting family.[7] Similar to Child's antebellum "Mary French and Susan Easton" (1834), a white character's temporary experience of enslavement only emphasizes the disparity of condition meted out in a racist society. For Jessie, as for the other crew members, the slaves serve as a repository of projected white angst, guilt, frustration, and self-loathing.

As much as these texts focus on abolition as eyewitness testimony, they also explore who is watching whom. In *The Slave Dancer*, although Jessie describes how he "could gaze without restraint at the helpless and revealed forms of these slaves" (75), when he observes the first kidnapped African brought aboard the ship, he realizes she is also watching them. Jessie recounts how later that night, "before my tightly closed eyelids floated the face of the child who had, after that one glance at us all, seemed to comprehend her whole fate" (65). Jessie also becomes aware of a boy he later knows as Ras, "close to my own age, staring at me from among the group of silent slaves" (67). Unsettled and "aware of his eyes, [Jessie . . .] tried to move out of their range"; unable to avoid the African's observation, Jessie finally whispers his name to the boy (86). Such moments complicate representations of power by revealing the active counterwitnessing of slaves who watch white oppressors.

More complex than antebellum radical abolition in its understanding of slave subjectivity, in neoabolitionist eyewitness stories, white narrators double gaze, aware that they are under slaves' observation. At such moments, white narrators looking at the slave "other" imagine themselves as that other, and also perceive (or imagine) ways in which that other views them. The discomfort of white characters under this gaze acknowledges their complicity in slavery. In this way, the ideology of these neoabolitionist novels is reminiscent of radical abolitionist antebellum literature which disrupts the complacency of its white audience by reminding them not only of their privilege but also of the ways ostensibly innocent whites supported slavery either in buying goods produced by slave labor or through inaction. From Jessie, who had enjoyed going to slave auctions to "peek" at the (presumably exposed female) slaves, to Nettie, ensconced in the economic privilege of her lace and furs, these white characters had been insensible to slavery's exploitation.

White protagonists in these fictionalized eyewitness accounts are neither activists nor heroic; instead, they ultimately flee the site of slavery. Yet, while they physically escape what they have seen, it has made such an indelible impression on them that they cannot psychologically escape it. Like Jessie, who tries to tightly close his eyes to stop the memory of the young girl brought aboard the ship, these white children cannot *un-see* what they have witnessed. Young Nettie has nightmares,[8] and although Jessie joins the Union army, he remains in emotional paralysis after his earlier experience aboard the slave ship. He is unable to listen to music, for, as he tells readers, "at the first note [. . .] I would see once again, as though they'd never ceased their dancing in my mind, black men and women and children lifting their tormented limbs in time to a reedy martial air" (152).

While antebellum abolitionist amanuensis texts, such as Jones's *The Young Abolitionists* (1848), evinced white authority in supplanting black testimony, the conclusions of neoabolitionist fictionalized eyewitness texts question or diminish that authority. They express an understanding that blacks in America have experienced an oppression that whites can only imagine and would rather both flee and forget. The reality of white power in a racist society is acknowledged here, but not taken for granted. Instead, power dynamics are interrogated and neoabolitionist eyewitness texts more often conclude with a sense of the irreconcilable separateness between white and black, free and slave, even despite the white protagonists' momentary empathy with slaves. It is not only slavery, but that separateness that haunts these protagonists.

In *The Slave Dancer*, as Jessie and Ras escape the foundering ship, Fox's reiterated designation of them in first-person plural—"we held each other's arms. [. . .] We slid down the deck [. . . .] We made for the shore" (130–131)—types them as a single entity. Whether alter ego or doppelgänger,[9] the two cross race and language barriers for a short while to find ways to communicate and survive. After the two swim to the American shore, they could represent a new version of republican childhood, a racial equality of two young men signaling new life arising out of death. But this beach is only liminal space, constricted, momentary, and necessarily secret; America supports legalized slavery and any hope that their tentative friendship or possible equality will survive quickly ends. When an escaped slave finds and tends to the boys, he is more affectionate to Ras. Jessie longs for similar attention, but recognizes the unassailable "distance between us" (145). That Ras answers something in Jessie's sense of self is clear when Ras leaves and Jessie feels "a hollowness" that is never repaired (143). In a world in which white Americans enslave, sell, and kill Africans, race crossing is a fragile thing and one another's lives ultimately unknowable.

That white protagonists who have seen slavery are numbed and sickened by it, left nightmare-ridden, and unable to resolve or act upon what they have witnessed bespeaks white America's inability to respond to slavery while nonetheless left haunted by it. Moreover, the representation of large groups of unnamed, unknown slaves who die (as in *The Slave Dancer*) or remain enslaved (as in *Nettie's Trip South*) also speaks to the unanswered magnitude of slavery. Not positioning white protagonists as hero or savior, these neoabolitionist eyewitness texts argue the ultimate ineffectiveness and inaction of whites against a slavery in which they (even in their inaction) are implicated. There are, ultimately here, no heroic or innocent white characters. Evoking a sense of survivor's guilt over what they have witnessed, these protagonists are paralyzed by the disparities in condition designated by race in a slave society. Such inaction stands in marked contrast to the confidence of antebellum abolitionist texts that argued the efficacy of eyewitness testimony in gaining abolitionist support. Allowing no closure, no rescue, no paradigm of white heroism, no promise of racial reconciliation, neoabolitionist eyewitness texts express white America's cultural trauma about slavery.

Although Fox's *The Slave Dancer* evokes a sense of racial pairing in the relationship of Jessie and Ras, theirs is a momentary connection and Ras largely remains a subsidiary character seen through the prism of white centrality. More developed neoabolitionist racial-pairing texts often present white and black characters as co-protagonists in order to disrupt long-standing literary representations of racialized hierarchies, as in the image of abolition as a state of white noblesse oblige and black passivity. Neoabolitionist racial-pairing texts explore the antebellum "Am I Not a Man and a Brother" image less as a petition than a declarative. By showing black and white protagonists who come together as comrades fighting a common enemy, racial-pairing texts argue inherent equality between black slave and free white. At the same time, they explore the tension between that equality and differences in condition determined by a society that defines value based on racial difference. In that contrast, these texts often present individual black heroism while arguing the near impossibility of its successful expression in a racist world.

In *Pink and Say* (1994), Patricia Polacco tells of a former young slave, Pinkus Aylee (Pink), who saves the life of a Northern white boy, Sheldon Curtis (Say). The relationship initially seems to evoke those depicted in Kirke's and Carleton's respective postbellum abolitionist stories, "The Little Prisoner" (1865) and "Winning His Way" (1865), where slaves save young white soldiers. Offering a more critical perspective of earlier white hero tropes, Polacco's story has the white boy-soldier admit that he was shot while abandoning his unit. Additionally, Polacco makes the escaped slave Pink the active abolitionist fighting against slavery. Unlike Kirke's and Carleton's postbellum stories where black adults save white boys, here Pink is a boy, the same age as Say. This similarity in age encourages young readers' identification with both characters and emphasizes a sense of the characters' parity. Moreover, Pink's youth is suggestive of hope and futurity; he is a new child of the republic, defending freedom and shaping a new nation.

Pink and Say's relationship offers tentative hope for the nation's racial future. As Say recuperates on an abandoned plantation, he and Pink occupy a fragile liminal space that allows a coexistence of races. It is here readers see the answer to the question "Am I not a man and a brother?," for the two are foster brothers under the care of Pink's mother. But such moments in a world marked by racial assault are only temporary. Pink's mother is murdered by marauding soldiers, and Pink and Say are captured and taken to Andersonville. Similar to their service in the Union army (where black soldiers were not issued guns), in prison the two are treated differently based on race. Months later, although weakened and sick, Say is released and later recovers. By contrast, readers learn that Pink "was hanged within hours after he was taken into Andersonville. His body was thrown into a lime pit."[10]

Although seeming to echo the absence of black characters found at the close of the pseudoabolitionist *Glory of the Seas* (1933) and *Swords of Steel* (1933), Polacco directly acknowledges that absence and answers it with the necessity of memory and testimony. In the story's final pages, the author reveals Say as her great-great grandfather and the story as family testimony passed from one generation to the next, telling readers, "*this book serves as a written memory of Pinkus Aylee since there are no living descendants to do this for him*" (u.p.). Acknowledging the genocidal underpinnings of racial exploitation, Polacco claims Pink's murder as part of her family history and also part of the reader's national history. The sentiment called for here is not the antebellum request to "pity the poor slave," but rather the acknowledgment that racial oppression and violence have been part of the white culture of both the Union and Confederacy.

In the end, Polacco uses the racial-pairing genre to interrogate stereotypes of racialized heroism and to question the nature of history: of what is remembered and how. Because *Pink and Say* is told from the perspective of the surviving white soldier's descendants, the story allows horrifying truths to be told while mitigating reader trauma by positioning him through the surviving character. Rather than the white amanuensis of antebellum literature who told the story of slavery in place of a living former slave, Pink's story is told by Say's white descendants, an acknowledgment of the attempted obliteration of black voice and presence. Here, a family narrative makes history more specific and the story traverses time to argue both the continuing legacy of the past in the present and the responsibility of current readers not to forget that past. Indeed, that one family survives and another does not demonstrates that contemporary white privilege is a result of racial exploitation and murder that has been indelibly grafted onto the nation's history.

Of neoabolitionist paradigms, rescuer stories tend to offer the most ostensibly happy endings because the narrative trajectory typically follows a young free protagonist aiding slaves along the Underground Railroad. These rescuer stories typically replace antebellum representations of children whose abolitionism is demonstrated through moral suasion and economic boycotts with more physical protagonists who help slaves in their journeys to freedom, action typically reserved for adults in antebellum texts such as *The Young Abolitionists*. Similar to pseudoabolitionist adventure novels of the early twentieth century such as Hewes's *Glory of the Seas*, the protagonist's participation in abolition marks his coming-of-age. It also provides the central adventure of the story, and similarly evinces a sense of anxiety about the safety of free (usually male) characters who endanger themselves on behalf of escaping slaves.[11] Yet, unlike in pseudoabolitionist novels, neoabolitionist protagonists do not ultimately reject, but rather accept, that fighting racial oppression is one's personal responsibility.

The paradigm of rescuer and rescued is often dependent upon an opposition of agency and passivity, power and need, noblesse oblige and gratitude, as well as oppositions of race, all of which typically populated radical antebellum abolitionist children's literature. Traditional neoabolitionist rescuer stories tend to reiterate the antebellum trope of supplicant slave and white hero-savior, yet often grant at least minimal revision to the oppositional paradigm of helpless, pitiful, passive slave and powerful, omniscient, active white savior. While developments in racial representations are not always neatly chronological, Jean Fritz's *Brady* (1960) and Christopher Paul Curtis's *Elijah of Buxton* (2007), separated by nearly fifty years, highlight ways in which the neoabolitionist rescuer paradigm has shifted to encompass a more interrogatory interaction with long-standing slavery tropes.

In *Brady*, Fritz offers a traditional rescuer story that largely reinstates antebellum representations of the white savior when the titled character meets Moss, a young runaway slave, and is unexpectedly initiated into abolitionism. While similar to earlier pseudoabolitionist novels in which aiding slaves is presented as an adventure, *Brady* also criticizes such banal insularity, as when Brady's brother cautions that the "Underground Railroad is nothing to fool with, Brady. *It's a matter of life and death*" (44).

Although pseudoabolitionist novels define coming-of-age for white protagonists in personal and global terms as racialized superiority, in neoabolitionist texts, coming-of-age also entails breaking out of the solipsism of one's childhood and racial insularity to recognize slaves as people. In this way, they echo radical abolitionist literature for children which encouraged free white children's active sympathy, often by presenting descriptions of enslaved children. Neoabolitionist rescuer novels for children often highlight the potential for that personal connection when the protagonist meets a slave of his (and the reader's) approximate age. When Brady comes upon the runaway Moss, for example, he realizes Moss "was not much older than he was" (137). That a free, white protagonist meets a runaway slave of his gender and approximate age does more than provide an easier identification between them. It also argues a sense of equality, especially when contrasted with earlier pseudoabolitionist and plantation literature for children, which constructed an immediate disparity through a contrastive pairing of young, white male protagonists with adult, black male slaves.[12] The genre implies that the two are racialized counterparts, and allows for an appreciation of the vagaries of racial exploitation since the determining marker of difference between the two and their conditions of life is race.

Yet unlike neoabolitionist racial-pairing texts, the traditional rescuer story typically situates free white and enslaved black characters in a hierarchical paradigm that is not narratively contradicted. In *Brady*, the sense of the boys' equality is transitory, and once Brady decides to help Moss, Brady's role as the novel's hero assigns Moss to subservience. When, for example, Brady says he will help with the escape, Moss's self-oblating declaration that "you can get into a peck of trouble. [. . .] A person like me ain't worth that big a risk" (197) seems intended to recalibrate the reader's sense of racial hierarchy. It also echoes the racial solipsism of the earlier pseudoabolitionist *Glory of the Seas*, when the white protagonist privileged white aide over black suffering, asserting that "it goes pretty hard with those [whites] who help you people [slaves]" (Hewes 221).

Hierarchy is also reinforced once Brady successfully aids Moss along the Underground Railroad. In gratitude, Moss, who had been searching for a last name, tells Brady "I got me my second name. I'm real proud of it. [. . . It's] Moss Brady" (204). Moss here redefines himself as a sign of gratitude for white aid, and in this, Fritz reflects the ideological ambivalences of antebellum white-authored radical abolitionist literature which ostensibly argued for racial equality at the same time that entrenched expectations of white agency rested upon countering images of assured black gratitude.[13] Representations of black need and white aid in neoabolitionist traditional rescuer novels reflect the antebellum trope of white benefactor and grateful slave iconographically represented in the twin emblems, "Am I Not a Man and a Brother?" and "Am I Not a Woman and a Sister?" (see fig. 1.2). The image created an irreconcilable tension in its call for racial equality and its depiction of white noblesse oblige and black supplication. Neoabolitionist white-hero rescuer texts occupy somewhat the same position as they affirm the need for equality yet focus on white agency and black gratitude. Unlike neoabolitionist white eyewitness stories that dramatize racial separation, the conclusions of rescuer texts with white protagonists are, in conservative terms, racially reconciliatory in the trope of grateful slave and heroic white abolitionist.

Although antebellum radical abolitionist children's literature often defined abolition as an opportunity for white action in the face of black passivity, neoabolitionist novels—even traditional white-hero rescuer texts—often shift that paradigm to present black agency as well. In *Brady*, for example, one sees this in the character of Tar Adams, a free black man who poses as a "cripple" (Fritz 70) to hide his abolitionist activities. Evoking images of antebellum slave narratives and the most radical of antebellum abolitionist children's literature (as, for example, in *The Youth's Emancipator*), Tar manipulates racialized expectations of the Sambo to enact and mask his disdain for white oppressors.

Living ten miles north of the Virginia border, Brady navigates contested borders: of abolition and enslavement, of childhood and adulthood, and of geographical boundaries marking legalized enslavement and freedom. Since the traditional neoabolitionist rescuer paradigm focuses on the successful escape of the runaway slave and ends with the protagonist committing himself to continued abolition, it implies an optimistic future for the specific runaway (unlike characters in pseudoabolitionist novels like Jasper of *Glory of the Seas*, who ends up reenslaved or Nicholas of *Swords of Steel*, who dies). Although traditional rescuer texts acknowledge the larger problems of slavery in the protagonist's determination to remain an agent on the Underground Railroad, the genre's typical narrative scope—of a specific escaping individual or family—both personalizes and tightly confines the representation of slavery. In such plots, slavery runs the risk of appearing finite and solvable since they avoid more direct representations, like plantation violence or the suffering of those who cannot escape. Instead, the narrative trajectory of and point of view through a character who is outside slavery provide a potential sense of emotional relief and distance to young readers.

By contrast, *Elijah of Buxton* (2007) counterpoints the genre expectations of traditional neoabolitionist rescuer novels by interrogating long-standing literary tropes about slavery. Christopher Paul Curtis's examination of the white savior figure is evident in more than an exchange of a U.S. white protagonist for a Canadian black protagonist. While the figure of a positive black protagonist welcomes a young African American readership, Curtis also reframes the supplicant slave/white hero trope to critique the very premise of the rescuer model and the racial paradigms that have underwritten much white-authored radical abolitionism.

Recipient of the Coretta Scott King Award and a Newbery Honor book, *Elijah of Buxton* tells the story of eleven-year-old Elijah, the first free child born in a community of former slaves who escaped to Canada from the United States. Elijah grows up hearing about slavery, but his exposure to it has always been secondhand until he journeys into the United States with Mr. Leroy, a neighbor, where they hope to recover the man's money and to reunite his family. When Mr. Leroy dies, young Elijah is suddenly alone and, because of his race, vulnerable to kidnapping by nearby slave catchers. It is then that Elijah witnesses slavery firsthand, and his developing comprehension of what he sees in a darkened barn provides a commentary on the objectification of slaves, particularly as, in Elijah's understanding, they move from indiscernible objects to slaves, and soon, from slaves to people. Elijah first thinks he sees five "bundles or sacks" (293), then "squatted-down demons" (296) who make a "terrorific" noise (295). Finally, the shapes chained to the wall become clear to Elijah and he realizes "these waren't no chained demons! These were five runaway slaves and a baby that had been caught!" (298). Although having grown up surrounded by others who had told him about slavery, Elijah realizes "seeing the chains real waren't the kind of thing you could imagine. It waren't the kind of picture that words could paint" (300).

While traditional white protagonist rescuer texts typically provide closure in the successful escape of slaves and the validation of the hero-rescuer, in *Elijah of Buxton*, Curtis does more than focus on black (rather than white) agency—although he does that as well. In a more pivotal reshaping of the genre, Curtis depicts slaves who will *not* escape to Canada, a protagonist who must realize that he cannot rescue them, and chained slaves who are not "sacks" only ennobled by freedom. In the typical activist model, to be the rescuer is to take power over another's life, even in their liberation from slavery. In *Elijah of Buxton*, Curtis critiques the imagined role of such a powerful hero, as well as the vacuity of texts that suggest an easy passage from slavery in the United States to freedom in Canada.

When Elijah comes upon these slaves, he recalls how he and friends "played abolitionists and slavers" as a game (307) and realizes that "our playing didn't have nothing to do with the truth." Looking at Chloe, the enslaved woman with a child, Elijah affirms: "I [. . .] swored to myself, shotguns and chains or not, I was gonna figure a way to get her and these Africans out of here!" (308). His plans for escape cascade one over the other. First, Elijah decides "I'll let you all loose and we'll have a shotgun too and when those other slave hunters come running we all could . . ." (309). He then determines that "maybe we could even borrow some of those horses there and wouldn't no one have to walk and . . ." (311); or that "it wouldn't make no noise if I cut that drunk one's throat and then took his shotgun and then we could . . ." (312). About the chains embedded in stone and impervious to his knife, he tells Chloe, "maybe if I pull the chains [. . .] I can tug 'em free. Sometimes if you want something bad enough, your dreams get answered, sometimes if you're scared enough, you get so strong you can do near anything . . ." (313).

Since neoabolitionist texts that present an individual's flight to freedom implicitly narrow the scope of slavery to a few select individuals, they often imply that if those individuals escaped slavery they either must be somehow better, smarter, braver, stronger, or more determined than slaves who did not escape and thus, that those slaves who did not escape were somehow responsible for their continued enslavement. Curtis signifies on those tropes—and the image of the hero-savior—by presenting Elijah's desperately unrealistic plans. That his dialogue repeatedly ends in ellipses suggests his ideas are unformed and uninformed impossibilities. Chloe corrects him: "Boy, stop! Them paddy-rollers ain't leaving nothing to chance. This ain't no 'musement to them. This how they live. This what they do. If they don't know nothing else, they knows how to hold slaves and they knows how to keep us held. [. . .] Don't you think if getting afeared and wishing something to happen would make it true, that these here chains would've turned to dust long ago? You think you wants to pull us free of these chains more than me and them Africans does? You think you got more strength and wanting in you than us?" (313–314).

Caught within an hour of Canada, unable to be rescued, naked, exhausted, and chained to stone, Chloe recasts the common trope of the passive slave rescued by another. Here, *she* is the slave-rescuer, for although Elijah cannot free her, she saves him, convincing Elijah that his various plans will fail and that he must leave before the slave catchers find him. With the gun she takes from Elijah, she may kill either herself and the other slaves or the slave catchers; although shackled, she can choose their life or death. It is she, the unemancipated slave, who returns Elijah to his mother, gains revenge upon slave traders, and, with Elijah's help, emancipates her daughter and gives another grieving mother a child. In a reciprocity that Chloe initiates,[14] Elijah will take her infant daughter back with him to freedom in Buxton.

In contrast to the traditional neoabolitionist rescuer paradigm, *Elijah of Buxton* refuses its readers the complacency of closure. With Mr. Leroy dead and the money unrecovered, his family remains lost in slavery and will never be reunited. The plight of the chained slaves is unknown; the last Elijah hears of them is when Chloe and her child's chained father tell each other of their love. Young Elijah realizes "their soft laughs [. . .] and those chains rattling and scraping are sounds I'm gonna be hearing for the rest of my life" (339). Unlike Jessie in *The Slave Dancer*, Elijah will remember pain but he is also a central figure in the recovery of hope. The novel ends just as Elijah reaches the edge of Buxton. Depriving the reader of Elijah's potentially heroic homecoming, in the conclusion's sense of quiet, Curtis holds in balance the joy of Elijah returning to safety with Chloe's child and the acknowledged loss of lives and freedoms left behind in the United States. Unlike novels that conclude with the celebratory success of the single hero-rescuer, in *Elijah of Buxton*, Curtis leaves readers with a more sobering sense that one known rescue holds within it the loss of many more unknown people still lost to slavery. Such an ending counters over a century's worth of white-hero rescuer tales as it disallows the illusion of a quick remedy to large-scale racial oppression.

Like *Elijah of Buxton*, even more traditional neoabolitionist stories in some measure reexamine the racially hierarchical tropes and underlying arguments of antebellum abolitionism and their reiterated appearances in children's literature. Although the exploration of those tropes obviously varies and racial hierarchies are still at times narratively supported, neoabolitionist stories often bring something new to presentations of abolitionism. They most often do this in their recognition of its limitations and their acknowledgment of a wider context of active abolitionism than that demonstrated by white hero and supplicant slave figures. Even *Brady*, for example, with its traditional representation of the young slave dependent upon the white hero's aid for freedom, nonetheless admits the coded resistance of Tar Adams, a black man who thwarts white slavers.

DIACHRONOUS FICTION AND FOLKTALES

When diachronous fiction—which typically moves between a normative time frame of the present day and a secondary time frame of the past—includes representations of slavery, it often does so to encourage interest in the past and to explore what history can mean to readers in a present-day context. Unlike rescuer and eyewitness paradigms, which usually (although not always) present white protagonists, diachronous fiction about slavery more often shows young African Americans coming to terms with a difficult or forgotten past. Such texts echo what Ashraf Rushdy has termed "palimpsest narratives." As Rushdy notes, a palimpsest is "either a parchment on which the original writing can be erased to provide space for a second writing or manuscript on which a later writing is written over an effaced earlier writing" (*Remembering* 7). This image of reinscribed texts is particularly evocative, for diachronous fiction about slavery often explores—as do palimpsest narratives—"the meaning of the past for the present" (Rushdy, *Remembering* 5).[15] While diachronous fiction about slavery includes realistic fiction and fantasy, both similarly destabilize the notion of history as time long past and recover stories of slavery as a way to make sense of the present.

African American–authored diachronous literature for children, particularly in fantasy stories, departs from earlier African American–authored representations of slavery for children which typically appeared as biography and nonfiction. Although American culture is still riddled with racial prejudice and prescriptions, by the late twentieth century, the inclusion of fiction assumes the acknowledgment of the historical existence of slavery and that a canonical group of slave figures—like Frederick Douglass and Harriet Tubman—has already been established. Fiction then allows new ways to tell about slavery, particularly in creating slave characters who would not otherwise have been able to tell their own stories. Moreover, although in the past, African American authors typically described slavery through nonfiction in children's literature, fantasy about slavery has a long tradition in African American and slave communities, particularly in the form of folktales. While folktales may seem more securely locked in a narrative past, collections of folktales—such as Virginia Hamilton's *The People Could Fly: American Black Folktales* (1985)—are metanarratively diachronous in their framing apparatus, particularly as authors establish themselves as storytellers who will recount folktales of the past for new audiences of children.

Slavery's appearance as an interpolated story in realistic fiction set in modern times allows an exploration of the legacy of American slavery in a twentieth-century context. Stories such as Lucille Clifton's *The Lucky Stone* (1979), Eleanora Tate's *The Secret of Gumbo Grove* (1987), and Sharon Dennis Wyeth's *The World of Daughter McGuire* (1994) focus on young African American—and, in Wyeth's text, biracial—protagonists of the late twentieth century who recover a deeper sense of identity by learning about the past. They also learn that an ostensibly closed, forgotten, or repressed history of slavery provides an informing context for current racism. To these protagonists—Tee listening to stories about a "lucky stone" from her grandmother; Raisin Stackhouse helping an elderly neighbor clean up a long-overgrown cemetery; and Daughter McGuire, facing the possible divorce of her parents—stories about slavery become a means of engendering personal, familial, communal, and historical regeneration.

Unlike stories set in antebellum times, the modern-day settings of these stories provide a century's buffer from slavery's violence. The intimate relationship between storyteller and auditor also mediates that violence. In *The Lucky Stone* and *The World of Daughter McGuire*, grandmothers become storytellers; in *The Secret of Gumbo Grove*, it is Miss Effie, an elderly woman in the community and a grandmother figure of sorts who passes on stories to young Raisin. Reframing the narrative rubric of Joel Chandler Harris's *Uncle Remus* tales to reflect the grandmother-narrator and African American child auditor of Julian Elihu Bagley's stories in *The Brownies' Book*, the interpolated stories about slavery in these three texts strengthen the young protagonists' self-esteem by recovering stories of (fictionalized) slaves who have otherwise been silenced. Functioning as modern-day amanuenses, these grandmother-storytellers fictionally signify on debates about who has a right to re-create history for coming generations. They also validate family stories over officially sanctioned history most often constructed by whites.[16] Indeed, in some ways these books are metanarratives, as they explore the role and power of storytelling and the refashioning of history.

Such diachronous fiction reiterates the ideological imperatives of *The Brownies' Book* and other African American biographies of the first half of the twentieth century in recovering black heroes to engender racial pride in contemporary children and to encourage their appreciation for those who preceded them. *The Secret of Gumbo Grove* notes those arguments as if verbatim from *The Brownies' Book* when Raisin complains that "when we read about people doing stuff in history class, [. . . .] nobody ever mentioned anybody Black. And when I asked [. . .] my teacher, how come we never studied about anybody Black who did stuff around here, she said nobody Black around here had ever done anything good worth talking about" (5).[17] Like the woman in *The Brownies' Book*'s "The Heritage" (Patterson), Miss Effie tells Raisin, "your ancestors are never too old to honor, Miss Lady. If it hadn't been for them you wouldn't be here now, and neither would nobody else" (15).

In *The Secret of Gumbo Grove*, the decrepit state of a cemetery stands as a metaphor for the suppression of memory and African

American history. Its graves long untended and overgrown with weeds, the cemetery is considered an eyesore, those buried there only "folks [who] died too long ago to worry about" (14). Yet the townspeople know that history is not long past, and their disregard of the cemetery seems intentional. When Raisin helps Miss Effie tend to the cemetery and learns about those buried there, Raisin's father warns her, "you're dragging up stuff nobody wants to hear about, [. . . . you'll be] opening up old sores" (135). Miss Effie's recounting of those buried in the cemetery reveals stories of slavery, segregation, discrimination, and racial violence. These are stories, some worry, that may aggravate race relations, and "make people, White and Black, have buckets of 'extended negative emotion'" (102). To avoid this anticipated "extended negative emotion," the residents of Gumbo Grove, according to Miss Effie, "don't talk much now about what used to happen to us back in the old days. [. . .] Are they all too shamed to tell it to you? Or are you all too shamed to hear it?" (17).

For the generation of Raisin's parents, slavery has become part of the "family secret," the "'symbol of shame' that black families historically attempt to hide, ignore, mute or deny" (Rushdy, *Remembering* 2, 17).[18] Indeed, the integration of Gumbo Grove's African American families into wider American society has been accompanied by a suppression of stories about America's violent racial history.[19] As Miss Effie recounts otherwise lost stories, cautioning Raisin, "don't be shamed of where you come from" (69), she expiates any guilt or shame about slavery that has been either ascribed to or adopted by African American characters. She also heals the protagonist's and the community's sense of alienation by connecting them to their past. In *The Secret of Gumbo Grove*, the effect of knowing one's past is immediate. Raisin feels "goose bumps of pride and amazement" as she hears Miss Effie's stories. Other characters also are changed, and when Big Boy, a local bully, learns of her own history, she feels redeemed and gains new purpose. Without parents, and once told that "nobody on [her . . .] daddy's side" ever did anything good (64), Big Boy now has an otherwise lost family returned to her in the names and stories of those buried in the cemetery.

As a group, these stories present new patterns of heroism that insist on the value of the lives and experiences of slaves who never wrote their own story and never became well known. The specific stories of slaves in these books are thus fictionalized to allow authors to create otherwise unknown ancestors for the protagonist and other characters. It also allows authors to imagine the lives of those whose stories were never told in antebellum accounts or narratives. These fictionalized recountings do not necessarily replicate the biographical entries in *The Brownies' Book* that described successful post-emancipation life. Instead, as in Virginia Hamilton's *The House of Dies Drear* (1968), these texts acknowledge that one could have been "brave and sold all the same" (230). Recovering slaves who did not escape as strong, valued people also addresses issues of cultural guilt and shame within African American communities. Here, the strength of those enslaved—their very existence—becomes a source of race pride, whether or not they were among the proportionally few who managed to escape. Moreover, post-emancipation success is shown not in individual slaves gaining freedom, as much as in the contemporary, modern African American protagonist and family who are the fulfillment of that earlier promise.

Learning of the history of slavery gives these protagonists a deeper cultural and historical context for current racism as well as the emotional legacy and resources to combat it. That those who were enslaved have something to tell the present both signals the long-lasting effects of racial exploitation in America and the strength of those who were enslaved. That those "dead" continue to affect the present, particularly through what young readers learn from them, also reframes the historical importance of the "slave" as a figure that still inhabits America's present.

The narrative objectives in realistic and fantastic diachronous literatures may be the same—particularly, of encouraging an appreciation for the past—but when contemporary protagonists are suddenly taken from their homes, transported back in time, immersed in slavery, and exposed to all its attendant dangers firsthand, the intensity of slavery's representation is amplified.[20] The involuntary remove to slavery in some ways hearkens back to antebellum kidnap stories like Lydia Maria Child's "Mary French and Susan Easton" to argue that the ways in which one feels protected from racial assault are more illusion than fact. The danger is all the more dire for African American characters who return to antebellum times; unlike Mary French, when the character taken into slavery is African American, rescue is not so easily achieved.

The immediacy of the protagonist's experience in the collapse of intervening time is meant to provide a more engaging experience of history for readers who identify with present-day protagonists. Kidnapped by time as well as by slavery, modern-day protagonists learn (as, presumably, so do readers) that, but for the happenstance of when they were born, they might be a slave. In some ways, the narrative effect of the time-travel story in this context is to simultaneously remove one's sense of the "otherness" of the figure of the slave while heightening (through sudden time contrast) the strangeness and horror of slavery itself.

In Faith Ringgold's fantastical picture book, *Aunt Harriet's Underground Railroad in the Sky* (1992), for example, young, modern-day African American Cassie and her brother find themselves runaway slaves in antebellum times. Not mediated by the storytelling of grandmotherly figures as in Clifton's, Tate's, and Wyeth's worlds, Cassie's experience of slavery comes without the protective veil of a century's time. With only the suggestion of a protective figure—Cassie hears Harriet Tubman give her clues along the Underground Railroad—Cassie must evade slave catchers as she makes her way to freedom. Finally arriving in Canada, Cassie reunites with her younger brother who tells her that he, too, now "know[s] what our great-great-grandparents survived when they were children" (u.p.). Time-travel books such as this, which move contemporary children back to a period when their ancestors suffered historical atrocities, puncture the insularity that surrounds what to contemporary children (and adults) may seem like time long past.[21] These characters come to understand prior suffering because they experience it; for the young reader, the experience seems fraught with danger—certainly so here as partially hidden ghost-white figures watch Cassie along her journey.

Tar Beach (1991), a necessary prelude and informing text to *Aunt Harriet's Underground Railroad in the Sky*, evidences the not fully erased legibility of slavery in the racial discriminations of contemporary society: Cassie's father has been excluded from joining a labor union. The overall effect in time-travel fantasies about slavery is to introduce "a bi-temporal perspective that shows the continuity and discontinuities from the period of slavery" (Rushdy, *Remembering* 5). In Ringgold's work, *Tar Beach* provides the normative contemporary world frame for the "bi-temporal perspective," just as the representation of slavery in *Aunt Harriet's Underground Railroad in the Sky* provides the defining context of the historicity of continued racial discrimination in America. As discrete physical texts linked by informing contexts, the simultaneous distinction and connection between *Tar Beach* and *Aunt Harriet's Underground Railroad in the Sky* is metaphorically representative of similar tensions between historical periods tied by slavery and continued racial discrimination.

The fluid relationship between different time periods also stands at the core of Walter Mosley's *47* (2005), although in this novel the time trajectory is reversed in that an antebellum slave journeys to modern times. As in *Aunt Harriet's Underground Railroad in the Sky*, in *47* slavery is depicted as a specific historical event and, at the same time, dialogically communicative to racial and national identity a century later. The novel's primary setting is a violent slave plantation in the antebellum South that realistically echoes representations of slave narratives. Mosley then overlays that realism with a blend of science fiction and magical realism presenting an intergalactic traveler, Tall John, who has spent three thousand years looking for the one expected to "grow into a man who will save the whole world" (165). He finds that person in the slave known as 47, bestows magical powers upon him, and readies him for the coming battle that will determine the fate of the universe.

Initially enacting a cataclysmic battle of good and evil against the backdrop of slavery situates slavery as a primary expression of evil. The physicality of that expression is shown when evil forces inhabit the cruel overseer and master who try to kill 47. Although the master's daughter is saved by Tall John and 47 and she later helps slaves in return, racial reconciliation is not at the forefront of the novel. Instead, 47 is a counterpoint to Stowe's Uncle Tom, who vowed to the murderous Legree that "if taking every drop of blood in this poor old body would save your precious soul, I'd give 'em freely" (582–583). In contrast, 47's task is not to convert or forgive slaveholders but to destroy them.

In *47*, Mosley refigures a seemingly insignificant slave as the hero. To initiate this move, 47 must first free himself from the psychological bonds of slavery—to cast off his belief in his own insignificance. Race pride stands at the core of Mosley's creation of the hero-slave. When 47 comes to the revelation that "the real chains that the slave wore were the color of his skin and the defeat in his mind" (146), he implicitly acknowledges the prevalence of the palimpsest (the present as an overlay of the past) and its expression in racism—that it assaults and attempts to infiltrate the self-perception of successive generations. In his fight against evil, 47 realizes he must battle the inculcation of racial self-loathing. As if evoking paradigms of cultural trauma, 47—who magically lives as a young man into the twenty-first century—knows that the "scar of slavery would never be gone from me. And as long as I lived that memory would be alive." While the memory will remain, he exorcises its more insidious effect, determining that "I would never be a nigger again" (173) to show that, like antebellum slave narrators, he has learned to distinguish between condition and personhood. 47 may have been a slave, but he would not keep the "*slavemind*" (101).[22]

So objectified that he is named only by the number branded into his skin, 47 is a cipher, both known and unknown, figured and unnamed, slave and prophesied savior of the universe. While Mosley retrieves the anonymity of the slave, he also argues that the "slave" is not ultimately a knowable object. Magical and ageless, the slave 47 is the only hope for the universe's survival; as Tall John declares, this "black-skinned, nappy-headed child who was born into slavery [. . .] shall ride into the greatest battle in the history of the world" to "save the universe" (107). A "slave"—by definition individually dispensable within the slave system—becomes, in Mosley's novel, not merely "destined for greatness" (85), but rather one without whom "there can be no future for anyone" (142). Through 47, Mosley thus signifies on tropes of the "slave."

Connected to his revisioning of the anonymous slave is an implicit critique of the canonicity of well-known historical figures, such as Frederick Douglass and Harriet Tubman, that seems to cast the millions of other people who endured slavery into an indifferent obscurity where they have often been represented as passive, foolish, unremarkable, and individually unimportant. Mosley criticizes how the hero-slave image has been culturally constructed by creating in 47 the ultimate hero-slave, a cipher upon whom the future of the universe depends. Situating the final battle in the contemporary reader's future—it has been prophesied as occurring in 2019—disrupts the possibility of narrative closure, or even, because so much is unknown about this battle, narrative definition. Readers are thus left with a reorganized pattern of present-day experience: around them walks a black child who has experienced more than one could imagine and who, far beyond an emblematic renewal of republican childhood, may be the world's savior. Mosley thus also imbues present-day experience with an understanding of the essential importance of a historical past to one's present and future.

* * *

Historical past and fantasy are also combined in Mosley's representation of the trickster figure, particularly as Tall John reveals 47 as the legendary black hero, "John the Conqueror," to evoke a sense of the respected and often-feared conjurer-slave on antebellum plantations. Folktales were a way the slave community expressed rebellion, found psychological respite, enjoyed the catharsis of besting masters, and shared survival strategies.[23] They are fantasy veiled in metaphor to explore power paradigms, conflict, and identity, and in *47*, as the lone "runt" (84) hero fights against slaveholders as a seemingly unbeatable foe, Mosley shows the ways folktales incorporate lived realities, and vice versa.

Although not obviously diachronous, slave and African American folktales have used fantasy to tell of slavery for generations. The tradition continues. Virginia Hamilton and Julius Lester, among others, have presented collections of slave folktales that return the tales more clearly to their black, slave, and African roots. Despite its title, in *The Tales of Uncle Remus: The Adventures of Brer Rabbit* (1987), Lester removes the Uncle Remus figure and Harris's use of dialect. In *The People Could Fly: American Black Folktales*, Hamilton reaffirms the primacy of black culture and honors her family history, as she tells readers the tales will "echo[. . .] the voices of slaves and fugitives, some of whom are my ancestors" (xii). Without the containment strategies of white reconstructionists, such as Joel Chandler Harris or Louise-Clarke Pyrnelle, these retellings of slave tales are situated within antebellum debates about the authority of black voice in telling stories about slavery. In their prefaces, Hamilton and Lester also position themselves as present-day storytellers of tales from the past.

Although not traditionally diachronous, newly created myths also represent ways of interpreting slave folktales and communicating images of black heroism to current generations of children. While Mosley presents a slave who may save the universe, Kim Siegelson's *In the Time of the Drums* (1999) and Julius Lester's *The Old African* (2005) tell of mythic heroes who counter the Middle Passage by leading Africans enslaved in America into the ocean to return home. Based on a Gullah story of slaves who walked into the water at Ibo (or "Ebo," "Ybo") Landing in Georgia, Siegleson's and Lester's collections differ on the gender of their hero, on the details of the protagonist's life in America, and whether the return to Africa is a physical or spiritual one. Yet in their descriptions of a slave who seeks to lead others out of slavery, they, along with Mosley, combine the hero of antebellum slave narratives and the folk hero of slave tales to define the "slave" as a figure holding unimaginable power and whose goal is rebellion, not reconciliation, with slaveholders. As in realistic and fantastic diachronous literature, such folktales and myths counter tropes of foolish and passive slaves to present new generations of readers with models of heroism, strength, and fortitude.

BIOGRAPHIES AND NEO-SLAVE NARRATIVES

Biographies and neo-slave narratives appear as fiction and nonfiction, both arguing a necessary respect for those who had been enslaved. While slave biographies reflect a more traditionally reiterated form in children's literature, recent biographies have continued to expand the genre, particularly in terms of those who are included among the list of biographical subjects. A distinguishing point between biographies and neo-slave narratives is the extent of subjectivity granted the main character; a principal element of neo-slave narratives is that subjectivity. Particularly as biographies take new innovative forms, they may overlap with neo-slave narratives; certainly the potential for crossover exists, perhaps most frequently in recent picture-book biographies. And while neo-slave narratives reflect the antebellum slave narrative in the subjectivity of the slave figure, they also often present innovative forms to "newly" reshape the slave narrative as a way to signify on antebellum abolitionist debates and recover lost voices.

Slave biographies for children (both nonfiction and fictionalized)[24] have overwhelmingly focused on several figures, particularly Frederick Douglass,[25] Harriet Tubman,[26] and Sojourner Truth.[27] Some recent series for young children—such as Fawcett Columbine's Great Lives, Patria Press's Young Patriots, and Chelsea House's Black Americans of Achievement—continue the objective of *The Brownies' Book* in recovering black heroes as a way to expand the often limited focus of children's education beyond histories of white Americans.[28]

Representations of slavery through biography are, of course, shaped as much by the choice of biographical subject as by how the biographer chooses to sculpt the subject's life story. Particularly in the cases of Douglass and Tubman, recounting episodes about their childhoods seems intended to engender young readers' identification and sympathy. In Alan Schroeder and Jerry Pinkney's Coretta Scott King Illustrator–awarded picture book, *Minty: A Story of Young Harriet Tubman* (1996), Minty's childlike love for her rag doll, the cruel treatment she receives from her mistress, and her determination to one day escape slavery, together synthesize the emotional arc of slave narratives, personalizing Tubman and moving her through oppression and rebellion. Narrowing down Tubman's story to her childhood years and calling her "Minty" would defamiliarize her to readers, so that the story seems to offer a fresh vantage point. It also concentrates the emotional focus of the biography to present Tubman's childhood as a "how she got there" story (A. Thompson 94).[29] Schroeder's focus argues the vulnerabilities of a child in slavery, the formative influence of childhood on one's later adulthood, and the resilience of exceptional children in the face of oppression. Yet this story ends before the typical turning point of escape found in antebellum slave narratives. Although Minty hopes to escape, at the last minute, "Minty lost her courage. She couldn't do it. Not now. [. . .] With tears in her eyes, she ran back [. . .] to the cabin" (u.p.). Although the child Minty does not escape, young readers are assured in the final pages that "someday she would run away [. . . .] and nothing would stop her. Nothing" (u.p.).

In slave biographies for children, escapes to freedom and, in the case of Tubman, continued returns to the South despite great personal danger, often serve as a story's narrative crux. They function, as did similar episodes in antebellum slave narratives, to engender a sense of adventure that would pique reader interest. Other earlier reiterated biographies—of, for example, Booker T. Washington and Phillis Wheatley—are less frequently published following the civil rights movement. Both lack the escape stories and adventure found in other, more frequently told slave biographies. Presumably Washington's "accommodationist" stance as well as Wheatley's amiable relationship with her masters and later difficulties in life make neither strong representatives of slave figures for late twentieth-century sensibilities.[30] By contrast, the trajectory of the life stories of Douglass, Tubman, and Truth as activist figures, who battled oppression in their move from slavery to freedom then to influence and renown in the national arena, places them as models of bravery, independence, and success for modern audiences, in some ways replicating the "progress-report autobiographies" (Gates and McKay 468) of the late nineteenth century.

In the case of these three figures in particular, literary canonization has resulted in often hagiographic biographies. As Nigel Hamilton has pointed out, "biography is [. . .] not simply human record but debate" (33), and biographies of slaves or former slaves offer inherent debates about slavery, personhood, and race.[31] In the Coretta Scott King Illustrator–awarded and Caldecott Honor picture book *Moses: When Harriet Tubman Led Her People to Freedom* (2006), author Carole Boston Weatherford presents the story of Tubman as a literal hagiography, a life of a saint. She incorporates Tubman's spirituality to frame escape as a conversation between Harriet (whose petitions and reflections are shown in italics and sentence style) and God (whose declarative promises are in uppercase and larger font). That Tubman makes the journey to freedom "holding God's hand" and later accedes to God's directive to "BE THE MOSES OF YOUR PEOPLE" and bring slaves to safety, defines her as God's daughter, messenger, and prophet (u.p.).

In accompanying illustrations, which open out to large double pages of 21″ × 11½″, Kadir Nelson represents Tubman's determination in a striking close-up of her face so dramatically scaled that it spills onto a second page as if grafted onto skyscapes visually suggestive of God's presence. Nelson's work exalts heroic portraiture of African Americans, like that of Charles Dawson's *ABC's of Great Negroes* (see fig. 4.1). At the same time, Weatherford authorizes Tubman's accounts of her spirituality, defines fighting racial oppression as a directive from God, and counters earlier tropes of weakened or unimportant slaves to present a quintessentially powerful figure: Harriet Tubman as one of God's saints, chosen to redeem those hurt by a fallen world. Such foci reflect the heroic slave biographies of earlier generations, such as those in *The Brownies' Book*. Yet, unlike many early twentieth-century depictions of biographical figures, Weatherford's Tubman is concerned with battling racial oppression rather than engendering racial amity. Such a return to the tenor of antebellum slave narratives that expose racial conflict is a common marker of post–civil rights biographies.

As much as an overwhelming number of these biographies focus on a select group, they run the risk of establishing a narrow canon, one which exclusively follows the "acceptable" life trajectory of the "slave"—from enslavement to escape, freedom, and lauded national contribution. Collections like Virginia Hamilton's *Many Thousand Gone: African Americans from Slavery to Freedom* (1993) counter this tendency by including a large number of biographical subjects with varied life experiences. That the range of subjects has grown to include new types of life stories is evidenced, too, by the success of Laban Carrick Hill and Bryan Collier's *Dave the Potter: Artist, Poet, Slave* (2010), recipient of the Coretta Scott King Award and a Caldecott Honor book. The title itself opens the sometimes flat designation of "slave" by defining the man first as potter, artist, and poet; the final term "slave" then comments on and stands in tension with the liberation evoked by the preceding descriptors. Together, they suggest untold stories lying within the generalized term "slave" to unearth the person held within that designation. Dave's life story does not follow the more typically told movement from slavery to legal freedom. Rather, Hill and Collier present the story of a slave few know much about, one who remained in slavery and whose story is largely told through the pots he made, upon which he sometimes inscribed brief lines: as Hill describes it, "before the jar / completely hardened, / Dave picked up a stick / and wrote to let us know / that he was here" (u.p.). Hill includes words found on some of Dave's recovered pots—"*I wonder where / is all my relation / friendship to all— / and, every nation*"—allowing a text that both speaks about and gives voice to the artist-slave (u.p.).

Even though in some ways Hill tells the reader both not much and very much about Dave, the racialized vision of *Dave the Potter* not only adds to the canon of slave biographies for children it more fundamentally adds to the definition of "slave." That expanded definition is the "very much" young readers learn—not that Dave was recognized as a national hero nor that he undertook a successful escape to the North, neither of which occurred—but that "he was here," he was talented and, although enslaved, nonetheless revolutionary. The book is an implicit response to Arna Bontemps's point that it is "hard to piece together the things one likes to know about interesting and gifted people, when they happen to have been slaves" (*Story* 41). *Dave the Potter* thus helps to recover the talents of this man from the historical anonymity accorded the vast majority of those who had been enslaved.

Neo-slave narratives also often recover otherwise lost voices, but as they do so, they reframe conventions of the antebellum slave narrative. Largely literal retellings of slave narratives, such as Mary Lyons's *Letters from a Slave Girl: The Story of Harriet Jacobs* (1992) or Ann Cameron's *The Kidnapped Prince: The Life of Olaudah Equiano* (1995), function more as re-created slave narratives than neo-slave narratives. Without the addition of anything particularly new, such texts largely adapt slave narratives by streamlining passages and modernizing language, and, as Cameron notes of her work, by "not add[ing] any ideas of my own to [Equiano's . . .] story, or fictionaliz[ing] it in any way" (ix).

By definition, a "neo-slave narrative" does something new with the antebellum slave narrative as a genre and focus. At the same time, it uses as its founding form of expression the antebellum slave narrative,[32] presenting the slave's voice as the authoritative perspective on slavery. It is, in many ways, the culmination of literary reiterations of the antebellum slave narrative. Neo-slave narratives often self-consciously call upon slave narratives, slave testimony, and slave studies as authenticating documents, in some ways signifying on issues of authentication in antebellum slave narratives. This is true, for example, in the ways neo-slave narratives typically refigure the peritextual apparatus of antebellum slave narratives. Authenticating letters that prefaced and appended antebellum slave narratives and were typically authored by white abolitionists to assure readers of the text's veracity are exchanged in neo-slave narratives. Here, framing documents—often an author's note or bibliography—cite slave narratives or slave studies as sources, thus reclaiming the slave's voice as the only necessary authentication for accounts about slavery.

Neo-slave narratives focus on the subjectivity of slaves in their recovery or fictive re-creation of the slave's perspective. Similar to antebellum slave narratives, these texts show the primacy of black agency over white aid to counter images of slaves as passive, foolish, content, or unloving of their children. Neo-slave narratives evoke the central motifs, ideology, and voice of the antebellum slave narrative while reshaping it in a variety of forms, often depending upon the age of the intended reader. Picture books about slavery provide the visual images that radical abolitionists had once asked children to imagine; narratives told in poetry—such as Marilyn Nelson's *Fortune's Bones* (2004)—echo antebellum abolitionist poetry that recounted incidents of slavery;[33] and polyphonic texts that include divergent perspectives reflect contesting antebellum debates about slavery.

Although antebellum slave narratives assured readers that their accounts were "no fiction" (Jacobs 1), neo-slave narratives make varying use of fiction in their re-creations. While some are solely nonfiction, others are fictionalized versions of whole pieces or even bits of historical information, and others are based on entirely fictionalized characters in a realistically depicted slave setting.[34] Even fictional neo-slave narratives aim for a verisimilitude with antebellum slave narratives in their depictions of slavery and point of view. Indeed, fiction often becomes a way not simply to "story" a scene of slavery, but to allow authors to imagine the lives that could not be fully expressed in antebellum slave narratives, particularly the lives of those who did not escape or survive slavery. In addition to depicting slaves who escaped or gained postbellum success, by means of fictional re-creation, neo-slave narratives are also able to grant subjectivity to slaves who stood only in the background or margins of antebellum slave narratives.

Representations of violence in neo-slave narratives for children are often sculpted depending on the intended age of the reader. In picture books for young readers, violence is often contained through point of view and plot focus.[35] Because neo-slave narrative picture books follow a slave's perspective, they frequently focus on a successful escape to freedom. As hopeful narratives, these escape stories balance symbolic representations of threat with a narrative trajectory that provides an optimistic resolution for very young readers. They also typically balance representations of racial interactions: the threat of white masters is often counterpointed by whites who offer aid along the Underground Railroad.[36]

Neo-slave narrative picture books for young readers often minimize direct representations of violence, sometimes suggesting violence through implication, other times sublimating it in symbol. One sees this, for example, in Jeanette Winter's *Follow the Drinking Gourd* (1988). In an early illustration, the master's threat and power are visually represented when he is scaled outside the frame of the picture. Whip in hand and so large he cannot fit on the page, the master need not be shown in the act of whipping a slave for young readers to understand his threat. Later images of violence are more symbolic: a sheep encountering a wolf with teeth bared and the changing texture and shape of grass and ground cover to signal the escaping slaves' danger or safety.

Although neo-slave narrative picture books for young children often avoid explicit images of violence, they nonetheless capture the essence of its representation in antebellum slave narratives, often encapsulating slavery's oppression in the threat of family separation. In *Follow the Drinking Gourd*, for example, the father is to be sold away, and is shown on an auction block, eyes downcast while surrounding white men bid for him. Particularly for young readers, the prospect of losing parents or of seeing them powerless can be terrifying; by focusing on these possibilities (rather than showing the whippings and physical torture described in many antebellum slave narratives), picture books often convey the essence and emotional trauma of slavery's violence without including more overt representations of physical abuse. Neo-slave narrative picture books that are told in the third person to provide some emotional distance to the reader nonetheless encourage reader sympathy (as did antebellum authors of slave narratives) by personalizing the slave by name and through family association; in *Follow the Drinking Gourd*, readers meet Hattie and George, as well as Molly, James, and their young son Isaiah.[37]

In their frequent focus on escape, neo-slave narrative picture books expand on a moment that in antebellum slave narratives often remained necessarily secret.[38] These picture books show the myriad resistance of slaves, much of which went unnoticed by white masters but predicated escape—from listening in on masters' conversations and passing that information along to others in the slave community to ferrying people to freedom. Escape stories are common neo-slave narratives for young audiences because they focus on the effectiveness of nonviolent rebellion. They also promise successful agency. Such stories, of course, risk suggesting that escape from slavery was always successful, potentially implying that if slaves had only enough determination they would have freed themselves. In the escape story of *Sweet Clara and the Freedom Quilt* (1993), author Deborah Hopkinson directly addresses this idea. When the protagonist, who has escaped slavery, reflects that "not all are as lucky as we were, and most never can come" (u.p.), she acknowledges the role of happenstance, even in the best of plans.

Neo-slave narrative picture books often reflect the antebellum slave narrative's representations of slaves contesting the hegemonic power of slaveholders in the slaves' creation of a vying, resistant community. Particularly in picture books where children serve as principal characters, depictions of black determination and resistance are often evinced within a support structure of familial love or faithfulness to the slave community. The choice of child protagonist heightens the sense of the slave's vulnerability, encourages reader identification with the young protagonist, and lauds the power of children. In rebelling against slavery, the child-slave protagonist refigures the antebellum trope of the white reformer child to a heroic black child capable of the most radical reform: emancipation.

Some more recent picture books present neo-slave narratives in which slaves remain on the plantation, but that is often accompanied by an implicit promise of eventual freedom.[39] In *The Listeners* (2009), for example, author Gloria Whelan tells of a group of slave children, "Bobby, Sue, and me, Ella May," who surreptitiously listen in on the master's conversations and carry news back to adults in the slave community. When the children bring back word of Lincoln's election, Ella May asks her father "is our listening over?" and he tells her "we see the road, but we don't see all the way to where the ending is. We got to know how long is that road and how we get down it. [. . . Your] listening is just begun" (u.p.). As in the conclusion to *Minty*, although freedom has not yet been achieved, the author implies its eventuality. Typical of the neo-slave narrative (rather than neoabolitionist) perspective, Whelan maintains a focus on black agency, although she uses Lincoln as a signal of coming emancipation. Not passively waiting for Lincoln to act, this slave community's children will continue their subversive spying to disempower slaveholders. It is they who are the heroes here.

While picture-book neo-slave narratives often present hopeful conclusions, neo-slave narratives for older children and adolescents more directly explore slavery's violence and the impossibility of its easy reparation. When just over a century after the Civil War Lester constructed the Newbery Honor book *To Be a Slave* (1968), he drew together testimonies from antebellum slave narratives and interviews of formerly enslaved people that were collected through the Federal Writers' Project (FWP) of the 1930s, counterpointing them with several proslavery excerpts, as in one by a white preacher who assured slaves that "your masters and mistresses are God's overseers" (78–79).[40] From slaves who rebelled to others who identified with their masters, from anguish to anger, from race theories that justified slavery to personalized accounts of the injustices suffered under enslavement, the collection of voices in *To Be a Slave* shows the way nonfictional testimony can be resculpted in a neonarrative form. As one of the most important authors in the development of neo-slave narratives for young audiences,[41] Lester's use of floating first-person testimony—as one excerpt stands beside another, only intermittently linked by narrative interpolation—implicitly debates *who* has the right to tell the history of slavery and argues the inseparability of race and enslavement in the American experience.

In *To Be a Slave*, Lester focuses not on a more well-known figure like Frederick Douglass, but instead breaks open the story of slavery to retrieve lost voices that might otherwise not be heard and in so doing, refigures the representation of the "heroic slave." There is not, here, only one journey that signals honor and there is no implicit condemnation of those who did not achieve physical freedom. Lester's recovery of many voices also gives further sense of the scope of experiences and people enslaved, as the accounts reveal grief, frustration, anger, and resistance. Moreover, he presents as main figures those who did not escape slavery and maintains their point of view at the close of the text, which prevents the reader from having any easy sense of closure about slavery. The narrative strategy thus more accurately depicts the vast majority of experiences endured by the millions of people who had been enslaved in America.

Lester exemplifies not only the refiguring of slavery in neo-slave narratives, but also important distinctions between neo-slave narratives written for young children (often in picture-book form) and those for adolescents. Neo-slave narratives for older readers, like *To Be a Slave*, typically avoid representations of racial cooperation and optimism commonly found in picture books. With Northern white readers as their primary audience, authors of antebellum slave narratives often had to navigate a minefield of reader expectations as they courted white sympathy while criticizing race oppression and Northern hypocrisy. By contrast, authors of neo-slave narratives for adolescents are less concerned with appeasing white readers than telling harsh truths as they reestablish the importance of slave testimony to encourage racial pride in African American children and to condemn historical and contemporary racial exploitation. Unlike the more conciliatory tone in picture books, Lester uses the testimony of those formerly enslaved to evoke the "blasting reproach" that Frederick Douglass had called for in describing slavery ("What to the Slave" 126). One hears this, for example, when Sallie Crane recalls of slave times that "we was cussed for so many bitches and sons of bitches and bloody bitches and blood of bitches. We never heard our names scarcely at all" (Lester, *To Be* 29). Far from the lauded supplicant slave in antebellum radical abolitionist children's literature or the reconciliatory tone in *The Brownies' Book* biographies, neoabolitionist accounts for adolescents often present the slave's racial outrage.

While neo-slave narrative picture books for young audiences mitigate violence most often through implied representations, neo-slave narratives for adolescents echo antebellum slave narratives in presenting unflinching accounts of slavery's violence enacted upon child and adult alike. In *To Be a Slave*, one reads of such violence during the Middle Passage when slavers took children from their mothers and "threw them over the side of the ship" (25). First-person accounts in *To Be a Slave* also convey the unrelieved trauma of slavery, as when Ben Simpson recalls witnessing the murder of his mother when he was just a boy. During a forced march from Georgia to Texas, his mother "give out [. . .]. Her feet got raw and bleeding, and her legs swoll plumb out of shape. Then massa, he just take out his gun and shot her, and while she lay dying, he kicks her two, three times, and say, 'Damn a nigger what can't stand nothing.' You know that man, he wouldn't bury Mother. Just leave her laying where he shot her" (55).

In stressing the subjectivity of the slave, neo-slave narratives, like antebellum slave narratives, depict slaves as neither deadened recipients of oppression nor supplicant slaves waiting for a white intercessor. As Lester notes in *To Be a Slave*, "*they who were held as slaves looked upon themselves and the servitude in which they found themselves with the eyes and minds of human beings, conscious of everything that happened to them, conscious of all that went on around them*" (28–29). As antebellum slave narratives revealed, both suffering and rebellion express that consciousness; and neo-slave narratives, too, use accounts of slaves' intellectual, psychological, physical, and at times even violent resistance to slaveholders to achieve the same effect. In *To Be a Slave*, for example, one reads of a slave responsible for whipping other slaves who "learned how to handle the whip with marvelous [. . .] precision, throwing the lash within a hair's breadth of the back [. . .] without touching" it (36); of slaves whose religious songs extolled the end of slavery (83–84);

of others who "*appear to be dumb* [. . . knowing] *the more ignorant he appeared to be, the less work he would have to do*" (98); and of Solomon Northup, who "*almost killed his owner after the latter had tried to kill him with an axe*" (128).

As much as antebellum slave narratives argued the heroism of those who stood against masters through subterfuge, escape, or psychological resistance, they also acknowledged slaves who were complicit with the master. Lester, too, shows that the "slave" is not a single figure, but a term that covers myriad individuals, including those who betrayed others in the slave community. Rather than the typically uniform representation that one finds in children's picture books of heroic and kind slaves, Lester instead describes slaves who identified with masters, as in the case of Edward Taylor, who recalled that "I thought [. . . . just] stay near the white folks and I had nothing to worry about. I thought white folks made the stars, sun and everything on the earth" (88–89).

While biographies of slaves in *The Brownies' Book* moved past slavery to focus on black success in emancipation and, particularly, on final images of racial cooperation configured as black service to interracial (but notably white) communities, neo-slave narratives instead focus on the experiences of those in slavery and often argue against both narrative closure and promises of racial cooperation. By recounting FWP interviews of former slaves, Lester not only makes known largely unfamiliar documents to young readers but also shows the long-lasting effects of slavery, as people recall events that occurred over half a century earlier. In contrast to the reconciliation stories and narratives of the postbellum years, here one learns that the pain of slavery is not so easily healed, as in the case of ninety-year-old Ben Simpson who as a child witnessed his mother's murder.

Contention—of different views, of the oppression of slavery upon an unwilling populace, of the struggle of slaves for freedom—stands at the core of these neo-slave narratives. Here, race warfare defines slavery. As a result, Stowe's paradigm of forgiveness and racial reconciliation has little presence in these texts. Eschewing nineteenth-century representations of romantic racialism, Lester includes a passage from Northup's slave narrative: "They are deceived who flatter themselves that the ignorant and debased slave has no conception of the magnitude of his wrongs. They are deceived who imagine that he arises from his knees with back lacerated and bleeding, cherishing only a spirit of meekness and forgiveness. A day may come—it *will* come, if his prayer is heard—a terrible day of vengeance, when the master in his turn will cry in vain for mercy" (129).

The view that slavery is embedded with promises of racial reconciliation is absent in neo-slave narratives for adolescents not only because they articulate the central struggles and tone of antebellum slave narratives, but also because they explore the reverberations of slavery in twentieth-century America. In *To Be a Slave*, for example, the inclusion of Alice Johnson's response to an FWP interview in the early twentieth century would surely resonate with late twentieth-century readers aware of continued racial segregation, discrimination, and violence in modern America: "You want to know what they did in slavery times. They were doing just what they do now. The white folks was beating the niggers, burnin' 'em and boilin' 'em, workin' 'em and doin' any other thing they wanted to do with them" (30). Through such testimony, Lester denies the sometimes neat classification of slavery as a closed historical event, refuting optimistic representations of postslavery's racial harmony. In so doing, neo-slave narratives for adolescents refuse readers the self-satisfied illusion of a repaired America.

Narrative techniques, such as polyphonic layering and the counterpointing of contrasting perspectives, reveal ways in which some neo-slave narratives explicitly reflect the clashing viewpoints of antebellum genres and later re-creations of slavery to provide commentary on the nature of story making and the construction of history. Polyphonic neo-slave narratives, in this way, both present and answer debates about authenticity. By offering varying points of view that can be traced to antebellum proslavery, slave narrative, and white abolitionist arguments, neo-slave narratives may subsume the responsive interaction of those antebellum genres, replicating the ways in which they vied for authority with readers. These neo-slave narratives also reflect the responsive interaction of post-emancipation slavery retellings that have countered, corroborated, and rewritten each other for over a century in their re-presentations of slavery. *To Be a Slave* is obviously polyphonic: accounts of former slaves include those who rebelled against and others who colluded with masters; proslavery testimony and pseudoscientific race theories are juxtaposed with accounts of slavery's violence. The contrasting—and often clashing—perspectives collectively stand as a type of narrative microcosm for the literary re-creation of slavery. Yet in polyphonic neo-slave narratives, the voice that has predominance is that of the slave, and the perspective remains undoubtedly an antislavery one. Against the emotional weight and narrative space of antislavery pieces, proslavery perspectives are presented in order to be discounted.

While neo-slave narrative picture books for young children usually show escape from slavery, neo-slave narratives for older children or adolescents are more likely to disrupt promises for happy conclusions by depicting figures who remained in slavery without hope of escape. Such neo-slave narratives expand the subject position of the antebellum slave narrative. One sees this in the fictionalized *Fortune's Bones: The Manumission Requiem* (2004), where author Marilyn Nelson gives voice to Fortune, an actual Connecticut slave in the late 1700s whose body, after death, was boiled down to a skeleton by his master, a doctor who then kept it for study and display. The skeleton was passed down for generations within the doctor's family, then became a museum exhibit, where, as one attendee said, it was "the *thing* to see when you go to the museum. I don't think anybody ever envisioned that this was truly a human being" (22, emphasis added). Both obvious and anonymous (people were unsure whose skeleton it was for a number of years), the public display of Fortune's skeleton was an unacknowledged sign of slavery as racial genocide.

In *Fortune's Bones*, Nelson creates subjectivity from what would seem irretrievable objectification; she also shows the necessity of fiction in telling about the lives of those enslaved who were unable to tell their own stories. In Nelson's imaginative recovery of a man otherwise "stripped of his name, his story, and his flesh" (13), she reinvests him with personhood and subjectivity so that the objectified use of his skeleton provides a multifaceted critique of slavery. In his persona poem, Fortune rebels against the slavery that had so grossly contained and catalogued him. As he declares, "you can own someone's body, / but the soul runs free. / [. . .] What's essential about you / is what can't be owned. / [. . .] glory hallelujah [. . .] / I am not my bones" (27), Fortune fictively becomes a recovered subject, despite death, dismemberment, anonymity, and skeletal objectification. The creation of Fortune's voice is here representative of the neo-slave narrative's reclamation of the slave's experiences as central to the portrayal of slavery. This subjectivity further serves as a comment on the literal objectification of slaves as well as on literary and cultural tropes that also contain him.

The polyphonic layering in *To Be a Slave* is also evident in *Fortune's Bones*, for not only Fortune but others are also given voice in persona poems. While Fortune speaks in a later poem, Nelson also gives voice to Fortune's wife and to his master. In one poem, Fortune's wife describes her grief as she dusts "the hands what use to stroke my breast; / [. . .] the arms what hold me when I cried; / [. . .] and his chest / what curved its warm against my back at night" (15). In another poem, the master/doctor who rendered Fortune's bones describes "my dissection of / the former body of my former slave," detailing how "death softens the human skin, / making it almost transparent, / so that under my reverent knife — / [. . .] / it feels like cutting the whole world —" (17). Simply by contrast, the emotional power of Fortune and his wife's poems, particularly their voiced connections to life and to each other, counter the self-serving eroticism of the physician. *Fortune's Bones* is further layered with nonfiction material, from photographs of generations of the physician's family to close-ups of Fortune's bones. Nelson's poems, appearing on each right-hand page, are counterpointed by facing pages that carry visuals and a nonfictional account of the disposition of Fortune's bones and what little is known of his life. Throughout the text, fiction and nonfiction meet and separate to provide often vying reflections on Fortune and his remains. The overall layering of genres and contrasting viewpoints suggests the panoply of often competing voices that both clash and intersect on the objectification, reclamation, and definition of what slavery was—and continues to be.

• • •

Neoabolitionist, diachronous, and neo-slave narrative texts ultimately evoke and interrogate antebellum tropes as a way to explore connections between contemporary racial politics and American slavery. Although each of these genres expresses images of slavery differently, they nonetheless similarly argue—and demonstrate—that slavery has had a lasting influence on American culture. In their depictions of the "slave," these authors show the responsive nature of literature about slavery as they variously sculpt antebellum representations that have been re-formed in children's literature through past generations. Their representations are, thus, both "new" and centuries old.

EPILOGUE

Sometimes it's better to forget.
—Eleanora E. Tate,
The Secret of Gumbo Grove (1987)

Sometimes people need to
remember the pain, so they won't forget.
—Eleanora E. Tate,
The Secret of Gumbo Grove (1987)

In Eleanora Tate's *The Secret of Gumbo Grove*, that Miss Effie recounts otherwise lost lives to young Raisin Stackhouse who writes them down as a recovered history argues the importance of memory, story, and historical reclamation. History, for Raisin, becomes personal and a means of making sense of her world. It is also conflicted, unresolved, problematic, painful, and liberating. The representation of recovering history in *The Secret of Gumbo Grove* offers a metaphor of the rewriting and retelling of slavery's history that has occurred in America for over the past two hundred years, although in that two-century time period authors' motivations for their retellings of slavery have varied drastically. Nonetheless, there has been in the American psyche something essential in trying to define what slavery has meant for the nation. In some sense, retellings of slavery explore not merely what slavery *was* in American history, but rather what slavery *is* (in the present tense) to American society and identity.

Embedded with issues of cultural trauma, racial fear and anger, debates about citizenship, and more fundamentally, definitions of humanity and personhood, slavery is the "pre-history" or "pre-text" (Carby 126) of black/white racial politics in America, inextricably bound to designations of race and prescriptions of racial characteristics that often posit "black" and "white" as "utterlye contrary" (qtd in Jordan 7), irrevocable opposites both defined by the other and separated by that opposition. In *Democracy in America* (1835), Alexis de Tocqueville argued that "the real inequality that is produced by fortune or by law is always succeeded by an imaginary inequality" (222); stories about slavery variously interrogate or reaffirm "imaginary inequality" in a system defined by racial difference. As much as by the end of the nineteenth century slavery is "reconstituted [. . .] as the primal scene of black identity" in America (Eyerman 16), it is also oppositionally constituted as the primal scene of white identity in America (Rushdy, *Remembering* 27). In sum, the story about slavery is a story about race—racial oppression, conflict, and meaning.

What the study of U.S. literature about slavery offers is an opportunity to disentangle racial myths that have been reconstructed for over two hundred years in America, and in so doing, to examine the ways slavery "haunts the peripheries of the national imaginary" (Rushdy, *Remembering* 2). That successive generations have reframed representations of slavery by—consciously or not—drawing upon the antebellum genres of the slave narrative, abolitionist novel, and plantation story, reveals a recursive dialectic about race in America. Literature shows us as a culture that is inextricably bound to antebellum tropes even as authors seek to rewrite them. In its exploration of how images of slavery are borrowed, reframed, and reshaped from antebellum literature, *Slavery in American Children's Literature* shows the literary recasting of slavery as a documentary fiction of sorts, as authors attempt to tell of the past by reflecting the anxieties and hopes of their present time.

Children's literature, in these expressions of race and slavery, is particularly important because it functions as an ideological primer for adult citizenship, a forum that would lay the groundwork for the country's racial future. In many ways, children's literature exposes what adults consider most important, what they hope to pass on to children as a way to bring about their own vision of futurity. While the prefatory epigraph of *A Sequel to Webster's Elementary Spelling Book* (1844) by William Webster, son of Noah Webster, extols the power of republican childhood in its admonition to "educate your children and the country is safe" (u.p.), one could easily argue the question is *how* one's children should be educated and *what* versions of slavery and race provide for a "safe" country. In American literary history, the country's "safety" has been variously constructed in the protection of a stringent racial hierarchy, the acknowledgment of racial equality, slavery, and emancipation. How purviews of sentience, subjectivity, agency, and citizenship are defined by racial tropes offers an education that encourages not only an "imaginary" equality or inequality, but fundamentally, an "imaginary America," a cultural means of creating ourselves and our political realities.

Despite the obvious disagreements between antebellum slavery opponents and supporters, they both believed that to win the child was to win the future of the nation. The generations following slavery have not been merely passive cultural victims of antecedent literature; each has actively re-created historical identity and reshaped racial figures as a way to explore America's past and present. As the fictional Raisin Stackhouse of *The Secret of Gumbo Grove* writes a history of her town, she represents how children reframe and reinterpret voices from the past, actively joining the chain of history makers to formalize a new vision for the future. Tate's fictional protagonist, like young readers and students of history before her, reframes the stories she hears to create a new version of her community's history. Like her, in determining which story we tell, we determine who we are and what our nation will be.

NOTES

INTRODUCTION

1. Francisco López de Gómara, in Peter Martyr (D'Anghera), *The Decades of the Newe Worlde. . . .* , trans. Richard Eden (London, 1555), reprinted in Edward Arber, ed., *The First Three English Books on America . . .* (Birmingham, UK, 1885) qtd in Jordan 7.

2. For population numbers, see Kolchin 991. Kolchin notes that throughout the antebellum years, one of every three people in the South was classified as a slave. Also see Gutman 340 and Curtin, especially chapter 1, who discusses the problems of ascertaining accurate statistics. Jordan, chapter 2, discusses early slavery in the colonies.

3. See MacLeod, especially chapters 1–2, for a discussion of education as "an indispensable protection for the Republic" (26). Avery and Murray provide important studies of early American children's literature. Also see Levander, who discusses the intersection of the child and nationhood, particularly regarding issues of race.

4. Throughout this study, I use "America" and "United States" as synonyms; in this context, "America" specifically refers to post-1788 literature authored and published in the United States. Because I seek to examine representations that reflect an American consciousness about race, I intentionally confine my discussion of children's texts to those authored and published in the United States (although some of those were also exported, published, or read abroad) as a way to distinguish a specifically "American" children's literary tradition.

5. "Juvenile Anti-Slavery Society" (1837), which comprises an entire issue of *The Slave's Friend*, models a "Constitution" for young antislavery activists. See Keller and Crandall, both of whom discuss how children were fictionally and socially constructed as "agents of reform" (Keller 86). Keller focuses on abolitionism, while Crandall provides a discussion of several reform movements that solicited children's attention, slavery being the most controversial. Also see De Rosa, *Domestic Abolitionism*, chapter 4, for further information on juvenile abolitionists.

6. Davis and Gates have described the slave narrative and its "narrative antithesis," the plantation novel, as "locked together in a bipolar moment, as it were, or signifying relationship" (xvii). I add to that by pointing out the impact of the white-authored abolitionist novel. By contrast, the antebellum black-authored novel—as seen in Frederick Douglass's *The Heroic Slave* (1853), William Wells Brown's *Clotel* (1853), and Harriet Wilson's *Our Nig* (1859)—is more closely aligned to the slave narrative in rhetorical stance, presentation of slavery, and images of race.

7. About the curse of Noah, see Gossett, *Race*, 5; Fredrickson 60–61, 87–88; and its origins in Genesis 9:25. For a discussion of race theories, see Gossett, *Race*, chapters 1–4; Watson 35–46; Jordan, especially chapters 1 and 6; and Fredrickson, chapters 1–3. Gossett points out that the number of races identified by early anthropologists ranged from three to sixty-three, with debates about the definitions of "species" and "races" making the matter all the more confused. One early anthropologist, for example, divided humans into "two 'species,' each containing three races" while another defined "seventeen races and thirty types" (82). Gossett argues how, in a Darwinian paradigm, "races were thought to represent different stages of evolutionary scale with the white race—or sometimes a subdivision of the white race—at the top" (144).

8. See Fredrickson, especially chapter 2, where he points out that "when politicians justified slavery, they almost invariably did so largely in terms of race" (68).

9. For examples of this in literature for adults, see discussions in Burnham; Samuels; and Morrison.

CHAPTER 1

1. About Child's abolitionist writings, and particularly their effect on the *Juvenile Miscellany*, see Karcher, especially chapter 8; Mills, chapter 2; MacCann, *White Supremacy* 51–55; MacLeod 33–37; and Murray 46–47.

2. In *White Supremacy in Children's Literature*, Donnarae MacCann delineates "reformist" and "cautious" abolitionist writers for children and points out that "the storytellers were spread across the political spectrum: radicals were agitating for emancipation, and conservatives were cautioning that the antislavery movement was 'extremist'" (22).

3. As Davis and Gates have argued, the slave narrative "represents the attempts of blacks to *write themselves into being*" (xiii) in a society that sought their virtual obliteration. Over a hundred narratives were published by the close of the Civil War, and many reached what one could term "best-seller" status, enjoying repeated reprintings and appreciable sales. See Davis and Gates 319–330 for a bibliography of narratives; Olney, regarding common characteristics of the genre; and Andrews's *To Tell a Free Story* regarding the influence of white editors and reader expectations on the genre.

4. Slave narratives also countered proslavery fiction by arguing that the descriptions they offered of lived experiences under slavery were truthful. In her autobiographical *Incidents in the Life of a Slave Girl*, for example, Harriet Jacobs wrote, "reader, be assured this narrative is no fiction. I am aware that some of my adventures may seem incredible; but they are, nevertheless, strictly true" (1). "Truth" and "authentic voice" are, of course, problematic issues. For discussions of authentic voice in slave narratives see Andrews, "Novelization"; Kibbey; and Stepto 3–31.

5. Webster's *A Grammatical Institute of the English Language* (1783) was revised and retitled *The American Spelling Book* (1787), and later *The Elementary Spelling Book* (1829). It remained "a phenomenon by any standards," with

Webster estimating printings of nearly 10 million copies by 1829 (Monaghan 11). See Monaghan regarding Webster's speller as a "nationalistic tool" (13).

6. Webster was influential in the 1791 founding of the Connecticut Society for the Abolition of Slavery (Unger 173), served as secretary for the Hartford antislavery society in 1792 (Monaghan 66), and donated a percentage of the proceeds of one of his books to the Pennsylvania antislavery movement (Monaghan 96). He also authored an abolitionist tract addressed to slave owners, *Effects of Slavery, on Morals and Industry* (1793).

7. See Elson 89–93 for other early schoolbooks, published before 1830, that included criticism of slavery.

8. Since Cugoano was never enslaved in the United States and Equiano was taken from the United States to England, neither autobiography is specifically a narrative of "American" slavery. Yet they—and particularly Equiano's account—were important to the American abolitionist endeavor. Called by Gates the "prototype of the nineteenth-century slave narrative" (Introduction xiv), Equiano's narrative achieved immediate international attention. Originally published in England in 1789, its first American edition appeared in 1791. By 1850 it had gone through 36 editions (Davis and Gates xvi). For discussion of Cugoano and Equiano, see Paul Edwards, "Three West African Writers" and Andrews, *To Tell a Free Story*, especially chapters 1 and 2.

Questions about the accuracy of some narratives have been long-standing. Regarding the influence of other writers in Cugoano's narrative, see Paul Edwards, "Three West African Writers" 183–187. Regarding possible sources for Equiano's account, see Paul Edwards, who notes that Equiano acknowledged the influence of Anthony Benezet's *Some Historical Account of Guinea* (1762) in his narrative (Introduction x, xxi). Carretta, in "Questioning the Identity of Olaudah Equiano" and *Equiano, the African*, provides important analysis of Equiano's history and narrative.

9. Rollins notes that *The Little Reader's Assistant* "did not continue long in use in schools" (151) and Monaghan, that it "only ran to a few printings" (101). Its lack of popularity may have been due, as Monaghan argues, to its "heretical" nature (101), particularly in its use of unconventional spelling and its antislavery stance (200).

10. See L. Turner, who categorizes five periods of abolition: 1641 until 1808, when Congress prohibited international slave trade; 1808–1831, typified by calls for gradual emancipation; Garrisonian abolitionism of 1831–1850, marked by calls for immediate emancipation and buoyed by the religious fervor of the Second Great Awakening; 1850–1861, the "Second Period of Militant Abolitionism," with renewed abolitionist fervor following passage of the Fugitive Slave Law of 1850; and lastly, 1861 to the close of the war in 1865 (371). Children's literature does not always follow Turner's neat pattern. In children's literature, for example, calls for gradual emancipation can be found during what he calls the "Second Period of Militant Abolitionism." Also see L. Turner for an overview of abolitionist literature for adults. Regarding racial violence, particularly of the 1830s, see Curry, chapter 6.

11. While the idyll of life in Africa is often contrasted with enslavement in America, radical abolitionists nonetheless rarely swerved from notions of white Christian hegemony. Although in "Zamor and Hinda" (1838), the children "thank the Great Spirit who placed [them] in this beautiful world [Africa]" (5), in "Joggy and Lorina" (1838), as issues of colonization are played out (themselves fraught with racial and cultural prescriptions) one argument against returning once-enslaved girls to Africa was that it was "wrong [. . .] to send them away from this Christian land to a heathen country" (10).

12. To the religious sensibilities of radical abolitionists, slavery and racial bigotry were affronts to God, and children were instructed that differences in skin color may be obvious to people, but God saw no distinction; as the poem *The Anti-Slavery Alphabet* (1847) told its young readers: "B is a Brother with a skin / Of somewhat darker hue, / But in our Heavenly Father's sight, / He is as dear as you" (u.p.). Although *The Anti-Slavery Alphabet* was published anonymously, Hannah and Mary Townsend have been identified as its authors (De Rosa, *Into the Mouths* 71). The *Alphabet* was sold at antislavery fairs to raise money for the cause. See De Rosa, *Into the Mouths* 71–72 and Sledge for estimated amounts raised.

13. Black children were not incidental to slavery; Duane notes research that records a slave ship in 1790 listing ninety percent of its captives as children and that on the *Henrietta Marie*, recovery experts found "over eighty pairs of shackles designed expressly for children's hands" (143). Duane cites Wilma King's work, *African Childhoods* (Palgrave Macmillan, 2005), as her source. Also see Duane 14–15, 125–164.

14. Jacobs also warned against appropriation of the slave's suffering, arguing that "only by experience can any one realize how deep, and dark, and foul is that pit of abominations [slavery]" (2). White abduction stories often momentarily create the illusion of such "experience" for white readers reading through white characters.

15. The story was also reprinted in *The Slave's Friend* (1836) as a rare single piece for the issue, although Child is not acknowledged as its author. There are minor, but intriguing differences in the two versions. *The Slave's Friend*, for example, adds to Child's story with a preface to readers regarding a newspaper account of a young white girl "stained black and sold for a SLAVE" (1). For other critical views on "Mary French and Susan Easton," see Crandall 15, Karcher 165–168, and Taketani. For further discussion of Child's work at *Juvenile Miscellany*, see Avery 83–84 and Karcher, especially chapters 3 and 7, where she examines the *Miscellany* in terms of Child's commitment to abolition.

16. See Genovese and Gutman regarding the moral codes of slave communities, distinct from those expected from white masters. For the somewhat problematic identification of Henson as model for the Uncle Tom character, see Gossett, *"Uncle Tom's Cabin" and American Culture*, 107–109; Andrews, *To Tell a Free Story*, 122; Winks; and Fisher. The 1858 edition of Henson's narrative included an introduction by Stowe (Bontemps, "Slave Narrative" xvii–

xviii) and following that, Henson was permanently identified as the model for Uncle Tom.

17. Despite Christian prohibitions, suicide was often one avenue of agency that radical abolitionists literarily allowed slaves, even more so than escaping to the North. Suicide is represented as an escape from slavery and a hope for reunion and rebirth. One sees this, for example, in "Zamor and Hinda," which tells of two siblings kidnapped from Africa and taken aboard a slave ship. When the young girl dies, her body thrown overboard by sailors, her brother "sprang over the side of the vessel, exclaiming, 'I will meet thee, sister, in the land of souls'" (12). Choosing suicide over enslavement obviously expresses one's anguish, but in presenting it as the central alternative to acquiescing to slavery, radical abolitionists erased a plethora of other rebellious responses found in narratives.

18. See, for example, "Bowie Knife" (1838), and for descriptions of mob violence, see "Mobs," "How to Get Up a Mob," and Garrison's "Mob in Philadelphia," all of them published in 1839.

19. See Crandall; Murray 42–44; and MacLeod 104–108. Radical abolitionists often aligned themselves with the peace movement and criticized any violent action. *The Slave's Friend* reiterates admonitions for nonviolence and forgiveness: "Abolitionists should all be peacemakers. [. . .] We want all the slaves to be peaceful and forgiving" ("Peace-Maker" 5). When Reverend Lovejoy was killed by an angry mob, radical abolitionist writers for children simultaneously lauded his abolitionism and criticized how he and friends had tried to defend themselves with guns, telling readers, "I wish he had died without having a gun in his hands" ("Elijah P. Lovejoy" 5).

20. See the illustrations accompanying "The Bond Slave" (1836); "The Poor Mother" (1836); "The Afflicted Mother" (1836); "Prayer of the Colored Mother" (1837); "The Slave's Address" (1838); and the untitled front page of 1.2 (1836), all in *The Slave's Friend.* The image of the female supplicant seems particularly positioned to evoke an emotional response from child readers, since the female adult slave in *The Slave's Friend* is often a mother, begging for her child's life. The white-activist agenda underlying the image inaugurates *The Slave's Friend*: in the magazine's first essay, a two-year-old white girl who has been taught to "pity the poor slaves" collects money for abolition in a box that holds an image of a chained African woman on her knees ("Collection Box" 3).

21. This image appears in the 1790 and 1791 editions of *Little Reader's Assistant* discussed here; this copy, however, comes from the 1798 fourth edition of *Little Reader's Assistant* (Northampton, MA: Butler), chosen for its visual clarity. For a visual image of violence in *The Slave's Friend* see, for example, the illustration accompanying "An Affecting Story" (1837).

22. See Yellin's chapter "The Abolitionist Emblem" in *Women and Sisters* (3–26) regarding the image as material culture. Yellin's analysis of the image provides clues to its popularity: The religious demeanor of the figure with hands and eyes raised to heaven; the tension between the human figure and

the shackles that imprison him/her (7); the "appeal to the heart" by figuratively expressing "the speechless agony of the fettered slave" (qtd in Yellin 5); its appearance in both male and female forms, which allowed female abolitionists an image that spoke directly to their own vulnerabilities; and the emotional impact of a visual image. Yellin argues that the male version of the supplicant slave suggests not passivity, but instead potential power (8–9).

23. See Andrews, *To Tell a Free Story*, regarding the role of amanuensis-editors. Andrews points out that "most early Afro-American autobiographies seem intended by their [white] editors and publishers to celebrate the acculturation of blacks into the established categories of the white social and literary order" (38). Slave narratives were often framed by authenticating letters written by white abolitionists who assured readers of the truth of the account and the reputable character of its author, as if the testimony of those formerly enslaved would not be believed without a white interlocutor. Regarding forms of authentication in slave narratives, see Stepto, chapter 1. Also see Matilda Thompson for a children's story in which a white mother functions as amanuensis for a formerly enslaved woman's account of slavery.

24. See De Rosa, *Domestic Abolitionism*, for representations of mother-abolitionists in children's literature, especially 99–103 for discussion of *The Young Abolitionists*.

25. First published as a serial, then in book form, *Uncle Tom's Cabin* was "the best-seller of the nineteenth century" (Douglas 9), the "first American novel ever to sell over a million copies" (Tompkins 124). Regarding the cultural effect of the novel, see Gossett's *"Uncle Tom's Cabin" and American Culture* and Bernstein, especially 92–133.

26. The children's version did not sell well (Murray 124), but that may be partly attributed to the fact that Stowe's original *Uncle Tom's Cabin* may have been their (and their parents') version of choice. The book's introductory note directs that the "verses have [. . .] been written [. . .] for the capacity of the youngest readers" while the "prose parts of the book [. . .] will claim the assistance of their older brothers or sisters" (Stowe, *Pictures and Stories* 2). The requested intercession of older family members is understandable since—with the exception of some vocabulary changes and major excising of text—the prose sections are often taken, verbatim, from the original novel.

27. *The Youth's Emancipator* faced financial problems almost immediately. Its second number urged subscribers to support the paper, and within a year editors wrote that they would have to cease publication without an increase in (and prompt payment of current) subscriptions. The periodical's content may have contributed to its lack of success: nearly "90 percent of its most significant material" was reprinted from other publications (Murphy 521), thus much of it may already have been familiar to readers. The magazine had the added disadvantage of not being visually engaging for young readers; it had no woodcuts and its pages featured three tightly printed columns of text. See Murphy for further background on the magazine.

28. Regarding black abolitionist activities, see J. Bacon 14–19; Curry 216–238; and Quarles.

29. See Curry 147–173; *History of Schools for the Colored Population*; and Murray 28.

30. For a study of *Freedom's Journal*, see J. Bacon.

31. Goodrich's publications included trade book, textbook, and magazine markets. Roselle points out that "Peter Parley books enjoyed almost unprecedented worldwide sale" (53). See Roselle 53–54, 71–72, 81 for publication statistics and a bibliography of Goodrich titles. About the appeal of the Parley character, see Roselle, chapter 3; and Carpenter 274–275.

32. See Elson, chapter 4, for a discussion of racist images in geographies. Elson points out that typically much of "the space devoted to each country was taken up by a description of what was considered to be the inherent mental and personality characteristics of a nation" (4). See Roselle 44, 73 regarding Goodrich's detractors.

33. Sold as volume 10 of *Parley's Cabinet Library*, this book was not written by but instead "prepared under the direction of Samuel G. Goodrich" (Roselle 170). Its title page nonetheless assured readers that the text was "by the Author of Peter Parley's Tales." Goodrich did not author all of the books that were attributed to him or "Peter Parley." Regarding other authors, including Nathaniel Hawthorne, whom Goodrich enlisted to write some of the schoolbooks, see Roselle 76–79, 115–126, 170 and Carpenter 200–201.

34. Such conflicted representations were not uncommon in children's geographies of the time. In *A Compend of History from the Earliest Times* (1840), for example, Samuel Whelpley denounced slavery as "the deepest abhorrence [meriting . . .] the heaviest curse of Almighty God" (156) while asserting the "merciless barbarity of those faithless savages [Africans]" (155). For further discussion of Goodrich's abolitionism see MacCann, *White Supremacy* especially 12–13, 58–69. Murray describes Goodrich's "cautious critique of slavery" (45); also see Crandall 13.

35. For discussion of black-authored antebellum fiction, see Andrews's Introduction, where he describes Brown's novel as drawing "substantially on the slave narrative tradition" (14).

36. Hatchie's power is also clear in the novel's two other illustrations of Hatchie striking a white man and saving Emily from drowning.

37. In an interesting parallel to Tom saving Eva from drowning, Hatchie also rescues Emily from the water. His adoration for Emily echoes Tom's for Eva when Hatchie describes her as "an angel of goodness" (111). MacCann, who categorizes Adams as part of "the cautious group" (13) of abolitionist writers, describes Hatchie as "a secular messianic figure in contrast to Stowe's evangelical 'Tom'" (*White Supremacy* 16–17). A psychoanalytic reading would find much to explore in the shifting relationship of the hero (Hatchie) and heroine (Emily); at times it hints at the erotic—of Emily as "the fair being whom he worshipped with all the lover's fondness, without the lover's sentiment"

(Adams 192). As Hatchie defends Emily's virginity, he is "almost maddened at the thought" (193) of men finding her defenseless. Then, at the close of the book, Adams describes Hatchie as a "fond father" (312) at Emily's wedding. The main title and subtitle of the book, *Hatchie, the Guardian Slave; or, The Heiress of Bellevue*, also emphasize the linkage between the two characters.

38. For discussion of the "Nat" stereotype, see Blassingame 230–248. Blassingame argues that "Nat, the actual and potential rebel, stands at the core of white perceptions of the slave" (230).

39. Broderick and MacCann each provide persuasive readings of *Cudjo's Cave*. See MacCann, especially for a discussion of Trowbridge's views about abolition and race (*White Supremacy* 61–64) and an analysis of the Toby character (20–21). MacCann describes *Cudjo's Cave* as "a quintessential collection of white supremacist beliefs" (20). Also see Broderick for a discussion of Toby and Barber Jim, a free black character (46–49), and of Cudjo (96, 105), whom she describes as "the prototype of the ugly black" (105) and discusses in terms of anthropological racial stereotyping.

CHAPTER 2

1. Regarding Jones County, see Bynum. Freehling cites the number of Southerners fighting for the Union (*Reintegration* 233). See Roark 1–32 regarding Southern whites' class conflicts and varying views about secession. Roark argues that while Southern planters disagreed over succession, they were united on the matter of slavery (2).

2. See E. Moss 20; F. Gaines 18; Charles Nichols 201; Yellin, *Intricate Knot* 60. For a discussion of Kennedy and *Swallow Barn*, see F. Gaines; Yellin, *Intricate Knot*, especially 49–62; and Ridgely.

3. The plantation novel, as a genre, functioned as an ideological "movement for defense" (F. Gaines 33) in the face of abolitionist representations of slavery. Author William Gilmore Simms, a contemporary of Kennedy's, praised Kennedy's work as "the most conclusive answer to the abolitionists that could be made" (qtd in Yellin, *Intricate Knot* 63). Kennedy understood the responsive role of the genre and cited the abolitionist debate—which he defined as "mawkish sentimentality [. . .] inventing sympathy for the pretended oppression of the negroes" (qtd in Osborne xl)—as the motivating force for publishing a second edition of his book in 1851. See Yellin, *Intricate Knot* regarding how plantation novels responded to political events at the same time that they narratively appeared to suppress them. The responsive nature of slavery literature is evident in the publication of proslavery anti–Uncle Tom novels following Stowe's *Uncle Tom's Cabin* in 1852; see Gossett, *"Uncle Tom's Cabin" and American Culture*, chapter 12.

4. See, for example, Daniell, who advises that slave mothers' breast milk be forcibly taken and withheld from their infants during the first ten days of the child's life. Stowe's *A Key to "Uncle Tom's Cabin"* (1853) catalogues published notices of and solicitations for the sale of slaves (129–130, 134–136, 144–147), reward notices for the return of runaway slaves (176–183), and advertise-

ments for dogs trained to hunt runaway slaves (109, 130–131). Weld's *American Slavery As It Is* (1839) includes announcements and reward notices for runaway slaves (152–156, 164–168). Such collections demonstrate how notices in Southern papers that revealed the actual workings of plantation life could be used by abolitionists.

5. For a discussion of the proslavery domestic novel, see E. Moss, who also contrasts the genre with the plantation novel (20–29). As Moss argues, proslavery Southern domestic fiction was "clearly influenced by the indigenous tradition of plantation fiction [and . . .] essentially duplicated its setting and cast of characters" (20).

6. Radical abolitionist authors for children also represented slavery issues through animal stories (particularly in stories that encouraged readers to treat their pets kindly), and thus also contributed to comparisons of animals and slaves. For discussion of this use of symbol, see Ginsberg.

7. See Blassingame for discussion of the "Sambo" and "Nat" stereotypes (223–248); Blassingame argues that the Sambo figure resulted from whites' "psychological repression" of fears of the "Nat" figure (233). Boskin examines the evolution of the Sambo image into the twentieth century. See Fredrickson for a range of slave stereotypes, and White regarding female slave stereotypes.

8. Regarding the master's valuing of slaves as attachment rather than commerce see, for example, Mary Eastman's *Aunt Phillis's Cabin* (1852), an anti-Uncle Tom adult novel written in response to Stowe's novel. There, a master describes how "we have a servant woman named Phillis, her price is far above rubies. Her industry, her honesty, her attachment to our family exceeds every thing" (137). For a historical analysis of attachment, paternalism, and "courtesy" between master and slave, see Genovese. Genovese argues that "paternalism's insistence upon mutual obligations [. . .] implicitly recognized the slaves' humanity. [It also . . .] undermines solidarity among the oppressed by linking them as individuals to their oppressors" (5).

9. A Northerner who moved to Charleston with her minister-husband, Gilman would become the most well-known female author of the antebellum South, her domestic fiction popular with women on both sides of the Mason-Dixon Line (Bakker 273; E. Moss 19–20). See E. Moss for further discussion of Gilman's work.

10. The nullification debates centered around South Carolina senator John Calhoun, who sought to protect cotton production and slavery by arguing states' rights to "nullify" federal intervention, especially federal tariffs. See E. Moss 72–74 for a discussion of Gilman's response to the nullification controversy; E. Moss points out Gilman's aversion to succession; also see Kenny 69.

11. *The Rose Bud, or Youth's Gazette* ran from 11 August 1832 to 24 August 1833. In 1833, Gilman announced a change both of the paper's title (to *Southern Rose Bud*) and main audience (to adults) ("Prospectus"). In *Southern Rose Bud*, which ran from 31 August 1833 to 1835 and comprised volumes 2 and 3 of the magazine, Gilman retained a column specifically for children which she titled, "For My Youngest Readers." She changed the paper's title again

in 1835, this time to *The Southern Rose*. The paper was also geared to adults, with one column titled "The Bud" for young readers. *The Southern Rose* ran from 5 September 1835 to 17 August 1839 and comprised volumes 4–7. Bakker notes the "widespread circulation of the Rose magazines" from New England to Cuba (273).

12. Regarding the fictional representations of plantations as separate, protected spaces, also see E. Moss, who describes how Southern authors sought "to quarantine the South from pernicious northernism" (19). For other discussions of Gilman's work in *The Rose* newspapers, see Bakker and especially Kenny. Regarding Gilman's "A Ballad," Kenny describes the plantation as a "retreat" (70) and "escape from the city" (69), and also points out that "the narrator's encounters with slaves only add to the plantation's peaceful ambiance" (70).

13. Although in "The Country Visit" series slaves do speak, Kenny points out that in Gilman's "A Ballad" "slaves appear as scenery rather than as speaking characters" (70).

14. For contrasting depictions of this, see John Pendleton Kennedy's plantation novel *Swallow Barn* (39) and Douglass's *Narrative* (49).

15. Bakker and Kenny discuss the socializing objectives of Gilman's fiction for children. See, for example, Kenny regarding Clara's socialization by her mother (73–75) and Clara's use of dialect (75–76). Kenny provides insightful analysis of Gilman's writing for children, particularly this scene of Clara on the plantation; several of my points here echo his.

16. Both Bakker (276–277) and Kenny (76–78) discuss "The Planter's Son." Bakker describes Gilman's presentation of "grateful dependents [i.e., slaves] who were capable [. . .] nonetheless, of a sly needling of their masters" (276). Kenny argues that Jim is a "realistic character in his subtle expression of resistance" and that his "apology at the story's end signaled that Gilman could not accept him as an incorrigible character incapable of improvement" (79). Regarding Gilman's stories about white girls who treat slaves badly, see Bakker who discusses "The Selfish Girl" (277) and Kenny, "The Mask Fairy" (79–83). Kenny argues that "Gilman's anxiety that white children [might be violent to slaves . . .] reveals the degree to which her plantation myth of genteel paternalism was false" (78). By contrast, I connect Gilman's fiction for children to her later domestic novels for women, showing their ideological alignment with the more pedagogically driven domestic plantation novel written by women rather than the male-authored plantation novel.

17. For an example of a slave's momentary independence, even rebelliousness, as a site of narrative humor in plantation novels for adults, see *Swallow Barn*, where the slave Carey makes fun of Ned's romance of Bel. Plantation novels generally depict slaves resistant to their master's authority as only hurting themselves or others in the slave community, as in Mary Eastman's *Aunt Phillis's Cabin*, where Phillis's dissolute husband finally accepts the master's stabilizing authority. Many slaveholders guessed that slaves were not as psychologically pliable as they outwardly appeared or as plantation novels

depicted. When slaveholder Mary Boykin Chesnut wrote in her diary of the war's initiating battle at Fort Sumter which she could hear from her home in Charleston, she noted: "Not by one word or look can we detect any change in the demeanor of these Negro servants. [. . .] You could not tell that they even hear the awful noise that is going on in the bay, though it is dinning in their ears night and day. [. . .] Are they stolidly stupid, or wiser than we are, silent and strong, biding their time" (38).

18. This illustration appears in Gilman's collection, *The Rose-Bud Wreath* (1841), which includes an edited version of "The Planter's Son." While Jim is described as a "small negro boy" (17) in the story's original publication (suggesting he is a child), in this reprint he is only described as a "negro boy" (63), which, in proslavery parlance, could refer to any black male, regardless of age, and he is not visually depicted as a child here.

19. In *The Religious Instruction of the Negroes*, Reverend Jones argues the importance of instructing children: "The great hope of permanently benefiting the Negroes is laid in Sabbath schools, in which children and youth may be trained up in the knowledge of the Lord. [. . .] If ministers are bound to assemble the *white* children, they are equally bound to assemble the *colored* children" (229, 231). He recommends that "if a people are to be instructed *orally*, let the instruction be communicated to them in *early life*" (229). Jones also offers instruction to ministers on the "manner of conducting Plantation Meetings" (267). While some Southern localities prohibited gatherings of free or enslaved black people during evening hours, one occasionally admitted exception was for meetings of "religious instruction, conducted by white men of good character" (*History of Schools* 309).

20. For the often-secret education of enslaved children, see King 74–80 and Genovese 561–566; Genovese also discusses different Southern state responses to slave literacy (562). He cites Du Bois's assertion that five percent of the enslaved population may have been literate, but notes that the figure may have been "too low" (563). Fox-Genovese estimates illiteracy rates as "well over 90 per cent" (156). See Freehling for conflicts about the religious education of slaves (*Prelude* 72–76). Regarding accounts of slaves who secretly learned or taught other slaves how to read, see Anderson 16–17 and also Douglass's *Narrative* (78–87).

21. The ordinance continues that "subscribers to or receivers of a newspaper called 'The Liberator,' are emphatically proscribed." Punishment for infractions included fines or imprisonment up to thirty days; free negroes and mulattoes unable to pay fines "were liable to be sold to service not exceeding four months." Such regulations "upon the colored people [. . . .] almost absolutely shut them up from all reading, as they were afraid to have any book in their possessions, scarcely even the Bible." Rights of assembly were also tightly controlled. An 1845 ordinance declared that "all assemblages, day or night, of black or colored persons [. . .] except meetings for religious instruction, conducted by white men appointed by either or any of the established churches of the town [, . . .] are hereby prohibited" (*History of Schools* 310).

22. Regarding the number of freed blacks in the South, the 1860 Louisiana Census, for example, documented that nearly half of the population—350,373—was black, and of that number, 18,647 (or 5.32%) were free (*History of Schools* 349). Regarding education available to, and often financially supported by, free blacks, see Curry (145–173), who describes New Orleans as "the site of one of the most substantial and financially secure private institutional educational undertakings" for free blacks of the antebellum South (157). Curry notes that by 1820 both private and public schools in all major cities were racially segregated, "with the possible exception of New Orleans" (150). Also see Curry regarding black educators in these schools (169–170); in the face of legal restrictions, many black teachers in Charleston worked in secret while white teachers of black students worked more openly (161).

23. Also see, *Little Eva: The Flower of the South* (c. 1853), which places Stowe's Eva on a plantation in "the bright sunny South" (2). A model young mistress, this little Eva enjoys teaching "the little colored boys and girls" of the plantation their alphabet (3). The proslavery plantation ideal of the mistress' noblesse oblige and slaves' adoration is depicted in a scene of religious education as Eva reads the Bible "to the colored people; [. . .] they would rather hear Eva read than read themselves, for they say her voice is so sweet; and she always explains all the questions they ask her so pleasantly, that it is a greater pleasure to hear her" (5). As De Rosa rightly points out, *Little Eva* is an "embattled text" in its presentation of slavery (*Domestic Abolitionism* 128). While, as De Rosa argues, the slaves' literacy suggests an abolitionist impetus (29), under the religious tutelage of Eva, these slaves enjoy life on the plantation. The Tom character (here named Sam) is given freedom after having saved Eva from drowning, "but he never left them, he loved them all too well" (*Little Eva* 8).

24. See Levine regarding coded language of slaves. For discussion of Christianity both taught to and revisioned by slaves, see Genovese 163–284. Kenny also discusses this prayer scene from "The Country Visit" (71–72).

25. In later editions, the book became more popularly known as *The Young Marooners*. Eight editions of the novel were printed in the United States before the Civil War (Kennerly 232).

26. Also see "The Goblin Swamp" chapter in *Swallow Barn*, where two white characters are lost in a nearby swamp (J. Kennedy 248–262). As Yellin argues, the "image is suggestive. There was indeed someone lurking in Southern swamps in the 1830s—perhaps [. . .] an escaped slave—perhaps old Nat Turner himself" (*Intricate Knot* 57–58). For a discussion of racialist discourse in American literature, see Morrison. The chapters "A Negro Mother" and "Abe," near the conclusion of *Swallow Barn*, present a more ambivalent description of plantation life: once the slave Abe leaves what is to him the stifling environment of the plantation, he becomes a heroic leader but dies at sea (J. Kennedy 461–490).

27. See Duane, who studies the antebellum conflation of slaves with chil-

dren. Duane argues that "fusing the child with the slave had become a common ploy of slavery apologists (as well as abolitionists such as Harriet Beecher Stowe). [. . .] As part of this shift, the temporal orientation of childhood—as a Lockean investment in futurity—realigned backwards. Rather than an emblem of yet-unrealized potential, the child came to embody a level of permanent dependence" (140). Her historical reading can inform the literary trope of adult male slave and young white child, as in *Robert and Harold*, where Sam is defined as regressively childlike; however, a necessary understanding of the trope's contrastive pairing lies in an appreciation of the inescapability of racial effect. Representations of white childhood still express the hope that a new generation will energize the (here, Southern) nation, while they define black adulthood in an oppositional paradigm of childhood marked by powerlessness and dependence. MacCann also argues that authors "hint at Black mental deficiency [. . .] by juxtaposing an adult Black character with White children and by demonstrating that the latter have more competence" (*White Supremacy* 135).

28. Broderick notes that a technique common to "the most biased of the southern white writers [. . .] was to put the most denigrating comments about blacks into the mouths of black characters" (116). Although Broderick was referring to postbellum writers, it was not uncommon of antebellum authors.

29. An antebellum term familiar in the South, "marooning" was further domesticated when it became "almost a synonym for 'picnicking.' Servants would row a youthful party to an uninhabited island and leave, or maroon, them there for a day of fun before returning late in the afternoon to bring them home" (Kennerly 231). One chapter of Gilman's serialized "The Country Visit" that describes a picnic is also titled "A Maroon."

30. The inaugural edition of *Southern Literary Messenger* called for the development of a purely "Southern Literature" ("Southern Literature"). Also see "The Duty of Southern Authors" and "Disenthralment of Southern Literature," the latter which acknowledges "it may be difficult [. . .] to exorcise the spell of Yankee supremacy" (360), but the South "must rid [itself . . .] of Yankee newspapers and periodicals (356).

31. The Reverend Marshall asserted that Southern states paid "the sum of nearly $5,000,000 per annum as tribute money, for books, and education, and abuse" to Northern authors and publishers ("Home Education" 664). Critics were concerned about a triple threat of Northern influence: of Southern students educated in the abolitionist North; of those educated in the South by Northern teachers; and of students reading Northern-authored books (see Marshall, "Home Education"). Of the three, schoolbooks seemed to be the most contentious issue. Regarding proposals to support Southern authorship and schoolbooks, particularly through legislative aid and intervention, see Heriott and also Marshall, "Home Education" and "Southern Authors." Calls for Southern-authored and -published schoolbooks escalated with the success of abolitionist literature, particularly the 1852 publication of *Uncle Tom's Cabin* (Heriott 652).

32. Kennerly points out that how one calculates the number of Confederate juvenile imprints depends upon whether one counts "every different edition of a title as a separate publication" (314). If one does, she estimates that between 150 and 175 books and periodicals were published for juveniles during the Confederacy. For publishing conditions during the Confederacy, see Parrish and Willingham's introduction, especially 11–22; Fahs, especially chapter 1; and Marten's *The Children's Civil War* 50–54, where he also discusses Southern determination to counter Northern publications in the schoolroom. For comprehensive listings and locations of Confederate imprints, including juvenile imprints, see Parrish and Willingham; also Kennerly 347–485. As Parrish and Willingham point out, the generally accepted definition of a "Confederate imprint" is a work "published in Confederate-held territory. Confederate imprints date from the time of a state's secession to the surrender of troops by a military commander or governmental official in any given locale" (23).

33. Wartime publishing conditions are sometimes acknowledged in the schoolbooks themselves, as in *Our Own First Reader*, which notes in its preface that "we are obliged to issue this volume without engravings, usually found in Primary School Books. Such illustrations could not be furnished in the Confederate States, and we would not have them from any other source" (Sterling and Campbell iv). Kennerly (325–328) and Carpenter (56) also point out that some Confederate books were bound in wallpaper because other printing materials were not available. Southern schools suffered the effects of war as well. Marten points out that "throughout most of the Confederacy [. . .] public and private schools fell victim to tightened budgets, invading Union armies, and patriotic teachers deserting classrooms for battlefields. Hundreds of schools closed, some for good; terms were shortened; attendance declined precipitously; and women and elderly men increasingly took over as instructors" (*Children's* 53).

34. The cover of the fifth edition of *Chaudron's Spelling Book, Carefully Prepared for Family and School Use* (Mobile, AL: S. H. Goetzel, 1865) notes "fortieth [*sic*] thousand" copies had been printed of the book thus far. The title page of Chaudron's *Second Reader* (1863) announces that it had been "adopted for use in the Public Schools of Mobile."

35. Also see Marten, *The Children's Civil War*, especially 50–61, regarding Confederate children's books. In his discussion of schoolbooks used to justify slavery, he notes racism in geographies and the depicted "beneficence of slavery" in a speller (58).

36. See Roark 35–67.

37. Kennerly points out that *The First Dixie Reader* was "popular enough to be reprinted at least twice during the war and even to appear once again in 1866" (118).

38. In response to abolitionist arguments about the exploitation of slave labor, proslavery writers often argued the financial independence of slaves, as did M. B. Moore, who described how Southern field slaves "often have as much pocket money as their mistresses" (*Geographical Reader* 14).

39. Marten explores the focus on war and patriotism in the few recreational books and magazines published during the Confederacy (*The Children's Civil War* 50–52). Also see Kennerly, chapter 4, regarding Confederate recreational books. The title page of *Boys and Girls Stories of the War* does not list a publication date or author. The Online Computer Library Center (OCLC) lists the publication date as 1863 and the author as Edward M. Boykin.

40. Fahs also discusses this story and points out how Ned's power in this scene is "diminutize[d]" (283). Also see Fahs regarding images of the returning slave in Southern-authored literature for adults during the war (181–189).

41. By 1863, "several hundred thousand former slaves had become free people within Union lines" (McPherson, "Civil War" 188). Following the 1863 Emancipation Proclamation, 190,000 former slaves joined the war to fight in the Union army and navy (McPherson, "Emancipation" 352). See Roark for analysis of "planter anxiety" (15) during the war, particularly masters' fears of slave revolt as slaves fled the plantation or were freed by Northern soldiers (68–108).

42. About the importance of elocution in Southern education, which was largely the prerogative of children of the planter class, see Kennerly 154–155; also Marten, *The Children's Civil War*, 56. See Carpenter regarding children's books on elocution (168–176). Chaudron offers elocution lessons throughout her *Third Reader*.

43. Confederate geographies differ from moderate and conservative abolitionist texts in that they do not discuss the Middle Passage, the culpability of white slave traders, or acknowledge African culture or the cruelties of slavery—topics that can be found, at some level, in abolitionist geographies. Racialized stereotypes that reflect widely accepted race theories of the time are common to moderate abolitionist and proslavery geographies. For comparison with Moore's *Geographical Reader*, see Goodrich's geographies (discussed in the previous chapter), where Africans are "characterized by great indolence [. . . and] gross barbarism" (*World* 207), as well as "improvidence [. . .] and thoughtless gaiety" (*Manners* 287).

CHAPTER 3

1. The Freedmen's Bureau was also charged with aiding Southern white refugees (Foner 69). About black student attendance, Anderson notes: "In Louisiana over 60 percent of all black children from five to twelve years of age were enrolled in school by 1865. [. . .] In the entire South in 1870, about one-fourth of the school-age ex-slaves attended 'public' schools" (19). For studies of the freedmen's schools, see Morris; Anderson, especially 4–32; Foner 97–102, 142–153; and M. Mitchell 188–230.

2. Teachers in freedmen's schools faced a myriad of obstacles, including little to no salary; uncertain living conditions; overcrowded classrooms, some numbering one hundred students (Foner 145); and threats of abuse from whites angered at the prospect of black education. About conflicts between former slaves and planters regarding education, see Anderson 18–23.

Regarding ex-slaves' financial support for schools, see Anderson, especially 5–12, 21–22, and Foner 97–100. As Anderson argues, former slaves' "self-determination [in gaining education] has escaped the attention of all but a few historians" (15). Foner points out that by "1870, blacks had expended over $1 million on education" (98). Regarding black teachers outnumbering white teachers, see Foner 145. The increase was also due to the opening of black colleges in the South—Fisk, Hampton, Berea—"all initially designed to train black teachers" (Foner 145). About black teachers in freedmen's schools, see Foner 98–101, 145–147; and Morris 85–130. Regarding problems faced by teachers and students of freedmen's schools, see M. Mitchell 188–190, 198–203.

3. Morris offers a sample of a typical day's curriculum at a freedmen's school (174–177).

4. Butchart points out that many freedmen's schools used common textbooks of the time, such as *McGuffey* readers and *Webster* spellers (135–136). Anderson also points out that "black leaders and educators adopted the New England classical liberal curriculum, so the subjects taught in post-Civil War black elementary, normal, and collegiate schools did not differ appreciably from those taught in northern white schools" (28).

5. See Mary Niall Mitchell for a discussion of the "civilizing mission" of many white Northerners involved in freedmen's education (91–142) and for debates about black postbellum education (188–230). She argues that "black children's education was often viewed by white politicians in terms of how it would affect white people. Schooling for black children would cause a race war, or it would stave off one, but it would not be, in these politicians' view, about the interests of the black child, but rather, the white race" (196). Also see Morris, who notes that white educators of freedmen often saw themselves as "raising the level of 'civilization'" of those formerly enslaved (173). Regarding the *Freedman's* schoolbooks, particularly how they served as models of "racial accommodation" (Morris 199–200), see Morris 198–202; Butchart 135–139; Karcher 502–503; Marten, *Children's* 61–66; and Anderson 30–31.

6. See Avery 98 and Morris 189. The ATS had edited out antislavery passages from antebellum schoolbooks they thought might offend Southerners (Morris 189); Butchart argues that the "ATS had equivocated on slavery right up to the war" (136). In the 1860s, the ATS began publishing materials specifically for newly freed people, beginning with large scripture cards which taught the alphabet, simple words, and short scriptural passages to gathered crowds (Morris 188–189). The ATS became the principal publisher of all freedmen's schoolbooks. As Butchart points out, "freedmen's education was not a sufficiently large field to attract major commercial publishers" (136).

7. Interesting in terms of gender representations, although single, white women made up the freedmen's schools' primary teaching force from the North, these covers emphasize the contributions of white male reformers.

8. See M. Mitchell for a study of the image of the black child in postbellum America. Mitchell argues that "as members of the first generation of African

Americans to grow up in the former slaveholding republic, the black child—freedom's child—represented the possibility of a future dramatically different from the past, a future in which black Americans might have access to the same privileges as whites: landownership, equality, autonomy. [. . .In debates about the] problem of freedom [. . .] the black child became both muse and metaphor" (5).

9. Compare to Henson's narrative, 132–137.

10. For other comparisons of Child's *The Freedmen's Book* to *Freedman's Third Reader*, see Karcher 502–507; Butchart 151–154; and Morris 202–209. That *The Freedmen's Book* is intended for adult readers is also evident in that it requires more sophisticated reading skills than does the *Freedman's* series. Moreover, its representations of rebellion and more strident tone differ from *Freedman* schoolbooks.

11. Peter Parley's *Universal History on the Basis of Geography* (1837) was published under the authorship of "Samuel G. Goodrich," but actually written by Nathaniel Hawthorne; it enjoyed over two dozen printings between 1837 and 1886. That the ATS used material from a Peter Parley book is ironic, since, as Roselle points out, the ATS had previously rejected the Parley books (81).

12. Page's *Two Little Confederates* was first serialized in *St. Nicholas* magazine from May to October 1888; Harris's "Daddy Jake, the Runaway" was serialized in the same magazine from March to May 1889. For further discussion of Page and *Two Little Confederates*, see MacCann (*White Supremacy* 136, 167–169). MacCann points out that the "plantation myth as a whole owes much to Page's defensive attitude toward the South and his skills as a mythmaker" (93). Goulding's antebellum *Robert and Harold* continued to be reprinted after the war, and in 1870 he published a sequel, *Marooner's Island*. Not as successful as *Robert and Harold* (probably because its focus shifted from the shipwrecked children to their father's attempts to locate them), its racial ideology remained the same. Simultaneously published in the North and South, it describes characters in racially disparaging and stereotyped terms: Judy's face is "homely as African faces ordinarily are" (20); her husband is "decidedly stupid" (20); and when Sam, who had been saved by the children in the first book, is shot in the head, he survives because his "skull[. . .] is very thick and hard" (474), a sure sign, in contemporaneous race science, of low intellect.

13. Even Pyrnelle's *Diddie, Dumps and Tot*, which takes place in the 1850s, ultimately shatters its plantation idyll. In its final chapter, Pyrnelle relates the war's catastrophic effect on the children: their father dies in the war; their mother, whose brain was "sickened" by "loss of her husband and home" is now a resident of "the State Lunatic Asylum" (213); the youngest girl, Tot, died before the war began; Diddie is a war widow; and Dumps is "an 'old maid'" (216) trying to support her mother. Their family home burned down during the war and the plantation remains desolate and abandoned, "just lying there useless, worthless" (214).

Pyrnelle also offers a paradigm for determining "good" and "bad" former slaves. "Good" slaves are apolitical or inept, like Uncle Snake-Bit Bob, who "does not meddle with politics" (238), and Aunt Nancy, who tried to learn to read, but then soon forgot what she had learned (216). By contrast, the violent Jim, who had once thought of killing the woman he would marry, "has been in Legislature, and spends his time in making long and exciting speeches [. . .] against the Southern whites, all unmindful of his happy childhood and of the kind and generous master who strove in every way to render his bondage (for which that master was in no way to blame) a light and happy one" (238).

14. MacCann, *White Supremacy* 159–161. MacCann points out that the novel was "immensely popular with White audiences" (97). For further discussion of *Diddie, Dumps and Tot,* see Broderick 12–13, 116–118, 136–137 and MacCann, *White Supremacy* 95–97, 217–219. Also see MacCann, *White Supremacy* for a seminal discussion of racist images and white supremacy in postbellum children's literature.

15. See Roark, who describes the effect of the war on the planter class, especially 35–108. He argues that the plantation "was the heart of the master's world. It was the source of wealth, status, power, and often identity itself [. . . . ,] the concrete expression of what was for many others an elusive abstraction—'the Southern way of life'" (35). Roark explores the postwar proslavery position of plantation owners, pointing out that "when abolition arrived, planters were engaged in both an intellectual and a military defense of their slave-plantation system. War destroyed slavery, but it did not provide masters with a common, workable set of ideas to replace their old beliefs" (107). This intellectual intractability underpinned the cult of the Lost Cause, which glorified the Confederacy and antebellum Southern life. Regarding early constructions of race in the United States, see Jordan; also see Rushdy, who argues that "the culture of slavery gave birth to whiteness" (*Remembering* 27).

16. See White regarding the myth of the "Mammy" and the lived reality of female slaves (especially 46–61). White points out that the Mammy figure was more glorified in the postbellum years (165). At the same time, the violence of Mammies against black children escalates in postplantation books, perhaps expressing postbellum white authors' need to idealize white charges and denigrate black children. Also see MacCann, who discusses the Mammy figure in Pyrnelle's novel (*White Supremacy* 95–96).

In contrast to the Mammy figure, Pyrnelle also introduces a slave mother devoted to her child, but Pyrnelle notes that such devotion "was unusual in a slave" (102); her devotion may be attributed to race, since she is "almost white" (101). The children meet this woman at a speculator's camp described as "a very bright scene [. . . . where] numbers of little negroes were playing about" (98). For discussion of this scene, see Broderick 116–118.

17. Compare how young Rip orders slaves about in the antebellum *Swallow Barn* (J. Kennedy 118–119, 310). Some postplantation novels present scapegoating violence toward young slaves as cathartic for unrepentant slaveholders. One sees this in Thomas Bailey Aldrich's *The Story of a Bad Boy* (1869): the young white protagonist describes how, in a fit of irritation, "I instantly kicked over the little negro boy who happened to be standing

by me at the moment" (5). Unlike the lessoning in Caroline Gilman's antebellum plantation fiction, the protagonist is not chastised for his bullying. After all, as he tells us, "as for kicking little Sam—I *always* did that, more or less gently, when anything went wrong with me" (7). For a fascinating discussion about nineteenth-century "scripting" of black dolls, including white violence enacted upon them, see Bernstein, especially chapter 5. Such violence, Bernstein argues, "both masked and delivered the powerful libel that African Americans were doll-like and insensate, and were appropriate objects for white violent fun" (221).

18. For discussion of the racialized "beast" or "brute" stereotype, see Fredrickson 275–280. Broderick discusses this stereotype in children's literature (93–102).

19. In chapter 1 of *Diddie, Dumps and Tot*, for example, the white children enjoy going to the quarters to watch slave children in prayers or receiving supposed health potions, but the central descriptions of each entail violence. Slave children receive "a sharp cut with a long switch" (Pyrnelle 16) during prayers, and the health potions are often accompanied with a "whipping" (18) or painful hair pulling (18–19).

20. See MacCann, *White Supremacy* 96–97 regarding minstrelsy in *Diddie, Dumps and Tot*. For discussion of minstrelsy in American culture, see Lott, who describes how the form is dependent upon a "'borrowing' of black cultural materials for white dissemination, a borrowing that ultimately depended on the material relations of slavery, [while] the minstrel show obscured these relations by pretending that slavery was amusing, right, and natural" (*Love* 3). One could argue that the various plantation genres become minstrel shows in their white creation of black slave characters.

21. See Gossett, who examines representations of Indians and Africans (*Race* 198–252).

22. See Roberts for a study of "subversive behaviors" (32) and folk heroes within slave communities. For studies of "conjurer" slaves whose power was feared, see Genovese, especially 215–227, and Blassingame 109–113. As a contrast, Uncle Balla in Page's *Two Little Confederates* is a stereotypical "Uncle" and uncomplicated Sambo—loyal to his mistress and her two sons, but rarely competent. Although an adult, he often functions as a "companion" (91) to the boys, implicitly affirming their (and white readers') sense of racial superiority.

23. The tales met with great popular success; ten *Uncle Remus* collections by Harris were published, totaling two hundred twenty tales in all. For background on Harris and the development of the Remus character, see Bickley, especially chapter 3, and Hemenway. Francis Gaines argues that "among masters of plantation literature, Harris must be given highest rank" (75). See Bernstein for a discussion of how Harris rescripted elements of Stowe's *Uncle Tom's Cabin* in his creation of *Uncle Remus* (133–141).

24. The tales reflect the coded world one sees in antebellum slave narratives. Like Frederick Douglass, who rebelled against his master by feigning "carelessness" and letting the master's horse run away (*Narrative* 42), or

Harriet Jacobs, who engaged in a battle of wits with her master, the most well-known character of the collection, Brer Rabbit, stands as the preeminent trickster. See Blassingame 127–130 and Levine 81–135 regarding the coded language and purposes of folktales within the slave community. Levine argues that slave tales "created the necessary space between the slaves and their owners and were the means of preventing legal slavery from becoming spiritual slavery" (80). See Roberts regarding the use of trickster stories in slave culture and Connolly, "Crossing Borders" regarding multiaged audiences of the tales. Kibbey describes the "linguistic virtuosity" of slave language (180); Genovese describes how slaves' language "throve on ambiguity and *double-entendre* and passed into para-language" (436).

25. See Watson, who discusses the "aristocratic myth" which included "the conviction that the region's slaveholders had descended almost entirely from the English Cavalier aristocracy" (15). In *Diddie, Dumps and Tot,* even the slave whom the girls return to his master recognizes that master is "no born gemmun [gentleman]" but instead "only er oberseer wat made 'im er little money, an' bought 'im er few niggers" (173). This distinction of class (and ultimately racial subcategories), which is dependent upon bloodline and not money, becomes important, particularly postslavery, as a way to reestablish the "true" master class when that former master class is impoverished.

26. The refashioning also benefits business activities on the plantation itself. As much as the proslavery position typically denies the fitness of slaves to support themselves, antebellum plantation stories as well as postplantation ones nonetheless depict slaves as inventive capitalistic entrepreneurs who trade, sell, or buy goods. In the antebellum "The Country Visit," when Clara's mother distributes fish and tobacco to the slaves, "many of the negroes came back with eggs, groundnuts, poultry of their own raising, [. . .] to purchase more of her" (Gilman, "little Negroes"). Similarly, in Page's *Two Little Confederates,* the "negroes [slaves] all had hen-houses and raised their own chickens, and when a camp was near them they used to drive a thriving trade on their own account, selling eggs and chickens" (19).

27. *The Adventures of Huckleberry Finn* was published in December 1884 in England, and February 1885 in the United States. For a sampling of varied critical views of the novel's racial politics, see Trites, especially 35–44; Graff and Phelan 279–479; D. Smith; and Lott, "Mr. Clemens." For reviews of the novel at the time of its publication, see Budd 259–280. For discussions of its audience, especially how the text functions as children's or adolescent literature, see Trites; also B. Clark 77–101.

28. Mary Niall Mitchell, for example, points out that many former abolitionists turned their attention to issues facing American Indians (139–140).

29. About the fracturing of the women's movement and the racism of Stanton's and Anthony's rhetoric, see E. DuBois, especially 78–104. Also see the Buhle, especially 1–30.

30. W. E. B. Du Bois described those enslaved as believing that slavery was the "sum of all villainies, the cause of all sorrow, the root of all prejudice"

(*Souls* 47); he goes on to describe the disillusionment faced by freedmen because of the broken promise of emancipation. Eyerman argues that African Americans of the late nineteenth century and early twentieth felt "the cultural trauma of the failure of emancipation to emancipate black Americans" (20).

31. See, for example, a series in *The Youth's Companion* titled "Eye and Ear Notes," especially "A Note of Introduction," "Old Uncle Abe," "A Peep into Slave Life," "A Slave Sale," and "The Slave Sale Again," all published in 1865, as well as Trowbridge's "A Visit to Mount Vernon" (1866) in *Our Young Folks*. In "How June Found Massa Linkum" (1868), Elizabeth Stuart Phelps explores the failure of Reconstruction. Also see Parris for a counterpart to Lesley Ginsberg's argument about antebellum literature; Parris explores animal stories in *Our Young Folks* that metaphorically call upon the reader's sympathy for freed blacks.

32. These stories are nonetheless infiltrated with racial stereotypes, as in the romantically racialist description of Uncle Peter who "loved to pray, and shout, and sing" (Carleton 735). Fahs identifies "Edmund Kirke" as James Roberts Gilmore (159).

33. Historian William Freehling has argued that the number of former slave and free black soldiers "made the Civil War a black man's no less than a white man's fight" with approximately 146,000 ex-slaves and 34,000 Northern free blacks joining the Union army (*Reintegration* 237). See Fahs 150–224 about popular representations of contraband soldiers, particularly for adult audiences. See Marten, *Lessons of War* 8–9, 41–46, 166–177, 187–190 for examples of contraband representations in children's magazines. For contrastive depictions of free blacks, see Lessels and Sterling about Jacob Abbott's antebellum series, *Stories of Rainbow and Lucky* (1859–1861).

34. A popular magazine with antislavery leanings, *Our Young Folks* ran during much of the Reconstruction period, from 1865 until its merger with *St. Nicholas* in 1873. Friedberg notes that the magazine's readers ranged from ten to eighteen years of age and that its circulation exceeded seventy-five thousand (330). I am grateful to Friedberg for her notations of stories from *Our Young Folks* related to slavery.

35. Many postbellum memorials—literary and otherwise—depict slaves' gratitude for the heroic white emancipator, particularly President Lincoln. In the schoolbook *A History of the United States for Schools* (1894), for example, authors John Fiske and Frank Alpine Hill include a photograph of a statue titled "Emancipation Group," where a former slave is free of his shackles but nonetheless remains on his knees at the feet of Lincoln, whose extended arm both liberates and contains him (405). "Emancipation" is represented here (as in Dolly Dixie's and Elizabeth Kilham's stories) as white acts of noblesse oblige more than black independence.

36. A response in the black abolitionist journal, *Provincial Freeman*, protested the options Stowe afforded her black characters: "Uncle Tom must be killed,—George Harris exiled! Heaven for dead negroes . . . Liberia for living mulattoes! Neither can live on the American continent!" (*Provincial Free-*

man, 22 July 1854, qtd in Banks 222). Burnham also discusses the role of the black body and emancipation in *Uncle Tom's Cabin* (118–146).

37. See Mary Niall Mitchell for an important analysis of visual representations of, and viewer interest in, young "white slaves," including viewers' sexual fascination with such images (51–90). Nigel Hamilton points out that the "precision of photography made it possible to extend the documentary scope of biographical depictions in the nineteenth century" (120). *The Youth's Companion*'s "White Slaves" image is meant to approximate original photography, and hence to claim a perceived authority of truth.

38. Regarding white fascination with "white slave" photographs, Mary Niall Mitchell argues the photographs served "as an augur of the racial implications of emancipation, [for they . . .] hinted at the uncertain future of the 'Anglo-Saxon' race [. . .]. A population of people [. . .] who looked 'white' but were not, would cast doubt on the alleged racial purity of all 'white' people" (56).

39. According to the *Dictionary of North Carolina Biography, A School History of the Negro Race in America* was the first textbook by an African American that was "approved by the North Carolina State Board of Education for use in public schools," although it is unclear how widespread its use was (Gatewood 288). The OCLC lists ten editions of the book between 1890 and 1911. Children in many schools across the country would not have had ready access to Johnson's text (or earlier *Freedman's* books), so it was unlikely this reclamation of slave figures reached wide (including white) audiences. Regarding racial terms, Johnson uses "Negro" and specifies that "*Negro* is written with a capital *N*. It deserves to be so enlarged and will help, perhaps, to magnify the race it stands for in the minds of those who see it" (5).

40. Elson notes that, following the Civil War, "the Negro, having been granted freedom, disappears from the schoolbooks" (96). See Elson 93–98 for a discussion of postwar schoolbooks. Elson argues that the "child influenced by these books would be unlikely to see the Negro as a participant in and a contributor to American culture" (98).

41. Johnson-Feelings notes that with variations in its title, *Floyd's Flowers* was "printed in at least three editions through 1925" (135). Other than the original 1905 edition, the OCLC records *The New Floyd's Flowers: Short Stories for Colored People Old and Young* (1922) and *Charming Stories for Young and Old: (Formerly Floyd's Flowers)* (1925).

42. About postbellum narratives, particularly their contrast with antebellum narratives, see Andrews, "Representation of Slavery" and McDowell's "Telling Slavery." Of the post-Reconstruction years, Eyerman argues, "for blacks, this rejection after the raised expectations engendered by emancipation and reconstruction forced a rethinking of their relationship to American society. This was traumatic not only because of crushed expectations but also because it necessitated a reevaluation of the past and its meaning regarding individual and collective identity. [. . .] Once again it would be necessary to attempt to transform tragedy into triumph with the uncovering of new strate-

gies in the struggle for collective recognition, in the face of the threat of marginalization" (24).

43. Gates argues that Douglass was "the most representative colored man both because he represented black people most eloquently and elegantly, and because he was the race's great opportunity to re-present their public selves in order to reconstruct their public, reproducible images" ("Trope" 129). Turning away from slavery is central in the image; Gates traces the figure of the New Negro from 1895 to 1925, a period he calls "the era of the myth of the New Negro" ("Trope" 132), and argues that the term "New Negro" simultaneously suggests "a temporal order of succession and an ahistorical American experience" (133). Also see Eyerman 61–75. For visual images of the "New" and "Old" Negro, see Gates, "Trope." For a nostalgic description of "The Old-Time Negro," see Page, *Negro*, especially chapter 6.

CHAPTER 4

1. The race of the children is read through illustrations; the verbal text never defines their race. Julia Mickenberg notes that *Two Is a Team* is "often considered the first interracial picture book" (129). The book has also been described as a counterpoint to *Dick and Jane* books, "with a black boy replacing Jane" (qtd in Dianne Johnson 47). Dianne Johnson notes that "this replacement is what renders the book a breakthrough" (47).

2. See Deane for discussion of racial stereotypes in series fiction; Murray, regarding racial images in the first Nancy Drew book, *The Secret of the Old Clock* (161–165); and MacCann, "Nancy Drew," regarding racial stereotypes in original and revised editions of the Nancy Drew series. Murray points out that "even though children's literature [. . .] had become a flourishing business by the 1920s, the America that these stories reflected was culturally, ethnically, religiously, and racially extremely narrow" (116).

3. Helen Bannerman's *The Story of Little Black Sambo* enjoyed much success in the United States. Murray notes its U.S. editions by Frederick Stokes (1900), Reilly and Britton (1905), Cupples and Leon (1917), and the "extremely popular" edition by A. Whitman and Company (1925) (134). See Michelle Martin for an analysis of *Little Black Sambo*, particularly distinguishing between its illustrations and story in terms of racial stereotyping. Also see Martin regarding racist depictions in picture books from the late nineteenth through the twentieth century (19–46).

4. The pervasiveness of plantation ideology is also evident in cartoons of the time that revealed a hostility to emancipation. Stowe's *Uncle Tom's Cabin* was a favorite subject for parody, as in *Uncle Tom and Little Eva* (1932), *Mickey's Mellerdrammer* (1933) featuring Mickey Mouse in blackface, *Eliza on the Ice* (1944) featuring Mighty Mouse, and *Uncle Tom's Cabaña* (1947). In *Uncle Tom and Little Eva*, slave characters—as monkeys, mice, and dogs—shuffle and dance their way through field work and on the auction block. A forced slave coffle transforms into a dancing, singing group of chained animals that follow

a placard announcing, "Slave Auction To-Day," as if participating in a celebratory parade; its contrast with the slave coffle scene from Webster's abolitionist "Story of the Treatment of African Slaves" (1790) is striking. Eliza's desperate flight across the frozen river in *Eliza on the Ice* becomes a comedy in choreography, with dancing dogs chasing Eliza, who performs *grands jetés* across the ice. While Legree remains the quintessential villain, once he is defeated—in *Uncle Tom and Little Eva* by Tom and in *Eliza on the Ice* by Mighty Mouse—Eliza and her child happily return to the plantation, which, these animated shorts assure their child and adult audiences, is the home of choice for slaves. Also see *Ethnic Notions* (1987) regarding racial stereotypes, particularly of the Mammy and Sambo, in cartoons and popular media.

5. The first *Miss Minerva* book, *Miss Minerva and William Green Hill* (1909), was the only one of the series written by Frances Boyd Calhoun, who died several months after its publication. The book was an immediate success and by the 1950s had undergone fifty printings (J. Wilson 69). After Calhoun's death, the series' publishers hired Emma Speed Sampson to continue the series; she authored ten more *Miss Minerva* books (1918–1939) that similarly enjoyed publishing success.

6. In *Miss Minerva Broadcasts Billy*, Sampson acknowledges racial discord in Fat Molly, a "negress" who "had no use for white folks" (77). A counterpoint to Deci and Aunt Cindy, Aunt Molly lives at The Dump where she picks over trash and is aggressive—"scream[ing]" at Billy when he calls her "Aunt Molly": "I ain't yo' Aunt Molly nor nobody's Aunt Molly" (79). Sampson situates Fat Molly's poverty, alienation, and anger as a result of the fact that Molly "had no regard for the 'quality,' never having lived with them or known them. Molly had been born in the midst of slavery, but of free parents. As was often the case in the southern states, what was known as a 'free nigger' had no standing with the better class of his or her own race and was, in consequence, somewhat of an outcast" (77–78). Danger to amicable race relations, here, comes from those who had never known the supposed civilizing effects of slavery. (See also J. Wilson 71–72.)

7. See Gossett for discussion of exaggerated naming as minstrel humor (*Race* 283). Regarding the choice of "Iovory" as a name, see M. Mitchell, who discusses late nineteenth-century soap advertisements that illustrated "before-and-after scenario[s . . .]—'black' adults or children with part of their face or arms scrubbed 'white' with the advertiser's product" (120). M. Mitchell describes such advertisements as representative of "evolutionary racism" (131).

8. For another example of a neoplantation novel, see Laura Lee Hope's *The Bobbsey Twins in the Land of Cotton* (1942). When the Bobbsey family travels to a Southern plantation, they find "a darling old mammy who looked like someone right out of a story book" (131) and "Negro" workers who all "looked healthy and happy, and each of them [. . .] was fond of the 'master,' as [. . . their employer, the Colonel] was affectionately called" (125). The Colonel assures the children that "cotton picking is healthful exercise" (134). Young Flossie Bobbsey feels that "it would seem funny—and nice—to have a servant all their

own," but acknowledges "'course we have Dinah and Sam at home, but they belong to Mother and Daddy, too" (127).

9. See MacCann, *White Supremacy*, especially 97–108 regarding representations of race in boys' adventure stories, including those by British author George Henty. MacCann notes that the boys' story was "the primary means of conveying the Black brute stereotype to the young" (98).

10. Also see Goldner regarding Uncle Tom and Little Eva as sexual fetish.

11. For popular adult representations of the fear of black men raping white women, see D. W. Griffith's *The Birth of a Nation* (1915) or the novel upon which it was based, Thomas Dixon's *The Clansman: An Historical Romance of the Ku Klux Klan* (1905). Fredrickson recounts pseudoscientific race studies of the "sexual madness" of black men for white women (275–282).

12. See Blassingame regarding the Nat stereotypes, especially 230–248.

13. Regarding racism and race theories of the 1920s, including eugenics debates, see Gossett, *Race* 370–408, Watkins 24–40, and Fredrickson, who discusses theories of black extinction and stereotypes of the black brute (256–282).

14. A number of literary critics have pointed out the narrow racial representations (in terms of both story lines and authors) and conservative racial politics of Newbery and Caldecott books, until recent decades. See Kidd; and Martin 85.

15. Dianne Johnson-Feelings writes that "the substantive development of African American children's and young adult literature began about 1920, the publication date of the *Brownies' Book*" (135). Katharine Capshaw Smith argues that Du Bois "reinvented conceptions of black childhood and instituted the genre of black children's literature" (1). Editors of *The Brownies' Book* were conscious of their historical role in the development of children's literature. After its first year of publication, the editors announced, "did you know that 98% of the articles appearing in THE BROWNIES' BOOK have been written by *colored* men, women and children? You see we are really creating modern Negro literature" (Editors).

16. In his announcement of *The Brownies' Book*, Du Bois listed the magazine's objectives: "(*a*) To make colored children realize that being 'colored' is a normal, beautiful thing. (*b*) To make them familiar with the history and achievements of the Negro race. (*c*) To make them know that other colored children have grown into beautiful, useful and famous persons. (*d*) To teach them delicately a code of honor and action in their relations with white children. (*e*) To turn their little hurts and resentments into emulation, ambition and love of their own homes and companions. (*f*) To point out the best amusements and joys and worth-while things of life. (*g*) To inspire them to prepare for definite occupations and duties with a broad spirit of sacrifice" ("True Brownies" 286). Also see an editorial in the magazine's "The Grown-Ups' Corner" (February 1921), which argues the dearth of positive black representations in popular culture: "The effect [on a child] can readily be imagined. He unconsciously gets the impression that the Negro has little chance to be

good, great, heroic or beautiful" (63). About Du Bois's views of children, see Diggs. Also see K. Smith 1–52 regarding Du Bois and *The Brownies' Book* and for an important discussion of "the centrality of childhood to the New Negro Movement" (3). For letters published in the magazine from young readers or their parents asking for or thanking *The Brownies' Book* for representations of black heroes, see Holland, Seymour, C. Moore, and Bradford.

17. Although for nine years the October issue of the NAACP's magazine, *The Crisis*, had been dedicated to children and family issues, Du Bois was concerned about the effect of the paper's explicit accounts of race violence on child readers ("True Brownies" 285). *The Brownies' Book* still reported on racial conflict, particularly in its current events column, "As the Crow Flies," which included reports on the Ku Klux Klan and current numbers of lynchings; as an example, see the magazine's February 1921 column ("As the Crow Flies" 53). See K. Smith for an analysis of how images of contemporary racial violence are represented and contained in *The Brownies' Book* (27–28).

18. See Kory for a study of the ways fairy tales in *The Brownies' Book* contrast Eurocentric fairy tales, especially ones appearing in *St. Nicholas*. As Kory points out, these tales signify upon the *Uncle Remus* tales in that Bagley "directs African American children back to their cultural roots and their elders" (107).

19. *The Brownies' Book* does not present an exclusively positive or "heroic" representation of slaves. Like slave narratives, some of its biographies acknowledge the complexity of the slave community, as in Aunt Katy, who was cruel to Douglass and other slave children (Wilkes 266); or slaves who betray Douglass (Wilkes 268) and Denmark Vesey (Allison 58).

20. In the preface to Frederick Douglass's 1855 autobiography, *My Bondage and My Freedom*, Douglass's editor also argued this distinction of truth and fiction: "the reader is [. . .] assured [. . .] that his attention is not invited to a work of ART, but to a work of FACTS—Facts, terrible and almost incredible, it may be—yet FACTS, nevertheless" (5). (This quotation comes from the original 1855 "Editor's Preface," written by an anonymous editor, not from the 2005 edition edited by John D. Smith.)

21. A number of the slave biographies in *The Brownies' Book* carry the subtitle "A True Story," such as "Katy Ferguson: A True Story"; "America's First Martyr-Patriot: A True Story," about Crispus Attucks; "The Story of Phillis Wheatley: A True Story"; "The Story of Frederick Douglass: A True Story," by Wilkes; and "The Bravest of the Brave: A True Story," by Wyman about Betsy Blakesley.

22. For discussions of cultural shame regarding slavery, see McDowell; Gates, "Trope"; and Rushdy, *Remembering* 10–22. Katharine Capshaw Smith discusses how the amelioration of slavery's trauma in *The Brownies' Book* reveals a perceived cultural shame associated with enslavement (188–204). African American authors writing for children—as McDowell argues regarding African American authors writing for adult audiences post-Reconstruction

through the early Harlem Renaissance—sought to mediate representations of slavery's violence to "soften those horrors" (McDowell 151).

23. Katharine Capshaw Smith argues that "*The Brownies' Book* was undoubtedly a response to the NAACP's antilynching agenda and to the 'Red Summer' of 1919 [. . .]. Tellingly, the first announcement of the children's magazine appears in August 1919, the month after the Chicago riots" (26–27).

24. From the antebellum years to the twentieth century, contrasting iconographic images of the American Indian as "noble savage" and the African slave as dim-witted and acquiescent were common. For an antebellum example, see M. Thompson 119–120. For a twentieth-century example, see Leo Huberman's widely read history for children, *"We, the People"* (1932). Considered a liberal text (Mickenberg 236–238) and although it described the horrific conditions of the Middle Passage (Huberman 16–19), it nonetheless argued that "when the early settlers found it practically impossible to make good slaves of the Indians [. . .] because the red man was too proud to work under the lash, they turned to Africa, where Negroes could be obtained" (16). Although American Indians faced near genocide, to an Anglo-American society that praised its revolutionary leaders for their proclamations of "give me liberty, or give me death!" the representation of American Indians as proud, fiercely independent, and rebellious caught white readers' imaginations in ways depictions of servile slaves did not. That mainstream publishers did not offer young readers stories of Frederick Douglass, Harriet Tubman, or many others who would have easily fit the American myth of fiercely independent revolutionary only reinforced that contrast. See Gossett, who examines representations of Indians and Africans (*Race* 198–252).

25. Regarding the "self-help ideology of racial uplift," Kevin Gaines notes, "believing that the improvement of African Americans' material and moral condition through self-help would diminish white racism, [African Americans . . .] sought to rehabilitate the race's image by embodying respectability, enacted through an ethos of service to the masses" (xiv). Gaines also explores conflicted representations of uplift, arguing that "racial uplift ideology constituted a complicated, contested appropriation of dominant racial discourses" (xix). Also see K. Smith who discusses its intersection with children's literature (xv–xix). See *Floyd's Flowers* and *A School History of the Negro Race in America* for examples of "racial uplift" messages to young readers.

26. Haynes's book *Unsung Heroes*, for example, was advertised in *The Brownies' Book* as a "new book of inspiration" for "the children of our time." (See the unpaginated advertisement section in *The Brownies' Book* 2.8 [August 1921].)

27. Dawson's book also serves as a corrective to earlier alphabet books like the Bontes's *ABC in Dixie: A Plantation Alphabet* (1900), which is a verbal and visual compendium of racialized tropes. Regarding the use of portraiture and photography as a means of biography, see N. Hamilton.

28. Regarding the African American–authored texts under discussion,

Haynes's collection was published by Du Bois and Dill, publishers of *The Brownies' Book*. Derricotte et al. and Shackelford were published by Carter Woodson's Associated Publishers. For an important critical study of the Associated Publishers and its books, see Katharine Capshaw Smith's *Children's Literature of the Harlem Renaissance*, especially chapter 4. Also see K. Smith for a study of representations of slavery in both Derricotte et al. and Shackelford (188–204).

29. Washington's assurances that former slaves "entertain no feelings of bitterness against the whites before and during the war" (13) would have been comforting to whites and probably an important reason why his autobiography was used in children's texts encouraging racial amity, particularly on the part of African Americans. Washington's *Up From Slavery* is a quintessential example of postbellum slave narratives that ameliorated the violence of slavery. For a discussion of postbellum narratives, see Andrews, "Representation of Slavery," where he argues that Washington's autobiography "signals a new wave of revisionism in post-bellum Afro-American literature" (64) and that Washington's position negotiates between accommodation and pragmatism. Also see McDowell. No biography of Washington appeared in *The Brownies' Book*. For Du Bois's condemnation of Washington's position, see "Of Booker T. Washington and Others" in his *Souls of Black Folk* (79–95).

30. Compare Washington's description in *Up From Slavery*, 3–4.

31. See K. Smith for an analysis of Shackelford's representations of slavery (173–180, 188–193). Smith points out how "Shackelford's denial of trauma becomes more ominous than any straightforward omission, for she frequently forces the reader to identify with the enslaver" (191).

32. The dedication of *Word Pictures of the Great*, "To Boys and Girls Everywhere," invites an integrated audience. Its preface also defines the book's content as "of interest to many children of third grade and above, and to adults. The book therefore may be used in intermediate grades and by classes in adult education" (ix). *The Child's Story of the Negro* was also meant for classroom use, and Shackelford hoped it would "find a hearty welcome from both pupils and teachers of the elementary grades in all sections of the country" (viii).

33. Haynes offers a contrasting representation in her biographical essay of Harriet Tubman, where Tubman first prays "oh, Lord, convert old Master; change that man's heart and make him a Christian." Then she "changed her prayer, saying: 'Lord, if you are never going to change that man's heart, kill him, Lord, and take him out of the way, so he will do no more mischief'" (91). An early version of this account is given in Sarah Bradford's biography of Tubman, *Scenes in the Life of Harriet Tubman* (1869).

34. See Eyerman 130–165. Eyerman also discusses the effect of 1940s'–1950s' "black-oriented radio" on the civil rights movement.

35. *Story of the Negro* also signifies on the first Newbery Award book, Henrick van Loon's *The Story of Mankind* (1921) both in title and content (for example, see Kidd, who calls it a "corrective" to the earlier history, 179). In van Loon's evolutionary paradigm, the "African" stands as a metaphor for pre-

historic man (473–474). When van Loon turns his attention to U.S. slavery, he condemns cruel treatment (422–423), but also argues that "negroes were strong and could stand rough treatment. Besides, association with the white man would give them a chance to learn Christianity and in this way, they would be able to save their souls, and so from every possible point of view, it would be an excellent arrangement both for the kindly white man and for his ignorant black brother" (422).

36. In the earlier *School History of the Negro Race in America*, Edward Johnson also notes the rebelliousness of the captives, but minimizes images of their violence. While Bontemps lauds Cinque's cultural independence as he testifies in his own language, Johnson recounts that the captives learned English "rapidly" and so gave their account of events in English (93). Also unlike Johnson's account, Bontemps never discusses nor commends the conversion of the *Amistad* slaves to Christianity, other than acknowledging the founding of an antislavery society in Africa under the auspices of the Union Missionary Society (*Story* 154).

37. Such complicity was not unknown among actual slaves. Josiah Henson, for example, had written in his autobiography how "heart and soul I became identified with my master's project" (48). Yet the emotional arc of Henson's autobiography is in his movement *away* from complicity with slaveholders. In Yates's novel, Amos has none of the complexity of the real-life Henson or even of Stowe's Uncle Tom, who tries to protect others in the enslaved community.

38. For a detailed reading of *Amos Fortune, Free Man*, see MacCann ("Racism"). For a fictionalized biography with contradictory representations of slaves, see Hildegarde Hoyt Swift's 1932 Newbery Honor book *The Railroad to Freedom*. Swift presents Harriet Tubman as courageous and intelligent, but unlike in *The Brownies' Book*, the slaves' physicality marks them as "grotesque" (82, 159). Heavily inflected dialect used only by slave or formerly enslaved characters also marks racial distinctions. Swift's ideological ambivalence navigates between abolitionism and a sentimental evocation of the plantation novel, particularly near the novel's close, when Harriet protects the son of her former master, then later grieves over his death. Swift's picture book, *North Star Shining* (1947), is more closely aligned with the perspective of *The Brownies' Book* in its sketch biographies (in poem form) that acknowledge the contributions of former slaves.

CHAPTER 5

1. As Carson points out about the *Brown v. Board of Education* decision, "black activism was necessary to compel the federal government to implement the decision and extend its principles to all areas of public life rather than simply in schools" (178).

2. See, for example, early significant studies such as Eugene Genovese's *Roll, Jordan, Roll: The World the Slaves Made* (1972), Herbert Gutman's *The Black Family in Slavery and Freedom* (1976), and Lawrence Levine's *Black Culture and Black Consciousness* (1977). Rushdy discusses this change in

historiography as a response to the Moynihan Report (1965) (*Remembering* 12–14) and traces cultural events of the 1970s that contributed to a revised representation of U.S. slavery (10–33), including Alex Haley's *Roots* (1976), which Rushdy describes as "the most significant seventies intervention into the discourse on the African American family" (14). Important analyses of race—such as Thomas Gossett's *Race: The History of an Idea in America* (1963) and George Fredrickson's *The Black Image in the White Mind* (1971)—also played a significant role in the revision of race studies.

3. See Wilkin for a study and annotated bibliography of African and African American images in Newbery Award–Winning titles. Also see Martin for an important study of children's literature authored by or featuring African Americans from 1950 to 2000 (50–72).

4. An 1838 essay in *The Slave's Friend*, for example, urged young readers: "Try to learn more about slavery. The more you *learn* about it the more you will *feel*. And the more you feel on the subject, the more useful you can be" ("To Juvenile Anti-Slavery" 9).

5. Compare, for example, Equiano's description of the Middle Passage: "The stench of the hold [. . .] was so intolerably loathsome [. . .]. The closeness of the place, and the heat of the climate, added to the number in the ship, which was so crowded that each had scarcely room to turn himself, [and] almost suffocated us [. . . .] and brought on a sickness among the slaves [. . .]. The shrieks of the women, and the groans of the dying, rendered the whole a scene of horror almost inconceivable" (24–25).

6. See Mathis and B. Tate for criticism of racial representations in *The Slave Dancer*; Mathis also discusses Jessie's objectification of slaves.

7. The scene perhaps unwittingly reveals the problems of white appropriation of black experience, and in this way reflects antebellum reformer debates. Early nineteenth-century reformers, from those advocating workers' to women's rights, often appropriated the term "slave" for their own cause, sometimes claiming they were even more oppressed than slaves of the South. While such appropriation may have revealed underlying racist assumptions (that slaves were not oppressed or, more probably, that whites of whatever situation should not be as oppressed as blacks), it also engendered an essentialist view of oppression—that white women, for example, by virtue of their gendered oppression, could understand what black women faced in the South. See Gallagher regarding how British industrial reformers used rhetoric about slavery to aid their own cause (especially chapter 1). In her narrative, Jacobs criticizes how the rhetoric of slavery was appropriated by reformers (see, for example, 31).

8. Compare the narrative frame of *Nettie's Trip South*, in which Nettie writes to a friend of her experiences, with "Soul-Drivers," *The Slave's Friend* (1837), where a boy writes his young cousin about witnessing a slave seller in possession of slave children.

9. See A. Moss for a discussion of this in *The Slave Dancer*.

10. Marten also points out how the treatment of soldiers depended upon

race: Black soldiers were paid less than white Union soldiers; if captured by Confederate troops, blacks risked being sold as slaves; there were also incidents in which black soldiers captured by Confederate troops were killed after surrendering (*Lessons* 221).

11. For an example of a neoabolitionist "rescuer text" with a white female protagonist, see M. Clark's *Freedom Crossing* (1980).

12. See, for example, the antebellum proslavery *Robert and Harold* (Goulding); the postplantation *Two Little Confederates* (Page); *The Adventures of Huckleberry Finn* (Twain); *Uncle Remus* and "Daddy Jake, the Runaway" (Harris); as well as the pseudoabolitionist *Glory of the Seas* (Hewes).

13. For a contrasting representation of racial interactions among peers, see the more recent picture book, *Friend on Freedom River* (Whelan 2004). When the young white protagonist agrees to take a family of escaping slaves across a river to freedom, he and the escaping boy Tyler are described as the same age, but depicted during the escape as working together as equals. Unlike Fritz's Moss assuming Brady's name, Whelan presents the black response as more than just an accolade to white agency, particularly from Tyler, who distrusts white people. Yet in the end, as the "two boys shook hands" (u.p.), Whelan offers a racially reconciliatory scene that also implies equality and mutual respect between young men.

14. For a similar account of a real-life infant given up by her captured mother, see "Little Adelaide Sabilia" in *The Youth's Emancipator* (1843).

15. Rushdy defines a "palimpsest narrative" as "a first-person novel representing late-twentieth-century African American subjects who confront familial secrets attesting to the ongoing effects of slavery" (*Remembering* 8). My explication of diachronous fiction also considers stories that focus on "family secrets," but includes third person narratives, particularly in picture books. See Rushdy, *Remembering* for a discussion of texts written for adults in the 1970s that represent palimpsest narratives.

16. See Dianne Johnson for further discussion of *The Secret of Gumbo Grove* (56–61); *The Lucky Stone* (83–91); and Virginia Hamilton's *The House of Dies Drear* (1968), which includes a present-day mystery about a house that was once a stop on the Underground Railroad (61–64). Regarding the storyteller role in contemporary adult literature about slavery, see Keizer, who discusses Margaret Walker Alexander's *Jubilee* (1966) and Ernest J. Gaines's *The Autobiography of Miss Jane Pittman* (1971).

17. Compare, for example, similar calls in *The Brownies' Book*: Seymour's letter (1920) and an editorial in "The Grown-Ups' Corner" (1921).

18. See Rushdy for a discussion of cultural shame regarding slavery (*Remembering* 10–22).

19. Dianne Johnson points out that *The Secret of Gumbo Grove* and Hamilton's *The House of Dies Drear* "relate histories in the form of mystery novels" (56) as these protagonists seek to discover secrets about the past. While slavery's history is suppressed in *The Secret of Gumbo Grove*, in *The House of Dies Drear* the father of protagonist Thomas is a history professor, thus

Thomas has been steeped in history throughout his childhood. As the novel begins, Thomas's father has bought a house that had once served as a station on the Underground Railroad; the house becomes a living history for young Thomas.

20. Although changing the race of the intended audience, such diachronous literature sharpens antebellum radical abolitionist calls to imagine oneself enslaved, as in "The Cart-Whip" (1837): "How should you like to have a cruel man follow your dear father or mother, about, all day, with one of these whips [. . .] striking them with it on their bare flesh? [. . .] You should try to put yourself in their [enslaved children's] place; think that it is *your* father or *your* mother that is whipped" (5–6).

21. Ringgold's use of time travel to develop an understanding of historical atrocity is evocative of Jane Yolen's Holocaust time-travel book, *The Devil's Arithmetic* (1988). For a discussion of contemporary adult fantasy fiction about slavery, see Spaulding, who argues that such texts "critique traditional history's reliance on objectivity, authenticity, and realism as a means of representing the past." He further posits that such texts "defamiliarize both the history of slavery and traditional approaches to writing that history. By deploying elements of the fantastic [. . .] in their texts, these writers force us to question the ideologies embedded within the 'realistic' representation of slavery in traditional history and historical fiction" (2).

22. See Eyerman and Caruth for discussions of cultural trauma. Regarding the difference between condition and personhood, note Jacobs's narrative, where she describes how her mother "had been a slave merely in name, but in nature was noble and womanly" (7).

23. About the slave-conjurer figure, see Genovese, especially 215–227, and Blassingame 109–113. For further discussion of slave tales, see Blassingame 127–130 and Levine 81–135.

24. Of *Minty: A Story of Young Harriet Tubman*, for example, author Alan Schroeder discusses the balance of fiction and nonfiction in biography, noting that he included "scenes [. . .] invented for narrative purposes, [although] the basic facts are true" (u.p.).

25. Biographies for young readers of Frederick Douglass include Margaret Davidson's *Frederick Douglass Fights for Freedom* (1968); Ossie Davis's Coretta Scott King Award–winning *Escape to Freedom: A Play about Young Frederick Douglass* (1978); Eric Weiner's *The Story of Frederick Douglass, Voice of Freedom* (1992); David Adler's *A Picture Book of Frederick Douglass* (1993); and Elisabeth Myers's *Frederick Douglass: Young Defender of Human Rights* (2007).

26. Some of the many biographies of Harriet Tubman, ranging from early through middle-grade readers, include: Dorothy Sterling's *The Story of Harriet Tubman: Freedom Train* (1954); Ann McGovern's *"Wanted Dead or Alive": The True Story of Harriet Tubman* (1965); Jeri Ferris's *Go Free or Die: A Story about Harriet Tubman* (1988); Judy Carlson's *Harriet Tubman: Call to Freedom* (1989); Kate McMullan's *The Story of Harriet Tubman, Con-*

ductor of the Underground Railroad (1991); Catherine Nichols's *Harriet Tubman* (2002); Maryann Weidt's *Harriet Tubman* (2003); and Thomas Allen's *Harriet Tubman: Secret Agent* (2006). See Sernett for a discussion of children's biographies about Tubman (11–40).

27. Sojourner Truth biographies for children include: Jacqueline Bernard's *Journey toward Freedom: The Story of Sojourner Truth* (1967); Jeri Ferris's *Walking the Road to Freedom: A Story about Sojourner Truth* (1988); Peter Krass's *Sojourner Truth: Antislavery Activist* (1988), and David Adler's *A Picture Book of Sojourner Truth* (1994). Biographies of other former slaves include Florence Freedman's *Two Tickets to Freedom: The True Story of Ellen and William Craft, Fugitive Slaves* (1971).

28. In the introduction to a Black Americans of Achievement biography, Coretta Scott King writes, "reading the stories of these courageous men and women not only helps us discover the principles that we will use to guide our own lives, but it teaches us about our black heritage and about America itself. It is crucial for us to know the heroes and heroines of our history and to realize that the price we paid in our struggle for equality in America was dear. [. . .] We are still struggling with racism and prejudice. But the great men and women in this series are a tribute to the spirit of our democratic ideals and the system in which they have flourished" (qtd in Krass 8). Biographical material for these books is largely drawn from antebellum narratives or earlier biographies, although the immediacy of voice found in slave narratives is often neutralized, both through the use of third person and through a frequent mitigation of rebellion. In the Young Patriots Series' *Frederick Douglass: Young Defender of Human Rights*, for example, author Elisabeth Myers quiets representation of slave narratives; when she describes Douglass's fight with Covey, she notes that "['Fred's'] aim was not to injure Covey but to keep Covey from injuring him" (91).

29. See A. Thompson for a discussion of picture books that focus on Tubman.

30. There are a few recent books about Wheatley and Washington for children. See, for example, Borland and Speicher's *Phillis Wheatley: Young Revolutionary Poet* (2005); and the picture books, *Phillis Sings Out Freedom: The Story of George Washington and Phillis Wheatley* (2010) by Ann Malaspina and Marie Bradby's *More Than Anything Else* (1995) about Booker T. Washington. Malaspina's and Bradby's picture books focus on their protagonists gaining literacy. For a discussion of other children's books about slavery that focus on literacy, see Chandler.

31. See N. Hamilton for a discussion of biography as hagiography (33–59). For a study of how hagiographic representation works in a children's text, see Cormier.

32. As Rushdy has defined it, neo-slave narratives are "contemporary novels that assume the form, adopt the conventions and take on the first-person voice of the antebellum slave narrative" (*Neo-slave Narratives* 3); Bernard Bell is largely credited with coining the term (289). For discussions of

the neo-slave narrative in adult literature, see Rushdy, *Neo-slave Narratives*; Valerie Smith, who provides an overview of the genre and the critics who have variously defined it; and Angelyn Mitchell, who prefers the term "liberatory narrative," arguing that the genre is "more than 'new': [it is . . .] more complex in form and content than the eighteenth- and nineteenth-century slave narratives" (4). Also see Ryan, who places current literature about slavery for adults as a responsive refutation of earlier literature (65–90). I use the term "neo-slave narrative," arguing that "newness" comprehensively defines the genre's re-creation and revision of the antebellum slave narrative, although I do not argue the necessary use of the first person.

33. See, for example, the antebellum poetry of African American author Frances Ellen Watkins Harper, such as "The Slave Mother" (58–59) and "The Slave Auction" (64–65).

34. See, for example, Lester's *Day of Tears* (2005), based on an account of "the largest auction of slaves in American history" (172). Lester describes his book as one in which "history and fiction have been blended" (175). In Raven's *Night Boat to Freedom* (2006), characters were inspired by interviews from the Federal Writers' Project's collection of narratives in the 1930s. Most neo-slave narratives include author's notes that point to a historical source for their story.

35. In contrast, see Tom Feelings's *The Middle Passage* (1995), the core text of which is told completely in wordless pictures, but—particularly in its scenes of beatings, rapes, and murders—is intended for an adult audience. Also see Lester's *From Slave Ship to Freedom Road* (1998), illustrated by Rod Brown, for a picture book with images of explicit violence.

36. Neo-slave narrative picture books are often told in the third, rather than first person, probably to mitigate potential reader anxiety about the protagonist's plight. Pamela Duncan Edwards's *Barefoot* (1997) and Vaunda Micheaux Nelson's *Almost to Freedom* (2003) demonstrate another technique to mitigate reader anxiety about the escaping slave. They situate the point of view in animals and a doll, respectively, to encourage the reader's engagement yet also to allow the child to maintain a measure of emotional separation from the scene.

37. Although *Follow the Drinking Gourd* begins with the arrival of a white abolitionist at the plantation, the point of view soon shifts to the escaping slaves; in this way, the text blends a neoabolitionist and neo-slave narrative perspective, but remains more focused on the escaping slaves' experiences. About narrative strategies used in picture books to balance representations of slavery's violence for a young audience, see Connolly, "Narrative Tensions" and Connolly, "Imagining the Escape."

38. In his *Narrative*, for example, Douglass criticized how the Underground Railroad has, because of the "open declarations [of some who know its secrets, . . .] been made most emphatically the *upperground railroad*. [. . . . Those] open declarations are a positive evil to the slaves remaining, who are

seeking to escape [because . . . .] they do much towards enlightening the master" (138).

39. For a contrasting picture book, see Dolores Johnson's *Now Let Me Fly* (1993), in which a mother and child remain—and expect to remain—enslaved.

40. Although Lester attributes this generally to "a white preacher to Virginia slaves" (*To Be* 79), the identical passage can be found in Thomas Bacon's *Two Sermons*. Also see discussion of proslavery religious education for slaves in chapter 2 herein.

41. Recipient of, among other awards, the Coretta Scott King Award and Honor, as well as the Newbery Honor, Lester's work in neonarrative and slave tales has ranged from folktales in his *Tales of Uncle Remus* series (the first of which was published in 1987); to his work for young adults in nonfiction and novel form, including *To Be a Slave* and *A Day of Tears* (2005); and to picture books, such as *From Slave Ship to Freedom Road* (1998) and *The Old African* (2005). Lester often moves outside expected narrative and storytelling boundaries in his work, as when he directly addresses readers in *From Slave Ship to Freedom Road* to call for an interactive response from readers; or when he deals with the sexual abuse of female slaves, as in "Where the Sun Lives" in *This Strange New Feeling*. See Connolly, "Still a Slave," about Lester's echoing of antebellum slave narratives in "Where the Sun Lives."

BIBLIOGRAPHY

Adams, Nehemiah. *A South-Side View of Slavery; or, Three Months at the South, in 1854*. Third Ed. 1854. Port Washington, NY: Kennikat, 1969.

Adams, William Taylor [Warren T. Ashton, pseud.]. *Hatchie, the Guardian Slave; or, The Heiress of Bellevue. A Tale of the Mississippi and the Southwest*. 1853. Freeport, NY: Books for Libraries P, 1972.

Adler, David A. *A Picture Book of Frederick Douglass*. Illus. Samuel Byrd. New York: Holiday House, 1993.

———. *A Picture Book of Sojourner Truth*. Illus. Gershom Griffith. New York: Holiday House, 1994.

"An Affecting Story." *The Slave's Friend* 2.12 (1837): 1–5.

"The Afflicted Mother." *The Slave's Friend* 1.8 (1836): 1–5.

Aldrich, Thomas Bailey. *The Story of a Bad Boy*. 1869. Hanover, NH: UP of New England, 1990.

Allen, Thomas B. *Harriet Tubman, Secret Agent: How Daring Slaves and Free Blacks Spied for the Union during the Civil War*. Illus. Carla Bauer. Washington, DC: National Geographic, 2006.

Allison, M. G. "Denmark Vesey: A Martyr for Freedom." *The Brownies' Book* 2.2 (February 1921): 57–58.

"Am I Not a Woman and a Sister?" *The Slave's Friend* 3.6 (1838): 1.

American Library Association (ALA). "The Coretta Scott King Book Awards for Authors and Illustrators: Selection Criteria." http://www.ala.org/emiert/cskbookawards/slction.

"America's First Martyr-Patriot: A True Story." *The Brownies' Book* 1.7 (July 1920): 216–218.

Anderson, James D. *The Education of Blacks in the South, 1860–1935*. Chapel Hill: U of North Carolina P, 1988.

Andrews, William L. Introduction. *Three Classic African-American Novels*. Ed. Andrews. New York: New American Library-Penguin, 1990. 7–21.

———. "The Novelization of Voice in Early African American Narrative." *PMLA* 105.1 (January 1990): 23–34.

———. "The Representation of Slavery and the Rise of Afro-American Literary Realism, 1865–1920." *Slavery and the Literary Imagination*. Ed. Deborah E. McDowell and Arnold Rampersad. Baltimore: Johns Hopkins UP, 1989. 62–80.

———. *To Tell a Free Story: The First Century of Afro-American Autobiography, 1760–1865*. Urbana: U of Chicago P, 1988.

The Anti-Slavery Alphabet. [Hannah Townsend and Mary Townsend]. Philadelphia: Merrihew and Thompson, 1847.

"As the Crow Flies." *The Brownies' Book* 2.2 (February 1921): 52–53.

Avery, Gillian. *Behold the Child: American Children and Their Books, 1621–1922.* Baltimore: Johns Hopkins UP, 1994.

Bacon, Jacqueline. *"Freedom's Journal": The First African-American Newspaper.* Lanham, MD: Lexington Books-Rowman and Littlefield, 2007.

Bacon, Thomas. *Two Sermons, Preached to a Congregation of Black Slaves at the Parish Church of S. P. in the Province of Maryland.* 1749. Reprinted in *Proslavery and Sectional Thought in the Early South, 1740–1829: An Anthology.* Ed. Jeffrey Robert Young. Columbia, SC: U of South Carolina P, 2006. 80–96.

Bagley, Julian Elihu. "How Mr. Crocodile Got His Rough Back." *The Brownies' Book* 1.11 (November 1920): 323–325.

Bakker, Jan. "Caroline Gilman and the Issue of Slavery in the Rose Magazines, 1832–1839." *Southern Studies* 24.3 (1985): 273–283.

Ball, Charles. "Charles Ball's Mother." *The Slave's Friend* 2.4 (1837): 11–14.

———. "The Mother and Babe." *The Slave's Friend* 2.4 (1837): 14–15.

———. *Slavery in the United States: A Narrative of the Life and Adventures of Charles Ball, A Black Man.* New York: John S. Taylor, 1837.

———. "A Slave's Cabin." *The Slave's Friend* 2.4 (1837): 15–16.

———. "A Slave's Dream." *The Slave's Friend* 2.4 (1837): 16.

Banks, Marva. "'*Uncle Tom's Cabin*' and Antebellum Black Response." *Readers in History: Nineteenth-Century American Literature and the Contexts of Response.* Ed. James L. Machor. Baltimore: Johns Hopkins UP, 1993. 209–227.

Beim, Lorraine, and Jerrold Beim. *Two Is a Team.* Illus. Ernest Crichlow. New York: Harcourt, Brace, 1945.

Bell, Bernard W. *The Afro-American Novel and Its Tradition.* Amherst: U of Massachusetts P, 1987.

Bernard, Jacqueline. *Journey toward Freedom: The Story of Sojourner Truth.* 1967. Introd. Nell Irvin Painter. New York: Feminist P at the City University of New York, 1990.

Bernstein, Robin. *Racial Innocence: Performing American Childhood from Slavery to Civil Rights.* New York: New York UP, 2011.

Bickley, R. Bruce, Jr. *Joel Chandler Harris.* Boston: Twayne–G. K. Hall, 1978.

Bingham, Jane, and Grayce Scholt. *Fifteen Centuries of Children's Literature: An Annotated Chronology of British and American Works in Historical Context.* Westport, CT: Greenwood, 1980.

Bird, Augusta E. "The Story of Harriet Tubman." *The Brownies' Book* 2.3 (March 1921): 84–86.

Blassingame, John W. *The Slave Community: Plantation Life in the Antebellum South.* 1972. Rev. Ed. New York: Oxford UP, 1979.

"The Bond Slave." *The Slave's Friend* 1.1 (1836): 11.

Bonte, Louise Quarles, and George Willard Bonte. *ABC in Dixie: A Plantation Alphabet.* New York: Dutton, 1900.

Bontemps, Arna. "The Slave Narrative: An American Genre." Introduction. *Great Slave Narratives*. Ed. Arna Bontemps. Boston: Beacon, 1969. vii–xix.

———. *Story of the Negro*. Illus. Raymond Lufkin. New York: Alfred A. Knopf, 1948.

Borland, Kathryn Kilby, and Helen Ross Speicher. *Phillis Wheatley: Young Revolutionary Poet*. Young Patriots Series. Illus. Cathy Morrison. Carmel, IN: Patria, 2005.

Boskin, Joseph. *Sambo: The Rise and Demise of an American Jester*. New York: Oxford UP, 1986.

"Bowie Knife." *The Slave's Friend* 3.2 (1838): 1–2.

[Boykin, Edward M.]. *Boys and Girls Stories of the War*. Richmond, VA: West and Johnston, [1863?].

Boylan, Grace Duffie. *Young Folks' "Uncle Tom's Cabin,"* Adapted for Children. New York: H. M. Caldwell, 1901.

Bradby, Marie. *More Than Anything Else*. Illus. Chris K. Soentpiet. New York: Orchard, 1995.

Bradford, George C. Letter. The Grown-Ups' Corner. *The Brownies' Book* 2.4 (April 1921): 126.

Branson, L[evi]. *First Book in Composition, Applying the Principles of Grammar to the Art of Composing; also, Giving Full Directions for Punctuation; Especially Designed for the Use of Southern Schools*. Raleigh, NC: Branson, Farrar, 1863.

Broderick, Dorothy M. *Image of the Black in Children's Fiction*. New York: R. R. Bowker, 1973.

Brown, William Wells. *Clotel; or, The President's Daughter: A Narrative of Slave Life in the United States*. 1853. *Three Classic African-American Novels*. Ed. William L. Andrews. New York: New American Library-Penguin, 1990. 113–283.

Budd, Louis J., ed. *Mark Twain: The Contemporary Reviews*. Cambridge: Cambridge UP, 1999.

Buhle, Mari Jo, and Paul Buhle. Introduction. "Woman Suffrage and American Reform." *The Concise History of Woman Suffrage: Selections from the Classic Work of Stanton, Anthony, Gage, and Harper*. Ed. Mari Jo Buhle and Paul Buhle. Urbana: U of Illinois P, 1978. 1–45.

Burnham, Michelle. *Captivity and Sentiment: Cultural Exchange in American Literature, 1682–1861*. Hanover, NH: UP of New England, 1997.

Butchart, Ronald E. *Northern Schools, Southern Blacks, and Reconstruction: Freedmen's Education, 1862–1875*. Westport, CT: Greenwood, 1980.

Bynum, Victoria E. *The Free State of Jones: Mississippi's Longest Civil War*. Chapel Hill: U of North Carolina P, 2001.

Caldwell, M. P., and W. W. Everett. *The Student's Arithmetic: A Collection of Concise Rules and Abridged Methods of Calculation, Adapted to the Use of Schools, Farmers, Mechanics, and Business Men Generally. With an*

Appendix, Containing Legal Forms, Bills of Sale, Deeds, Wills, etc. Athens, GA: J. H. Christy's Franklin Job Office, 1861.

Calhoun, Frances Boyd. *Miss Minerva and William Green Hill.* Illus. Angus MacDonall. Chicago: Reilly and Lee, 1909.

Cameron, Ann, adapt. *The Kidnapped Prince: The Life of Olaudah Equiano.* By Olaudah Equiano. Introd. by Henry Louis Gates Jr. New York: Alfred A Knopf, 1995.

Carby, Hazel V. "Ideologies of Black Folk: The Historical Novel of Slavery." *Slavery and the Literary Imagination.* Ed. Deborah E. McDowell and Arnold Rampersad. Baltimore: Johns Hopkins UP, 1989. 125–143.

Carleton. "Winning His Way." Chapter XX: "Dark Days." *Our Young Folks: An Illustrated Magazine for Boys and Girls* 1.11 (November 1865): 733–736.

Carlson, Judy. *Harriet Tubman: Call to Freedom.* Great Lives Series. New York: Fawcett Columbine, 1989.

Carpenter, Charles. *History of American Schoolbooks.* Philadelphia: U of Pennsylvania P, 1963.

Carretta, Vincent. *Equiano, the African: Biography of a Self-Made Man.* Athens: U of Georgia P, 2005.

———. "Questioning the Identity of Olaudah Equiano, or Gustavus Vassa, the African." *The Global Eighteenth Century.* Ed. Felicity A. Nussbaum. Baltimore: Johns Hopkins UP, 2003. 226–235.

Carson, Clayborne. "Civil Rights Movement." *The Reader's Companion to American History.* Ed. Eric Foner and John A. Garraty. Boston: Houghton Mifflin, 1991. 177–180.

"The Cart-Whip." *The Slave's Friend* 2.4 (1837): 5–6.

Caruth, Cathy. *Unclaimed Experience: Trauma, Narrative, and History.* Baltimore: Johns Hopkins UP, 1996.

A Catechism to Be Taught Orally to Those Who Cannot Read; Designed Especially for the Instruction of the Slaves, in the Prot. Episcopal Church in the Confederate States. Raleigh, [NC]: Office of "The Church Intelligencer," 1862.

Chandler, Karen Michele. "Paths to Freedom: Literacy and Folk Traditions in Recent Narratives about Slavery and Emancipation." *Children's Literature Association Quarterly* 31.3 (Spring 2006): 3–26.

Chaudron, A. de V. [Adelaide de Vendel]. *Chaudron's Spelling Book, Carefully Prepared for Family and School Use.* Mobile, AL: S. H. Goetzel, 1864.

———. *The First Reader, Designed for the Use of Primary Schools.* Chaudron's Series. Second Ed. Mobile, AL: W. G. Clark, 1864.

———. *The Second Reader, Designed for the Use of Primary Schools.* Chaudron's Series. Mobile, AL: Office of the Daily Advertiser and Register, 1863.

———. *The Third Reader, Designed for the Use of Primary Schools.* Chaudron's Series. Mobile, AL: W. G. Clark, 1864.

Chesnut, Mary Boykin. *A Diary from Dixie*. 1949. [Revised edition]. Ed. Ben Ames Williams. Foreword by Edmund Wilson. Cambridge, MA: Harvard UP, 1980.

Child, Lydia Maria. *The Freedmen's Book*. 1865. New York: Arno P and *New York Times*, 1968.

———. "Mary French and Susan Easton." *Juvenile Miscellany* 6.2 (May/June 1834): 186–202.

[———]. "Mary French and Susan Easton." *The Slave's Friend* 1.9 (1836): 1–15.

Chubb, Ida M. *Little Pickaninnies*. Racine, WI: Whitman, 1929.

Clark, Beverly Lyon. *Kiddie Lit: The Cultural Construction of Children's Literature in America*. Baltimore: Johns Hopkins UP, 2003.

Clark, Margaret Goff. *Freedom Crossing*. New York: Scholastic, 1980.

Clifton, Lucille. *The Lucky Stone*. Illus. Dale Payson. New York: Bantam Doubleday Dell, 1979.

"The Collection Box." *The Slave's Friend* 1.1 (1836): 1–3.

"Colored Children at Buffalo." *The Slave's Friend* 2.12 (1837): 16.

Connolly, Paula T. "Crossing Borders from Africa to America." *Transcending Boundaries: Writing for a Dual Audience of Children and Adults*. Ed. Sandra L. Beckett. New York: Garland, 1999. 149–164.

———. "Imagining the Escape: Picture Books and the Flight to Freedom." *Journal of Children's Literature* 22 (Spring 1996): 8–13.

———. "Narrative Tensions: Telling Slavery, Showing Violence." *The Presence of the Past in Children's Literature*. Ed. Anne Lawson Lucas. Westport, CT: Praeger-Greenwood P, 2003. 107–112.

———. "Still a Slave: Legal and Spiritual Freedom in Julius Lester's 'Where the Sun Lives.'" *Children's Literature* 26 (1998): 123–189.

Cormier, Emily Cardinali. "'Genius, Scientist, Saint': Carver as Hagiography." *Children's Literature* 38 (2010): 153–180.

Crandall, John C. "Patriotism and Humanitarian Reform in Children's Literature, 1825–1860." *American Quarterly* 21.1 (Spring 1969): 3–22.

Cremin, Lawrence A. *American Education: The National Experience, 1783–1876*. New York: Harper and Row, 1980.

Cugoano, Quobna Ottobah. *Thoughts and Sentiments on the Evil and Wicked Traffic of the Slavery and Commerce of the Human Species*. 1787. Ed. Vincent Carretta. Reprinted in *Thoughts and Sentiments on the Evil of Slavery, and Other Writings*. New York: Penguin, 1999. 1–111.

Curry, Leonard P. *The Free Black in Urban America, 1800–1850: The Shadow of the Dream*. Chicago: U of Chicago P, 1981.

Curtin, Philip D. *The Atlantic Slave Trade: A Census*. Madison: U of Wisconsin P, 1969.

Curtis, Christopher Paul. *Elijah of Buxton*. New York: Scholastic, 2007.

Daniell, W. C., MD. "Health of Young Negroes." *Debow's Review* 20.6 (June 1856): 746–747. University of Michigan. Making of America Journals Digital Library. http://quod.lib.umich.edu/m/moajrnl.

Davidson, Margaret. *Frederick Douglass Fights for Freedom*. New York: Scholastic, 1968.

Davis, Charles T., and Henry Louis Gates Jr., ed. *The Slave's Narrative*. New York: Oxford UP, 1985.

Davis, Ossie. *Escape to Freedom: A Play about Young Frederick Douglass*. New York: Viking–Penguin, 1978.

Dawson, Charles C. *ABC's of Great Negroes*. Chicago: Dawson, 1933.

Deane, Paul C. "The Persistence of Uncle Tom: An Examination of the Image of the Negro in Children's Fiction Series." *The Black American in Books for Children: Readings in Racism*. Second Edition. Ed. Donnarae MacCann and Gloria Woodard. Metuchen, NJ: Scarecrow P, 1985. 162–168.

"Declaration of the National Anti-Slavery Convention." *The Liberator* 3.50 (14 December 1833): 198.

DeMott, Benjamin. *The Trouble with Friendship: Why Americans Can't Think Straight about Race*. New York: Atlantic Monthly P, 1995.

Denenberg, Barry. *When Will This Cruel War Be Over?: The Civil War Diary of Emma Simpson*. Dear America series. New York: Scholastic, 1996.

De Rosa, Deborah C. *Domestic Abolitionism and Juvenile Literature, 1830–1865*. Albany: State U of New York P, 2003.

———, ed. *Into the Mouths of Babes: An Anthology of Children's Abolitionist Literature*. Westport, CT: Praeger, 2005.

Derricotte, Elsie Palmer, Geneva Calcier Turner, and Jessie Hailstalk Roy. *Word Pictures of the Great*. Washington, DC: Associated Publishers, 1941.

de Tocqueville, Alexis. *Democracy in America*. Vol. 1 (1835) and Vol. 2 (1840). Abridged edition. Ed. Thomas Bender. 1945. New York: Modern Library-Random House, 1981.

Diggs, Irene. "DuBois and Children." *Phylon* 37.4 (1976): 370–399. JSTOR Arts and Sciences Archive Collection Online. http://www.jstor.org/stable/274501.

"Disenthralment of Southern Literature." *DeBow's Review* 31.4 (October–November 1861): 347–361. University of Michigan. Making of America Journals Digital Library. http://quod.lib.umich.edu/m/joajrnl.

Dixie, Dolly. "The Colored Mammy and Her White Foster-Child: A True Story." *Our Young Folks: An Illustrated Magazine for Boys and Girls* 4 (March 1868): 137–140.

Douglas, Ann. Introduction. "The Art of Controversy." *Uncle Tom's Cabin; or, Life among the Lowly*. New York: Penguin, 1981. 7–36.

Douglass, Frederick. *The Heroic Slave*. 1853. Reprinted in *Three Classic African-American Novels*. Ed. William L. Andrews. New York: New American Library-Penguin, 1990. 23–69.

———. *Life and Times of Frederick Douglass, Written by Himself*. 1881. New York: Citadel-Carol, 1983.

———. *My Bondage and My Freedom*. 1855. Ed. John David Smith. New York: Penguin, 2003.

———. *Narrative of the Life of Frederick Douglass, An American Slave.* 1845. Ed. and Introd. Houston A. Baker Jr. New York: Penguin, 1982.

———. "What to the Slave Is the Fourth of July?" 1852. "Contexts" in *Narrative of the Life of Frederick Douglass, an American Slave, Written by Himself.* A Norton Critical Edition. Ed. William L. Andrews and William S. McFeely. New York: Norton, 1997. 116–127.

Duane, Anna Mae. *Suffering Childhood in Early America: Violence, Race, and the Making of the Child Victim.* Athens: U of Georgia P, 2010.

DuBois, Ellen Carol. *Feminism and Suffrage: The Emergence of an Independent Women's Movement in America, 1848–1869.* Ithaca, NY: Cornell UP, 1978.

Du Bois, W. E. Burghardt. "The Immortal Child." *Darkwater: Voices from Within the Veil.* 1920. New York: AMS P, 1969. 193–217.

———. "The Immortal Children." *The Crisis* 12.6 (October 1916): 267–268.

———. *The Souls of Black Folk.* 1903. New York: Signet–New American Library, 1969.

———. "The True Brownies." *The Crisis* 18.6 (October 1919): 285–286.

"The Duty of Southern Authors." *Southern Literary Messenger* 23.4 (October 1856): 241–247. Reprinted in *The Southern Literature Messenger: Devoted to Every Department of Literature and the Fine Arts.* Vol. 23. New York: AMS P, 1965.

Eastman, Mary H. *Aunt Phillis's Cabin; or, Southern Life As It Is.* 1852. Upper Saddle River, NJ: Gregg, 1968.

Editors. The Grown-Ups' Corner. *The Brownies' Book* 2.1 (January 1921): 25.

Edson, John R. "*Slave's Friend.*" *Children's Periodicals of the United States.* Ed. R. Gordon Kelly. Westport, CT: Greenwood, 1984. 408–411.

"Education of the Freedmen." *The North American Review* 101.209 (October 1865): 528–549. American Periodicals Series Online. http://www.proquest.com/en-US/catalogs/databases/detail/aps.shtml.

Edwards, Pamela Duncan. *Barefoot: Escape on the Underground Railroad.* Illus. Henry Cole. New York: Harper Collins, 1997.

Edwards, Paul. Introduction. *The Life of Olaudah Equiano; or, Gustavus Vassa, the African.* Ed. Paul Edwards. White Plains, NY: Longman, 1994. vii–xxxviii.

———. "Three West African Writers of the 1780s." *The Slave's Narrative.* Ed. Charles T. Davis and Henry Louis Gates Jr. New York: Oxford UP, 1985. 175–198.

"Elijah P. Lovejoy." *The Slave's Friend* 3.8 (1838): 1–5.

Eliza on the Ice. Animated short. Dir. Connie [J. Conrad] Rasinski. Terrytoons, 1944. http://www.YouTube.com.

Elson, Ruth Miller. *Guardians of Tradition: American Schoolbooks of the Nineteenth Century.* Lincoln: U of Nebraska P, 1964.

"Emancipated Slaves, White and Colored." *Harper's Weekly* 8 (30 January 1864): 69.

Equiano, Olaudah. *The Life of Olaudah Equiano; or, Gustavus Vassa, the*

African. Written by Himself. 1789. Ed. and Introd. Paul Edwards. White Plains, NY: Longman, 1994.

"Escape from Bondage in the State of New York." *The Youth's Emancipator* 1.1 (May 1842): 1–2.

Ethnic Notions: Black People in White Minds. VHS. Dir. Marlon Riggs. California Newsreel. San Francisco, CA: Marlon Riggs, in association with KQED, 1987.

"Eye and Ear Notes. From an Army Correspondent. A Note of Introduction." [By "Uncle James"]. *The Youth's Companion* 38.7 (16 February 1865): 26.

"Eye and Ear Notes. From an Army Correspondent. Old Uncle Abe." [By "Uncle James"]. *The Youth's Companion* 38.8 (23 February 1865): 30.

"Eye and Ear Notes. A Peep into Slave Life." [By "Uncle James"]. *The Youth's Companion* 38.35 (31 August 1865): 140.

"Eye and Ear Notes. A Slave Sale." [By "Uncle James"]. *The Youth's Companion* 38.50 (14 December 1865): 198.

"Eye and Ear Notes. The Slave Sale Again." [By "Uncle James"]. *The Youth's Companion* 38.51 (21 December 1865): 202.

Eyerman, Ron. *Cultural Trauma: Slavery and the Formation of African American Identity.* Cambridge: Cambridge UP, 2001.

Fahs, Alice. *The Imagined Civil War: Popular Literature of the North and South, 1861–1865.* Chapel Hill: U of North Carolina P, 2001.

Fauset, Arthur Huff. "A Story of a Former Slave Boy." *The Brownies' Book* 1.3 (March 1920): 95–96.

Feelings, Tom. *The Middle Passage: White Ships, Black Cargo.* Introd. John Henrik Clarke. New York: Dial–Penguin, 1995.

Ferris, Jeri. *Go Free or Die: A Story about Harriet Tubman.* Illus. Karen Ritz. Minneapolis: Carolrhoda, 1988.

———. *Walking the Road to Freedom: A Story about Sojourner Truth.* Illus. Peter E. Hanson. Minneapolis: Carolrhoda, 1988.

The First Reader, for Southern Schools. Raleigh: N.C. Christian Advocate, 1864.

Fisher, Walter. Introduction. *Father Henson's Story of His Own Life.* 1849. Second Ed. 1858. New York: Corinth, 1962. v–xi.

Fiske, John, and Frank Alpine Hill. *A History of the United States for Schools.* 1894. Boston: Houghton, Mifflin, 1899. http://books.google.com/books?id=nsE_AAAAYAAJ&pg=PR6&dq=history+of+the+united+states+%22fiske%22+1901&hl=en#v=onepage&q=history%20of%20the%20united%20states%20%22fiske%22%201901&f=false.

Floyd, Silas X. *Floyd's Flowers: Or, Duty and Beauty for Colored Children; Being One Hundred Short Stories Gleaned from the Storehouse of Human Knowledge and Experience.* Illus. John Henry Adams. [Atlanta]: Hertel, Jenkins, 1905. Internet Archive. Boston Public Library. http://www.archive.org/details/floyd'sflowers.

Foner, Eric. *Reconstruction: America's Unfinished Revolution, 1863–1877.* New York: Harper and Row, 1988.

Foner, Eric, and John A. Garraty, ed. *The Reader's Companion to American History*. Boston: Houghton Mifflin, 1991.

Fox, Paula. "Newbery Award Acceptance." *The Horn Book Magazine* (August 1974): 345–350.

———. *The Slave Dancer*. New York: Dell, 1973.

Fox-Genovese, Elizabeth. *Within the Plantation Household: Black and White Women of the Old South*. Chapel Hill: U of North Carolina P, 1988.

Fredrickson, George M. *The Black Image in the White Mind: The Debate on Afro-American Character and Destiny, 1817–1914*. New York: Harper and Row, 1971.

Freedman, Florence B. *Two Tickets to Freedom: The True Story of Ellen and William Craft, Fugitive Slaves*. Illus. Ezra Jack Keats. New York: Peter Bedrick, 1971.

The Freedman's Second Reader. 1865. Reprinted as *Freedmen's Schools and Textbooks*. Vol. 2. Ed. Robert C. Morris. New York: AMS, 1980.

The Freedman's Spelling-Book. 1866. Reprinted as *Freedmen's Schools and Textbooks*. Vol. 2. Ed. Robert C. Morris. New York: AMS, 1980.

Freedman's Third Reader. 1865. Reprinted as *Freedmen's Schools and Textbooks*. Vol. 2. Ed. Robert C. Morris. New York: AMS, 1980.

Freehling, William W. *Prelude to the Civil War: The Nullification Controversy in South Carolina, 1816–1836*. New York: Harper and Row, 1965.

———. *The Reintegration of American History: Slavery and the Civil War*. New York: Oxford UP, 1994.

Friedberg, Joan Brest. "*Our Young Folks: An Illustrated Magazine for Boys and Girls*." *Children's Periodicals of the United States*. Ed. R. Gordon Kelly. Westport, CT: Greenwood, 1984. 329–341.

Fritz, Jean. *Brady*. Illus. Lynd Ward. 1960. New York: Puffin-Penguin, 1987.

Gaines, Francis Pendleton. *The Southern Plantation: A Study in the Development and the Accuracy of a Tradition*. 1924. Gloucester, MA: Peter Smith, 1962.

Gaines, Kevin K. *Uplifting the Race: Black Leadership, Politics, and Culture in the Twentieth Century*. Chapel Hill: U of North Carolina P, 1996.

Gallagher, Catherine. *The Industrial Reformation of English Fiction: Social Discourse and Narrative Form, 1832–1867*. 1985. Chicago: U of Chicago P, 1988.

Garrison, W[illiam]. L[loyd]. "Mob in Philadelphia." *The Slave's Friend* 4.2 (1839): 4–10.

———. "No Union with Slaveholders: The Meeting at Framingham." *The Liberator* 24.27 (7 July 1854): 106.

———. "To the Public." *The Liberator* 1.1 (1 January 1831): 1.

Gates, Henry Louis, Jr. Introduction. *The Classic Slave Narratives*. New York: New American Library-Penguin, 1987. ix–xviii.

———. *The Signifying Monkey: A Theory of African-American Literary Criticism*. 1988. New York: Oxford UP, 1989.

———. "The Trope of a New Negro and the Reconstruction of the Image of the Black." *Representations* 24 (Fall 1988): 129–155.

Gates, Henry Louis, Jr., and Nellie Y. McKay, ed. "Literature of the Reconstruction to the New Negro Renaissance: 1865–1919." *The Norton Anthology of African American Literature.* New York: Norton, 1997. 461–472.

Gatewood, Willard B., Jr. *Dictionary of North Carolina Biography: Volume 3, H–K.* Ed. William S. Powell. Chapel Hill: U of North Carolina P, 1988. 288–289.

Genovese, Eugene D. *Roll, Jordan, Roll: The World the Slaves Made.* 1972. New York: Vintage-Random House, 1976.

Gilman, Caroline. "A Ballad. Part First: The Plantation." *The Rose Bud, or Youth's Gazette* 1.38 (18 May 1833): 149–150.

———. "Country Visit. Chapter I." *Southern Rose Bud* 2.35 (26 April 1834): 139.

———. "The Country Visit. Chap. II. 'The Ride.'" *Southern Rose Bud* 2.36 (3 May 1834): 113.

———. "The Country Visit. Chap. III. 'A Maroon.'" *Southern Rose Bud* 2.37 (10 May 1834): 147.

———. "The Country Visit. Chap. IV. 'The Arrival.'" *Southern Rose Bud* 2.42 (14 June 1834): 167.

———. "The Country Visit. Chap. VI. 'The little Negroes.'" *Southern Rose Bud* 2.46 (12 July 1834): 183.

———. "The Country Visit. Chap. VII. 'The Swing.'" *Southern Rose Bud* 2.47 (19 July 1834): 187.

———. "The Country Visit. Chap. VIII. 'The Frog Concert.'" *Southern Rose Bud* 2.48 (26 July 1834): 191.

———. "The Country Visit. Chap. IX. 'Second Visit to the Frog Pond.'" *Southern Rose Bud* 2.49 (2 August 1834): 195.

———. "The Country Visit. Chap. X. 'Singing Hymns.'" *Southern Rose Bud* 2.50 (9 August 1834): 199.

———. "The Country Visit. Chap. XI. 'Old Nelly.'" *Southern Rose Bud* 2.51 (16 August 1834): 203.

———. "The Country Visit. Chap. XII. 'The Return.'" *Southern Rose Bud* 2.52 (23 August 1834): 207.

———. "Editor's Address." *The Rose Bud, or Youth's Gazette* 1.1 (11 August 1832): 1.

———. "The Mask Fairy. An Original Tale." *Southern Rose Bud* 2.1 (31 August 1833): 1–2.

———. "The Mask Fairy. An Original Tale. Concluded." *Southern Rose Bud* 2.2 (7 September 1833): 5–7.

———. "The New Boots." *The Rose Bud, or Youth's Gazette* 1.15 (8 December 1832): 60.

———. "The Planter's Son." *The Rose Bud, or Youth's Gazette* 1.5 (29 September 1832): 17–18.

———. "The Planter's Son." *The Rose-Bud Wreath*. Charleston, SC: S. Babcock, 1841. 63–69.

———. "Prospectus of the *Southern Rose Bud*, Vol. II." *The Rose Bud, or Youth's Gazette* 1.51 (17 August 1833): 204.

———. *Recollections of a Southern Matron*. New York: Harper and Brothers, 1838.

———. "The Selfish Girl." *The Rose Bud, or Youth's Gazette* 1.33 (13 April 1833): 129–131.

———. "Sullivan's Island: No. 1." *The Rose Bud, or Youth's Gazette* 1.4 (22 September 1832): 13–14.

Ginsberg, Lesley. "'I am your slave for love': Race, Sentimentality, and Harriet Beecher Stowe's Fiction for Children." *Enterprising Youth: Social Values and Acculturation in Nineteenth-Century American Children's Literature*. Ed. Monika Elbert. New York: Routledge, 2008. 97–113.

Goldner, Ellen J. "Arguing with Pictures: Race, Class, and the Formation of Popular Abolitionism through '*Uncle Tom's Cabin*.'" *Journal of American and Comparative Cultures* 24.1 and 24.2 (Spring and Summer 2001): 71–84.

Goodrich, Samuel G. *Lights and Shadows of African History*. Boston: Bradbury, Soden, 1844.

———. *Manners and Customs of the Principal Nations of the Globe*. Boston: Bradbury, Soden, 1845.

———. *The Tales of Peter Parley about Africa*. 1830. Rev. Ed. Philadelphia: Desilver, Thomas, 1836.

———. *The Tales of Peter Parley about America*. 1827. Second Ed. 1828. Introd. Barrows Mussey, New York: Dover, 1974.

———. *The Tales of Peter Parley about Asia*. 1830. Rev. Ed. Philadelphia: Thomas, Cowperthwait, 1849.

———. *Universal History on the Basis of Geography*. [By "Peter Parley"]. New York: J. A. Hoisington, 1837.

———. *Universal History on the Basis of Geography*. [By "Peter Parley"]. Seventh Ed. London: William Tegg, 1860.

———. *Universal History on the Basis of Geography*. [By "Peter Parley"]. New York: Ivison, Blakeman, Taylor, 1875.

———. *The World and Its Inhabitants*. Boston: Bradbury, Soden, 1845.

"The Good Schoolmaster." *The Slave's Friend* 2.11 (1837): 1.

Gossett, Thomas F. *Race: The History of an Idea in America*. 1963. New Ed. New York: Oxford UP, 1997.

———. *"Uncle Tom's Cabin" and American Culture*. Dallas, TX: Southern Methodist UP, 1985.

Goulding, F[rancis] R[obert]. *Marooner's Island; or, Dr. Gordon in Search of His Children*. Philadelphia: Claxton, Remsen and Haffelfinger, 1870.

———. *Robert and Harold; or, The Young Marooners on the Florida Coast*. 1852. Third Ed. Philadelphia: William S. Martien, 1853.

———. *Robert and Harold; or, The Young Marooners on the Florida Coast.* First Confederate Ed. Rev. Macon, GA: Burke, Boykin, 1863.

Graff, Gerald, and James Phelan, ed. *"Adventures of Huckleberry Finn": A Case Study in Critical Controversy.* Boston: Bedford-St. Martin's, 1995.

"A Great Sailor." *The Brownies' Book* 1.2 (February 1920): 38–39.

The Grown-Ups' Corner. *The Brownies' Book* 2.2 (February 1921): 63.

Gutman, Herbert G. *The Black Family in Slavery and Freedom, 1750–1925.* New York: Random House, 1976.

Hamilton, Nigel. *Biography: A Brief History.* Cambridge, MA: Harvard UP, 2007.

Hamilton, Virginia. *The House of Dies Drear.* New York: Aladdin-Simon and Schuster, 1968.

———. *Many Thousand Gone: African Americans from Slavery to Freedom.* Illus. Leo Dillon and Diane Dillon. New York: Alfred A. Knopf, 1993.

———. *The People Could Fly: American Black Folktales.* Illus. Leo Dillon and Diane Dillon. New York: Alfred A. Knopf, 1985.

Harper, Frances Ellen Watkins. *A Brighter Coming Day: A Frances Ellen Watkins Harper Reader.* Ed. and Introd. Frances Smith Foster. New York: Feminist P at the City University of New York, 1990.

Harris, Joel Chandler. Introduction. *The Young Marooners on the Florida Coast; or, Robert and Harold, a New Edition: Illustrated and Enlarged.* By F. R. Goulding. New York: Dodd, Mead, 1887. i–v.

———. ["Uncle Remus"]. "Daddy Jake, the Runaway." *Daddy Jake the Runaway and Short Stories Told after Dark.* 1889. New York: Century, 1896. 1–82.

———. *Uncle Remus: His Songs and His Sayings.* 1880. Ed. and Introd. Robert Hemenway. 1982. New York: Penguin, 1986.

"Have the Negros Any Minds?" *The Youth's Emancipator* 1.2 (August 1842): 2.

Hawes, Charles Boardman. *The Great Quest: A Romance of 1826, Wherein Are Recorded the Experiences of Josiah Woods of Topham, and of Those Others with Whom He Sailed for Cuba and the Gulf of Guinea.* Illus. George Varian. Boston: Atlantic Monthly P, 1921.

Haynes, Elizabeth Ross. *Unsung Heroes.* New York: Du Bois and Dill, 1921.

Hemenway, Robert. Introduction. "Author, Teller, and Hero." *Uncle Remus: His Songs and His Sayings.* 1982. New York: Penguin, 1986. 7–31.

Henson, Josiah. *Father Henson's Story of His Own Life.* 1849. Second Ed. 1858. Introd. Walter Fisher. New York: Corinth, 1962.

[Heriott, Edwin]. "Education at the South." *Debow's Review* 21.6 (December 1856): 650–659. University of Michigan. Making of America Journals Digital Library. http://quod.lib.umich.edu/m/moajrnl.

Hewes, Agnes Danforth. *Glory of the Seas.* New York: Alfred A. Knopf, 1933.

Hill, Laban Carrick. *Dave the Potter: Artist, Poet, Slave.* Illus. Bryan Collier. New York: Little, Brown, 2010.

"The History of a Fugitive." *The Youth's Emancipator* 1.3 (September 1842): 4.

History of Schools for the Colored Population. 1871. New York: Arno P, 1969.

Holland, Eleanor. Letter. "The Jury." *The Brownies' Book* 1.1 (January 1920): 15.

Hope, Laura Lee. *The Bobbsey Twins in the Land of Cotton*. New York: Grosset and Dunlap, 1942.

Hopkinson, Deborah. *Sweet Clara and the Freedom Quilt*. Illus. James Ransome. New York: Alfred A. Knopf, 1993.

"How to Get Up a Mob." *The Slave's Friend* 4.2 (1839): 3–4.

Hubbard, Rev. F[ordyce] M[itchell]. *The North-Carolina Reader. Number I. Prepared, with Special References to the Wants and Interests of North Carolina*. 1855. New York: A. S. Barnes, 1866.

Huberman, Leo. *"We, the People."* Illus. Thomas H. Benton. New York: Harper and Brothers, 1932.

"Isabella." *The Slave's Friend* 1.12 (1836): 10–12.

Jacobs, Harriet A. *Incidents in the Life of a Slave Girl*. 1861. Ed. Jean Fagan Yellin. Cambridge, MA: Harvard UP, 1987.

Jefferson, Thomas. *Notes on the State of Virginia*. 1784/1861. Introd. Thomas Perkins Abernethy. New York: Harper and Row, 1964.

"Joggy and Lorina." *The Slave's Friend* 3.3 (1838): 9–10.

Johnson, Dianne. *Telling Tales: The Pedagogy and Promise of African American Literature for Youth*. New York: Greenwood, 1990.

Johnson, Dolores. *Now Let Me Fly: The Story of a Slave Family*. New York: Macmillan, 1993.

Johnson, Edward A. *A School History of the Negro Race in America, from 1619 to 1890, with a Short Introduction As to the Origin of the Race; Also a Sketch of Liberia*. Raleigh, NC: Edwards and Broughton, 1890.

Johnson-Feelings, Dianne. "Children's and Young Adult Literature." *The Oxford Companion to African American Literature*. Ed. William Andrews, Frances Smith Foster, Trudier Harris. New York: Oxford UP, 1977. 133–140.

Jones, Charles C[olcock]. *A Catechism for Colored Persons*. Charleston, [SC]: Observer Office P, 1834.

———. *The Religious Instruction of the Negroes. In the United States*. Savannah, GA: Thomas Purse, 1842; rpt. New York: Negro Universities P, 1969.

Jones, J. Elizabeth. *The Young Abolitionists; or, Conversations on Slavery*. Boston: Anti-Slavery Office, 1848.

Jordan, Winthrop D. *White Over Black: American Attitudes Toward the Negro, 1550–1812*. Chapel Hill: U of North Carolina P, 1968.

"Juvenile Anti-Slavery Meeting in Boston." *The Slave's Friend* 3.2 (1838): 12–14.

"Juvenile Anti-Slavery Society." *The Slave's Friend* 2.5 (1837): 1–16.

Karcher, Carolyn L. *The First Woman in the Republic: A Cultural Biography of Lydia Maria Child*. Durham, NC: Duke UP, 1994.

"Katy Ferguson: A True Story." *The Brownies' Book* 1.1 (January 1920): 27.

Keizer, Arlene R. *Black Subjects: Identity Formation in the Contemporary Narrative of Slavery*. Ithaca, NY: Cornell UP, 2004.

Keller, Holly. "Juvenile Antislavery Narrative and Notions of Childhood." *Children's Literature* 24 (1996): 86–100.

Kennedy, John Pendleton. *Swallow Barn; or, A Sojourn in the Old Dominion*. 1832. Rev. Ed. 1853. Introd. William S. Osborne. 1962. New York: Hafner, 1971.

Kennedy, Randall. "Racial Desegregation." *The Reader's Companion to American History*. Ed. Eric Foner and John A. Garraty. Boston: Houghton Mifflin, 1991. 898–900.

Kennerly, Sarah Law. "Confederate Juvenile Imprints: Children's Books and Periodicals Published in the Confederate States of America, 1861–1865." Diss. U of Michigan, 1956.

Kenny, Gale L. "Mastering Childhood: Paternalism, Slavery, and the Southern Domestic in Caroline Howard Gilman's Antebellum Children's Literature." *Southern Quarterly* 44.1 (Fall 2006): 65–87.

Kibbey, Ann. "Language in Slavery: Frederick Douglass's *'Narrative.'*" *Prospects* 8 (1983): 163–182.

Kidd, Kenneth. "Prizing Children's Literature: The Case of Newbery Gold." *Children's Literature* 35 (2007): 166–190.

Kilham, Elizabeth. "Tobe's Monument." *Our Young Folks: An Illustrated Magazine for Boys and Girls* 8 (February 1872): 80–87.

King, Wilma. *Stolen Childhood: Slave Youth in Nineteenth-Century America*. Bloomington: Indiana UP, 1995.

Kirke, Edmund. [James Roberts Gilmore]. "The Little Prisoner. Part II. Wounded." *Our Young Folks: An Illustrated Magazine for Boys and Girls* 1.4 (April 1865): 240–244.

Kolchin, Peter. "Slavery: The Institution of Slavery." *The Reader's Companion to American History*. Ed. Eric Foner and John A. Garraty. Boston: Houghton Mifflin, 1991. 990–992.

Kory, Fern. "Once upon a Time in Aframerica: The 'Peculiar' Significance of Fairies in the *'Brownies' Book.'*" *Children's Literature* 29 (2001): 91–112.

Krass, Peter. *Sojourner Truth: Antislavery Activist*. Black Americans of Achievement series. Introd. Coretta Scott King. New York: Chelsea House, 1988.

Lander, Rev. S[amuel]. *Our Own Primary Arithmetic*. Second Ed. Greensboro, NC: Sterling, Campbell and Albright, 1863.

———. *Our Own School Arithmetic*. Greensboro, NC: Sterling, Campbell and Albright, 1863.

Leigh, C. C. "White and Colored Slaves." *Harper's Weekly* (30 January 1864): 71.

Lessels, Jeannette Barnes, and Eric Sterling. "Overcoming Racism in Jacob Abbott's *'Stories of Rainbow and Lucky'* and in Antebellum America." *Enterprising Youth: Social Values and Acculturation in Nineteenth-*

Century American Children's Literature. Ed. Monika Elbert. New York: Routledge, 2008. 83–96.

Lester, Julius. *A Day of Tears: A Novel in Dialogue*. New York: Jump at the Sun-Hyperion, 2005.

———. Foreword. *The Tales of Uncle Remus: The Adventures of Brer Rabbit*. New York: Dial, 1987. xiii–xxi.

———. *From Slave Ship to Freedom Road*. Illus. Rod Brown. New York: Puffin-Penguin, 1998.

———. *The Old African*. Illus. Jerry Pinkney. New York: Dial-Penguin, 2005.

———. *The Tales of Uncle Remus: The Adventures of Brer Rabbit*. Illus. Jerry Pinkney. New York: Dial, 1987.

———. *This Strange New Feeling*. New York: Scholastic, 1981.

———. *To Be a Slave*. Illus. Tom Feelings. New York: Scholastic, 1968.

Levander, Caroline F. *Cradle of Liberty: Race, the Child, and National Belonging from Thomas Jefferson to W. E. B. Du Bois*. Durham, NC: Duke UP, 2006.

Levine, Lawrence W. *Black Culture and Black Consciousness: Afro-American Folk Thought from Slavery to Freedom*. Oxford: Oxford UP, 1977.

"Little Adelaide Sabilia." *The Youth's Emancipator* 1.9 (March 1843): 2–3.

Little Eva: The Flower of the South. New York: Philip J. Cozans, [1853?]. *Uncle Tom's Cabin* and American Culture: A Multi-Media Archive, The Harriet Beecher Stowe Center-Hartford, University of Virginia. www.utc.iath.virginia.edu/childrn/cbcbambt.html.

"Lot Cary." *The Slave's Friend* 3.4 (1838): 1–3.

Lott, Eric. *Love and Theft: Blackface Minstrelsy and the American Working Class*. New York: Oxford UP, 1993.

———. "Mr. Clemens and Jim Crow: Twain, Race, and Blackface." *The Cambridge Companion to Mark Twain*. Ed. Forrest G. Robinson. Cambridge: Cambridge UP, 1995. 129–152.

Lyons, Mary E. *Letters from a Slave Girl: The Story of Harriet Jacobs*. New York: Charles Scribner's Sons-Macmillan, 1992.

MacCann, Donnarae. "Nancy Drew and the Myth of White Supremacy." *Rediscovering Nancy Drew*. Ed. Carolyn Stewart Dyer and Nancy Tillman Romalov. Iowa City: U of Iowa P, 1995. 129–135.

———. "Racism in Prize-Winning Biographical Works." *The Black American in Books for Children: Readings in Racism*. Second Edition. Ed. Donnarae MacCann and Gloria Woodard. Metuchen, NJ: Scarecrow, 1985. 169–179.

———. *White Supremacy in Children's Literature: Characterizations of African Americans, 1830–1900*. New York: Routledge, 1998.

MacLeod, Anne Scott. *A Moral Tale: Children's Fiction and American Culture, 1820–1860*. Hamden, CT: Archon, 1975.

Malaspina, Ann. *Phillis Sings Out Freedom: The Story of George Washington and Phillis Wheatley*. Illus. Susan Keever. Chicago: Albert Whitman, 2010.

Marshall, Rev. C. K. "Home Education at the South." *Debow's Review* 18.5 (May 1855): 655–668. University of Michigan. Making of America Journals Digital Library. http://quod.lib.umich.edu/m/moajrnl.

———. "Southern Authors, School Books and Presses." *De Bow's Review* 21.5 (November 1856): 519–523. University of Michigan. Making of America Journals Digital Library. http://quod.lib.umich.edu/m/moajrnl.

Marten, James. *The Children's Civil War.* Chapel Hill: U of North Carolina P, 1998.

———, ed. *Lessons of War: The Civil War in Children's Magazines.* Wilmington, DE: Scholarly Resources, 1999.

Martin, Michelle H. *Brown Gold: Milestones of African-American Children's Picture Books, 1845–2002.* New York: Routledge, 2004.

Mathis, Sharon Bell. "'*The Slave Dancer*' Is an Insult to Black Children." *Cultural Conformity in Books for Children: Further Readings in Racism.* Ed. Donnarae MacCann and Gloria Woodard. Metuchen, NJ: Scarecrow P, 1977. 146–148.

McDowell, Deborah E. "Telling Slavery in 'Freedom's' Time: Post-Reconstruction and the Harlem Renaissance." *The Cambridge Companion to the African American Slave Narrative.* Ed. Audrey Fisch. Cambridge: Cambridge UP, 2007. 150–167.

McDowell, Deborah E., and Arnold Rampersad, ed. *Slavery and the Literary Imagination.* Baltimore: Johns Hopkins UP, 1989.

McGovern, Ann. *"Wanted Dead or Alive": The True Story of Harriet Tubman* [original title: *Runaway Slave*]. Illus. R. M. Powers. New York: Scholastic, 1965.

McMullan, Kate. *The Story of Harriet Tubman, Conductor of the Underground Railroad.* Illus. Steven James Petruccio. New York: Yearling–Bantam Doubleday Dell, 1991.

McPherson, James M. "Civil War." *The Reader's Companion to American History.* Ed. Eric Foner and John A. Garraty. Boston: Houghton Mifflin, 1991. 182–190.

———. "Emancipation Proclamation and Thirteenth Amendment." *The Reader's Companion to American History.* Ed. Eric Foner and John A. Garraty. Boston: Houghton Mifflin, 1991. 351–352.

Mickenberg, Julia L. *Learning from the Left: Children's Literature, the Cold War, and Radical Politics in the United States.* New York: Oxford UP, 2006.

Mickey's Mellerdrammer. Animated short. DVD. Dir. Wilfred Jackson. Walt Disney Studios, 1933. In *Walt Disney's Treasures: Mickey Mouse in Black and White.* Vol. 2. Walt Disney Productions, 2004.

Mills, Bruce. *Cultural Reformations: Lydia Maria Child and the Literature of Reform.* Athens: U of Georgia P, 1994.

Mitchell, Angelyn. *The Freedom to Remember: Narrative, Slavery, and Gender in Contemporary Black Women's Fiction.* New Brunswick, NJ: Rutgers UP, 2002.

Mitchell, Mary Niall. *Raising Freedom's Child: Black Children and Visions of the Future after Slavery*. New York: New York UP, 2008.

"Mobs." *The Slave's Friend* 4.2 (1839): 1–2.

Monaghan, E. Jennifer. *A Common Heritage: Noah Webster's Blue-Back Speller*. Hamden, CT: Archon, 1983.

Moore, Augusta. "Turn About, Fair Play." *The Youth's Companion* 38.15 (13 April 1865): 57.

Moore, Claudia. Letter. "The Jury." *The Brownies' Book* 1.3 (March 1920): 83.

Moore, Mrs. M. B. *The Dixie Elementary Spelling Book for the Use of Common Schools*. Raleigh, NC: Branson and Farrar, 1864.

———. *The First Dixie Reader; Designed to Follow the Dixie Primer*. Second Ed. Raleigh, NC: Branson and Farrar, 1864.

———. *The Geographical Reader for the Dixie Children*. Raleigh, NC: Branson, Farrar, 1863.

Morgan, Jo-Ann. *"Uncle Tom's Cabin" as Visual Culture*. Columbia: U of Missouri P, 2007.

Morris, Robert C. *Reading, 'Riting, and Reconstruction: The Education of Freedmen in the South, 1861–1870*. Chicago: U of Chicago P, 1976.

Morrison, Toni. *Playing in the Dark: Whiteness and the Literary Imagination*. 1992. New York: Vintage-Random House, 1993.

Mosley, Walter. *47*. New York: Little Brown, 2005.

Moss, Anita. "Captain Marryat and Sea Adventure." *Children's Literature Association Quarterly*. 8.3 (Fall 1983): 13–15.

Moss, Elizabeth. *Domestic Novelists in the Old South: Defenders of Southern Culture*. Baton Rouge: Louisiana State UP, 1992.

Murphy, Avon Jack. *"The Youth's Emancipator." Children's Periodicals of the United States*. Ed. R. Gordon Kelly. Westport, CT: Greenwood, 1984. 518–523.

Murray, Gail Schmunk. *American Children's Literature and the Construction of Childhood*. New York: Twayne-Simon and Schuster Macmillan, 1998.

Myers, Elisabeth P. *Frederick Douglass: Young Defender of Human Rights*. Young Patriots Series. Illus. Cathy Morrison. Carmel, IN: Patria, 2007.

"Near 307 Stolen Children." *The Slave's Friend* 2.4 (1837): 3–5.

Nelson, Dana D. *The Word in Black and White: Reading "Race" in American Literature, 1638–1867*. New York: Oxford UP, 1992.

Nelson, Marilyn. *Fortune's Bones: The Manumission Requiem*. Notes and annotations by Pamela Espeland. Asheville, NC: Front Street, 2004.

Nelson, Vaunda Micheaux. *Almost to Freedom*. Illus. Colin Bootman. Minneapolis: Carolrhoda–Lerner, 2003.

"Never Despair." *The Youth's Emancipator* 1.1 (1842): 1.

Nichols, Catherine. *Harriet Tubman*. Hello Reader! Level 2 series. Illus. Brian Denington. New York: Scholastic, 2002.

Nichols, Charles H., Jr. "Slave Narratives and the Plantation Legend." *Phylon* 10.3 (1949): 201–210. JSTOR Arts and Sciences I Archive Collection Online. http://www.jstor.org/stable/272382.

Odell, Margaretta Matilda. *Memoir and Poems of Phillis Wheatley, a Native African and a Slave*. 1834. Third Ed. Boston: Isaac Knapp, 1838.

Olney, James. "'I Was Born': Slave Narratives, Their Status as Autobiography and as Literature." *The Slave's Narrative*. Ed. Charles T. Davis and Henry Louis Gates Jr. New York: Oxford UP, 1985. 148–175.

Osborne, William S. Introduction. *Swallow Barn; or, A Sojourn in the Old Dominion*. 1962. New York: Hafner, 1971. xiii–xliii.

Page, Thomas Nelson. *The Negro: The Southerner's Problem*. New York: Charles Scribner's Sons, 1904.

———. *Two Little Confederates*. 1888. Harrisonburg, VA: Sprinkle, 1994.

Parris, Brandy. "Difficult Sympathy in Reconstruction-Era Animal Stories of *'Our Young Folks.'*" *Children's Literature* 31 (2003): 25–49.

Parrish, T. Michael, and Robert M. Willingham Jr., ed. *Confederate Imprints: A Bibliography of Southern Publications from Secession to Surrender [Expanding and Revising the Earlier Works of Marjorie Crandall and Richard Harwell]*. Austin, TX: Jenkins and Katonah; New York: Gary A. Foster, [1984].

Patterson, Blanche Lynn. "The Heritage." *The Brownies' Book* 1.8 (August 1920): 249–250.

"A Peace-Maker." *The Slave's Friend* 3.7 (1838): 5–6.

Perkins, Lucy Fitch. *The Colonial Twins of Virginia*. Boston: Houghton Mifflin, 1924.

Phelps, E. Stuart. "How June Found Massa Linkum." *Our Young Folks: An Illustrated Magazine for Boys and Girls* 4 (May 1868): 272–279.

"A Pioneer Suffragette." *The Brownies' Book* 1.4 (April 1920): 120–121.

Polacco, Patricia. *Pink and Say*. New York: Philomel, 1994.

"The Poor Mother." *The Slave's Friend* 1.3 (1836): 3–5.

"Prayer of the Colored Mother." *The Slave's Friend* 2.3 (1837): 13–14.

"Pronunciation in Singing." *The Rose Bud, or Youth's Gazette* 1.37 (11 May 1833): 145.

Pyrnelle, Louise-Clarke. *Diddie, Dumps and Tot, or, Plantation Child-Life*. 1882. Gretna, LA: Pelican, 2004.

Quarles, Benjamin. *Black Abolitionists*. New York: Oxford UP, 1969.

Raven, Margot Theis. *Night Boat to Freedom*. Illus. E. B. Lewis. New York: Melanie Kroupa Books; Farrar, Straus and Giroux, 2006.

Rev. of *A Southern Home*. *Debow's Review* 18.5 (May 1855): 668–669. University of Michigan. Making of America Journals Digital Library. http://quod.lib.umich.edu/m/moajrnl.

Ridgely, J. V. *John Pendleton Kennedy*. New York: Twayne, 1966.

Ringgold, Faith. *Aunt Harriet's Underground Railroad in the Sky*. New York: Crown, 1992.

———. *Tar Beach*. New York: Crown, 1991.

Roark, James L. *Masters Without Slaves: Southern Planters in the Civil War and Reconstruction*. New York: Norton, 1977.

Roberts, John W. *From Trickster to Badman: The Black Folk Hero in Slavery and Freedom*. Philadelphia: U of Pennsylvania P, 1989.

Rollins, Richard M., ed. *The Autobiographies of Noah Webster: From the Letters and Essays, Memoir, and Diary*. Columbia: U of South Carolina P, 1989.

"Rose and Miss Belle." *The Slave's Friend* 1.10 (1836): 11–12.

Roselle, Daniel. *Samuel Griswold Goodrich, Creator of Peter Parley: A Study of His Life and Work*. Albany: State U of New York P, 1968.

Rushdy, Ashraf H. A. *Neo-slave Narratives: Studies in the Social Logic of a Literary Form*. New York: Oxford UP, 1999.

———. *Remembering Generations: Race and Family in Contemporary African American Fiction*. Chapel Hill: U of North Carolina P, 2001.

Ryan, Tim A. *Calls and Responses: The American Novel of Slavery Since "Gone with the Wind."* Baton Rouge: Louisiana State UP, 2008.

S., Peter. Letter. *The Rose Bud, or Youth's Gazette* 1.7 (13 October 1832): 27.

Sampson, Emma Speed. *Miss Minerva Broadcasts Billy*. Illus. William Donahey. Chicago: Reilly and Lee, 1925.

———. *Miss Minerva on the Old Plantation*. Illus. William Donahey. Chicago: Reilly and Lee, 1923.

———. *Miss Minerva's Baby*. Illus. William Donahey. Chicago: Reilly and Lee, 1920.

Samuels, Shirley. "The Identity of Slavery." *The Culture of Sentiment: Race, Gender, and Sentimentality in Nineteenth-Century America*. Ed. Shirley Samuels. New York: Oxford UP, 1992. 157–171.

Schroeder, Alan. *Minty: A Story of Young Harriet Tubman*. Illus. Jerry Pinkney. New York: Dial–Penguin, 1996.

Sernett, Milton C. *Harriet Tubman: Myth, Memory, and History*. Durham, NC: Duke UP, 2007.

Seymour, Bella. Letter. The Grown-Ups' Corner. *The Brownies' Book* 1.2 (February 1920): 45.

Shackelford, Jane Dabney. *The Child's Story of the Negro*. Illus. Lois Mailou Jones. Washington, DC: Associated Publishers, 1938.

Siegelson, Kim L. *In the Time of the Drums*. Illus. Brian Pinkney. New York: Hyperion, 1999.

Singmaster, Elsie. *Swords of Steel: The Story of a Gettysburg Boy*. Illus. David Hendrickson. Boston: Houghton Mifflin, 1933.

"The Slave's Address." *The Slave's Friend* 3.12 (1838): 9.

Sledge, Martha L. "'A Is an Abolitionist': '*The Anti-Slavery Alphabet*' and the Politics of Literacy." *Enterprising Youth: Social Values and Acculturation in Nineteenth-Century American Children's Literature*. Ed. Monika Elbert. New York: Routledge, 2008. 69–82.

Smith, David L. "Huck, Jim, and American Racial Discourse." *Satire or Evasion? Black Perspectives on Huckleberry Finn*. Ed. James S. Leonard, Thomas A. Tenney, and Thadious M. Davis. Durham, NC: Duke UP, 1994. 103–120.

Smith, Katharine Capshaw. *Children's Literature of the Harlem Renaissance.* Bloomington: Indiana UP, 2004.

Smith, Valerie. "Neo-slave Narratives." *The Cambridge Companion to the African American Slave Narrative.* Ed. Audrey Fisch. Cambridge: Cambridge UP, 2007. 168–185.

"Soul-Drivers." *The Slave's Friend* 2.9 (1837): 1–4.

"Southern Literature." *Southern Literary Messenger* 1.1 (August 1834): 1–3. Reprinted in *The Southern Literature Messenger: Devoted to Every Department of Literature and the Fine Arts.* Vol. 1. New York: AMS P, 1965.

The Southern Primer; or, Child's First Lessons in Spelling and Reading. Improved Ed. Richmond, VA: A. Morris, 1860.

Spaulding, A. Timothy. *Re-forming the Past: History, the Fantastic, and the Postmodern Slave Narrative.* Columbus: Ohio State UP, 2005.

Stanton, Elizabeth Cady. "Address to the National Woman Suffrage Convention, Washington, D.C., January 19, 1869." *The Concise History of Woman Suffrage: Selections from the Classic Work of Stanton, Anthony, Gage, and Harper.* Ed. Mari Jo and Paul Buhle. Urbana: U of Illinois P, 1978. 249–256.

"The Starling." *The Slave's Friend* 1.4 (1836): 1–3.

Stepto, Robert B. *From Behind the Veil: A Study of Afro-American Narrative.* Urbana: U of Illinois P, 1979.

Sterling, Dorothy. *The Story of Harriet Tubman: Freedom Train.* New York: Scholastic, 1954.

Sterling, Richard, and J[ames]. D. Campbell. *Our Own First Reader, for the Use of Schools and Families.* Greensboro, NC: Sterling, Campbell and Albright, 1862.

———. *Our Own Third Reader, for the Use of Schools and Families.* Greensboro, NC: Sterling, Campbell and Albright, 1862.

"The Story of Phillis Wheatley: A True Story." *The Brownies' Book* 1.8 (August 1920): 251–253.

Stowe, Harriet Beecher. *A Key to "Uncle Tom's Cabin"; Presenting the Original Facts and Documents upon Which the Story is Founded. Together with Corroborative Statements Verifying the Truth of the Work.* 1853. Port Washington, NY: Kennikat, 1968.

[———]. *Pictures and Stories from "Uncle Tom's Cabin."* Boston: John P. Jewett, 1853.

———. *Uncle Tom's Cabin; or, Life among the Lowly.* Chapters 42–44. *National Era* 6.274 (1 April 1852): 53. American Periodicals Series Online. http://www.proquest.com/en-US/catalogs/databases/detail/aps.shtml.

———. *Uncle Tom's Cabin; or, Life among the Lowly.* 1852. Ed. Ann Douglas. New York: Penguin, 1981.

Swift, Hildegarde Hoyt. *North Star Shining: A Pictorial History of the American Negro.* Illus. Lynd Ward. New York: William Morrow, 1947.

———. *The Railroad to Freedom: A Story of the Civil War.* Illus. James Daugherty. 1932. New York: Harcourt, Brace and World, 1960.

Taketani, Etsuko. "The 'Omnipresent Aunt' and the Social Child: Lydia Maria Child's *'Juvenile Miscellany.'*" *Children's Literature.* Vol. 27. New Haven, CT: Yale UP, 1999. 22–39.

Tate, Binnie. "Racism and Distortions Pervade *'The Slave Dancer.'*" *Cultural Conformity in Books for Children: Further Readings in Racism.* Ed. Donnarae MacCann and Gloria Woodard. Metuchen, NJ: Scarecrow P, 1977. 149–153.

Tate, Eleanora E. *The Secret of Gumbo Grove.* 1987. New York: Bantam Doubleday Dell, 1988.

Thompson, Audrey. "Harriet Tubman in Pictures: Cultural Consciousness and the Art of Picture Books." *The Lion and the Unicorn* 25.1 (January 2001): 81–114.

Thompson, Matilda G. "Aunt Judy's Story: A Story from Real Life." *The Child's Anti-Slavery Book: Containing a Few Words about American Slave Children, and Stories of Slave-Life.* 1859. Miami: Mnemosyne, 1969. 106–153.

"To Juvenile Anti-Slavery Societies." *The Slave's Friend* 3.2 (1838): 7–11.

Tompkins, Jane. *Sensational Designs: The Cultural Work of American Fiction, 1790–1860.* New York: Oxford UP, 1985.

"Toussaint L'Ouverture." *The Brownies' Book* 1.5 (May 1920): 149–152.

Townsend, John Rowe. *Written for Children: An Outline of English-Language Children's Literature.* 1965. Fourth Rev. Ed. New York: Harper Trophy, 1990.

Trelease, Allen W. "Ku Klux Klan." *The Reader's Companion to American History.* Ed. Eric Foner and John A. Garraty. Boston: Houghton Mifflin, 1991. 625–626.

Trites, Roberta Seelinger. *Twain, Alcott, and the Birth of the Adolescent Reform Novel.* Iowa City: U of Iowa P, 2007.

Trowbridge, J[ohn]. T[ownsend]. *Cudjo's Cave.* Boston: J. E. Tilton, 1864.

———. *The Three Scouts.* [1865]. Boston: Lee and Shepard, 1888. http://books.google.com/books?id=cX8YAAAAYAAJ&printsec=frontcover&dq=three+scouts&hl=en#.

———. "A Visit to Mount Vernon." *Our Young Folks: An Illustrated Magazine for Boys and Girls* 2 (February 1866): 88–93.

Turner, Ann. *Nettie's Trip South.* Illus. Ronald Himler. New York: Macmillan, 1987.

Turner, Lorenzo Dow. "Anti-Slavery Sentiment in American Literature Prior to 1865." *The Journal of Negro History* 14.4 (October 1929): 371–492. JSTOR Arts and Sciences I Archive Collection Online. http://www.jstor.org/stable/2714189.

Twain, Mark. *The Adventures of Huckleberry Finn.* 1884. Ed. John Seelye. New York: Penguin, 1985.

"Two Good Boys." *The Slave's Friend* 2.12 (1837): 5–6.

Uncle Tom and Little Eva. Animated short. Dir. unknown. Van Beuren Studios, 1932. http://YouTube.com.

Uncle Tom's Cabaña. Animated Short. Dir. Tex Avery. Metro-Goldwyn-Mayer, 1947. http://YouTube.com.

Unger, Harlow Giles. *Noah Webster: The Life and Times of an American Patriot.* New York: John Wiley and Sons, 1998.

van Loon, Hendrick. *The Story of Mankind.* [New York]: Boni and Liveright, 1921.

Washington, Booker T. *Up From Slavery: An Autobiography*. 1901. New York: Carol, 1989.

"The Water-Melon Boats." *The Youth's Companion* 21.15 (12 August 1847): 57–58. American Periodicals Series Online. http://www.proquest.com/en-US/catalogs/databases/detail/aps.shtml.

Watkins, William H. *The White Architects of Black Education: Ideology and Power in America, 1865–1954*. Foreword by Robin D. G. Kelley. New York: Teachers College P, 2001.

Watson, Ritchie Devon, Jr. *Norman and Saxons: Southern Race Mythology and the Intellectual History of the American Civil War.* Baton Rouge: Louisiana State UP, 2008.

Weatherford, Carole Boston. *Moses: When Harriet Tubman Led Her People to Freedom*. Illus. Kadir Nelson. New York: Jump at the Sun-Hyperion, 2006.

Webster, Noah. *The Little Reader's Assistant*. . . . 1790. Third Ed. Northampton: William Butler, 1791.

———. "On the Education of Youth in America." 1788. Reprinted in *A Collection of Essays and Fugitiv Writings on Moral, Historical, Political and Literary Subjects*. By Noah Webster. 1790. Introd. Robert K. Peters. Delmar, NY: Scholars' Facsimiles and Reprints, 1977. 1–37.

Webster, William G. *A Sequel to Webster's Elementary Spelling Book; or, A Speller and Definer.* 1844. Philadelphia: J. B. Lippincott, [1845].

Weidt, Maryann N. *Harriet Tubman*. History Maker Bios series. 2003. New York: Barnes and Noble, 2006.

Weiner, Eric. *The Story of Frederick Douglass, Voice of Freedom*. Illus. Steven Parton. New York: Yearling–Dell, 1992.

[Weld, Theodore Dwight]. *American Slavery As It Is: Testimony of a Thousand Witnesses*. 1839. New York: Arno P and the *New York Times*, 1968.

Whelan, Gloria. *Friend on Freedom River*. Illus. Gijsbert van Frankenhuyzen. Chelsea, MI: Sleeping Bear P, 2004.

———. *The Listeners*. Illus. Mike Benny. Chelsea, MI: Sleeping Bear, 2009.

Whelpley, Samuel. *A Compend of History from the Earliest Times by Samuel Whelpley; With Corrections and Important Additions and Improvements, by Rev. Joseph Emerson*. Eleventh Ed. New York: Collins, Keese, 1840.

White, Deborah Gray. *Ar'n't I a Woman?: Female Slaves in the Plantation South*. New York: W. W. Norton, 1985.

"White Slaves." *The Youth's Companion* 38.10 (9 March 1865): 38. American Periodicals Series Online. http://www.proquest.com/en-US/catalogs/databases/detail/aps.shtml.

Wilkes, Laura E. "The Story of Frederick Douglass: A True Story." *The Brownies' Book* 1.9 (September 1920): 266–270.

Wilkin, Binnie Tate. *African and African American Images in Newbery Award-Winning Titles: Progress in Portrayals*. Lanham, MD: Scarecrow, 2009.

Willis, Nathaniel. "Editorial: Slavery." *The Youth's Companion* 2.8 (18 July 1828): 32. American Periodicals Series Online. http://www.proquest.com/en-US/catalogs/databases/detail/aps.shtml.

———. "Editorial: Slavery." *The Youth's Companion* 2.9 (25 July 1828): 36. American Periodicals Series Online. http://www.proquest.com/en-US/catalogs/databases/detail/aps.shtml.

Wilson, Harriet E. *Our Nig; or, Sketches from the Life of a Free Black*. 1859. Ed. Henry Louis Gates Jr. New York: Vintage Books-Random House, 1983.

Wilson, John Scott. "Race and Manners for Southern Girls and Boys: *'The Miss Minerva'* Books and Race Relations in a Southern Children's Series." *Journal of American Culture* 17.3 (Fall 1994): 69–74.

Winks, Robin W. "The Making of a Fugitive Slave Narrative: Josiah Henson and Uncle Tom—a Case Study." *The Slave's Narrative*. Ed. Charles T. Davis and Henry Louis Gates Jr. New York: Oxford UP, 1985. 112–146.

Winter, Jeanette. *Follow the Drinking Gourd*. New York: Dragonfly-Knopf, 1988.

Wright, Courtni C. *Jumping the Broom*. Illus. Gershom Griffith. New York: Holiday House, 1994.

Wyatt-Brown, Bertram. "Black Schooling during Reconstruction." *African Americans and Education in the South, 1865–1900*. Ed. Donald G. Nieman. New York: Garland, 1994. 426–445.

Wyeth, Sharon Dennis. *The World of Daughter McGuire*. New York: Bantam Doubleday Dell, 1994.

Wyman, Lillie Buffum Chace. "The Bravest of the Brave: A True Story." *The Brownies' Book* 1.11 (November 1920): 338–339.

Yates, Elizabeth. *Amos Fortune, Free Man*. Illus. Nora S. Unwin. 1950. New York: Puffin–Penguin, 1989.

Yellin, Jean Fagan. *The Intricate Knot: Black Figures in American Literature, 1776–1863*. New York: New York UP, 1972.

———. *Women and Sisters: The Antislavery Feminists in American Culture*. New Haven: Yale UP, 1989.

Young, Jeffrey Robert. Introduction. "A Transatlantic Perspective on the Problem of Proslavery Thought." *Proslavery and Sectional Thought in the Early South, 1740–1829: An Anthology*. Ed. Jeffrey Robert Young. Columbia: U of South Carolina P, 2006. 1–67.

"Zamor and Hinda." *The Slave's Friend* 3.10 (1838): 1–12.

INDEX